China's Participation in the IMF,
the World Bank, and GATT

China's Participation in the IMF, the World Bank, and GATT

Toward a Global Economic Order

Harold K. Jacobson and Michel Oksenberg

Ann Arbor
The University of Michigan Press

1993   1992   1991   1990   4   3   2   1

Library of Congress Cataloging-in-Publication Data

Jacobson, Harold Karen.
    China's participation in the IMF, the World Bank, and GATT :
toward a global economic order / Harold K. Jacobson and Michel
Oksenberg.
        p.   cm.
    Includes bibliographical references.
    ISBN 0-472-10177-3
    1. China—Foreign economic relations.   2. World Bank—China.
3. International Monetary Fund—China.   4. General Agreement on
Tariffs and Trade (Organization)—China.   I. Oksenberg, Michel,
1938–   .   II. Title.
HF3836.5.J33   1990
337.51—dc20   90-10727
                                                                    CIP

To the memory of
Alexander Eckstein
*whose devotion to understanding modern China and to bringing it
and the rest of the world closer together provided enduring
inspiration*

Preface

This is a study of the evolving relationship between the People's Republic of China (PRC) and the keystone international economic organizations (KIEOs): the International Monetary Fund (IMF), the International Bank for Reconstruction and Development (IBRD or World Bank) and its affiliated agencies, and the General Agreement on Tariffs and Trade (GATT). The PRC entered the IMF and the World Bank in 1980, and in 1986 it formally requested that negotiations be opened on its full participation in GATT.

These three multilateral organizations deserve to be called keystone international economic organizations because they play indispensable roles in giving a measure of coherence and stability to the international monetary, financial, and commercial systems. They are crucial to the functioning of the contemporary international political economy. When created in the immediate aftermath of World War II, their organizers envisioned that the membership in them would be universal, but until the early 1970s they were comprised almost exclusively of states with market economies. In the 1970s, various Eastern European countries with planned economies entered the KIEOs, but their inclusion pales in significance to that of China.

China has more than a fifth of the world's population. In 1980, when it entered the IMF and the World Bank, its gross national product was the eighth largest in the world, even though on a per capita basis China remained a poor country. Its textiles, metallurgy, and energy industries place China among the top five countries in total production of fabrics, steel, petroleum, and coal. China's economic potential is tremendous.

China's embracing of the KIEOs reversed its previous policies. From 1949, when the People's Republic of China was proclaimed, until the early 1970s, China pursued a largely autarkic economic policy outside the KIEOs. While China did have extensive economic relations with the Soviet Union and Eastern Europe in the 1950s, and cultivated commercial ties with Western Europe and Japan in the early 1960s, in both instances the purpose of the external involvement was to build an integrated and self-reliant national economy. Chinese officials regularly castigated the KIEOs as instruments of capitalist exploitation. Many Western governments—especially the United States—seemed equally hostile toward China. Not only did these governments express little desire to include China in the KIEOs, but for strategic reasons they applied an economic embargo against China.

In contrast, radicals throughout the world pointed to China as a virtuous example of autonomous, noncapitalist development, a course they urged all developing countries to emulate. In the 1970s, even as the radicals were still lauding China's autonomous course, China began a long, complicated process of reform that included opening China's economy to the outside world. China's decisions to seek inclusion in the KIEOs were an intimate part of a reform process that repudiated policies China had pursued for three decades.

China's involvement in the keystone international economic organizations moves these organizations in the direction of universal membership. The Soviet Union is the only large country still not involved, and it has indicated that it too may seek inclusion. Thus China's involvement, and what might follow, opens the prospect of a truly global economic order being organized under the auspices of the KIEOs, hence the subtitle of our book, *Toward a Global Economic Order*.

China's evolving relationship with the KIEOs raises fascinating and significant questions. How and why did such a sharp change in the relationship occur? What accounts for the Chinese decisions to seek inclusion in the KIEOs? How did the KIEOs, and their most important members, the Western states, come to welcome China's inclusion? What have the consequences of China's involvement in the IMF and the World Bank been for the two institutions and for China? Thus far, has China's emergence into the world economy been managed in ways that are minimally disruptive to China and the KIEOs, and indeed that strengthen the existing international financial institutions and reinforce China's domestic program of economic reform? Under what circumstances can the previous record of success be sustained? What are the issues involved in China's request for full participation in GATT? What are the implications of China's evolving relationship with the KIEOs for the prospects of the USSR's involvement in these institutions? This study seeks to answer these and similar questions. It is an analysis of the interaction between two sets of political-economic systems, those of China and those of the KIEOs, that independently are undergoing change. It shows how the interaction becomes an added ingredient in the processes of change on both sides.

More broadly, the analysis provides a case study for exploring the interactions between international institutions and their member states. It also provides a case study for considering the applicability of contemporary perspectives on international political economy, including dependency, hegemonic stability, classical liberal, and neomercantilist theories.

The study argues that until mid-1989 the evolving relationship between China and the KIEOs was managed with considerable success. The tragic events in Beijing in May and June, 1989, however, underscored that the process of Chinese inclusion in the neoliberal international economic order was far from complete, and that the challenges of the next decade were likely to be more complex than the previous decade. In response to the use of military force to suppress massive and sustained demonstrations in the capital city, with many resulting deaths, the executive directors of IBRD delayed processing of new loans to the Beijing government. The United States, Japan, and the countries of the European Economic Community applied a variety of economic sanctions against China, principally the withholding of concessional interest rate loans. The negotiations over full Chinese participation in GATT were postponed. The actions of China's leaders, justified on the alleged grounds of quelling an effort to topple the regime, raised questions around the world about their reliability, credibility, and judgment and about the prospects for social stability and political continuity in China. Subsequent signs in the summer of 1989 of a far-reaching political crackdown, of an abandonment of portions of the reform program, and of a campaign against foreign ideological influences created additional doubts over the Chinese leaders' commitment to abide by generally accepted, international norms about how leaders should treat their people. The Beijing spring of 1989 suggested that China's incorporation into the international economic community was likely to be more protracted, more difficult, and more internally divisive than the early and mid-1980s suggested. The study emphasizes the importance of the next segment of the journey. A most complicated, difficult, and important stage, China's full participation in GATT, has just been begun.

Our story is a reminder of the potentiality and necessity of purposeful political action, and the damage that can be done by ill-considered decisions that violate international norms. The successful Chinese participation in the KIEOs until June, 1989, was not an automatic outcome dictated by the structure of the international system. Rather, political leadership in the KIEOs, their member states, and China enabled the progress to occur and minimized the potentially harmful consequences to the participants. But political leadership was not enough. The context in which the leaders worked had to permit and encourage the cooperation we describe. Our study is also a reminder, therefore, that no simple theory of international affairs will suffice. To understand complex international events requires analyses of the interaction among processes on many levels: international, national, and subnational.

We completed our manuscript in July, 1989, when the tumultuous events associated with the prodemocracy movement in China dominated the news. It was impossible to foretell the implications of these events for the immediate relationship between China and the KIEOs. We remained convinced, however, of the validity of our analysis of the evolving relationship between China and the KIEOs through mid-1989, and we believe that whatever the immediate future brings, the trends that we identified in our analysis have long-term validity.

The research on which this study is based was supported by grant INT

8514847 of the National Science Foundation and by grants from the East-West Center and the Rockefeller Foundation. Harold Jacobson worked on the manuscript while he was a fellow at the Center for Advanced Study in the Behavioral Sciences. His fellowship at the center was supported by National Science Foundation grant BNS8700864. This research is part of a cooperative project jointly undertaken by the Center for Political Studies, part of the Institute of Social Research of the University of Michigan, and the Institute of World Economics and Politics of the Chinese Academy of Social Sciences.

In addition to being based on documents and other written materials in the public domain, this study is based on extensive interviews with approximately one hundred officials of governments and international governmental organizations in Beijing, Geneva, and Washington who have played a role in or observed China's evolving relationships with the keystone international economic organizations. We interviewed middle- and high-level officials in all the principal Chinese agencies that deal with the KIEOs, and in no instance did a Chinese agency refuse our request for an interview. The interviews in Beijing were conducted in the summers of 1986, 1987, and 1988, those in Geneva in the summer of 1986, the fall of 1987, the summer of 1988, and the spring of 1989, and those in Washington at various times during 1986, 1987, 1988, and 1989. The interviews were conducted on the condition that we would protect the identity of our interviewees and not quote them directly. Unfortunately, even to list the names of those whom we interviewed would risk identifying who gave us certain information. We can understand the frustration of our readers with our inability to be more revealing about our interviewees, but we feel obligated to obey the strictures placed upon us.

Beyond questioning them about the historical events in which they had been involved, we asked thirty-six of those whom we interviewed to respond to a set questionnaire. The items contained in this questionnaire are reproduced in Appendix 3. Eleven of these respondents were Chinese, twenty-five were of other nationalities. Four of the Chinese and twenty-one of those of other nationalities were professionally concerned with China's relationship with GATT, seven Chinese and four others were concerned with its relationship with IMF and IBRD. Although these respondents are neither a representative sample nor the universe of those whom we interviewed, many of their answers are revealing because of either the unanimity of views expressed or the sharp and uncontestable differences among the answers given. We use these data at various places in our analysis. We do not make great claims for their significance. Rather, we present them because they provide additional evidence in this fascinating story.

We also benefited greatly from several exceptionally candid, perceptive, and thoughtful informal discussions with Chinese colleagues in China and the United States. In addition to giving us specific criticisms of an earlier draft, these Chinese commentators encouraged us to place our topic in an appropriately broad strategic context, to stress the relationship between participation in the KIEOs and the domestic reforms, and to emphasize China's continued resolve to protect its national sovereignty. We hope our revisions adequately incorporate these thoughts. However, no Chinese read our treatment of China's political history, nor did any Chinese read the final draft, incorporating revisions after the June tragedy. We suspect many Chinese who helped us on this project would object to our interpretations.

The manuscript has been improved as a result of critiques of earlier versions in seminars and colloquia at the University of Michigan, the Council on Foreign Relations, the Woodrow Wilson International Center for Scholars, the East-West Center in Hawaii, and the University of Chicago. Barbara B. Crane, Bruce Dickson, Steven Goldstein, Ernst B. Haas, Leah Haus, Nina Halpern, Margaret P. Karns, Robert O. Keohane, Samuel S. Kim, Paul Kreisberg, Kenneth Lieberthal, Nicholas Lardy, Steven Norton, Alan Romberg, Michael Ryan, Benjamin Stavis, and Margaret Garritsen de Vries provided insightful comments on earlier drafts. We gratefully acknowledge our assistants, Merle Feldbaum, Sheree Groves, Barbara Opal, Ena Schlorfl, and Cheryl Shanks, without whose help the study would not exist.

Our book has deep roots. We both were privileged to have worked with Alexander Eckstein. His devotion to understanding modern China and its economy and to bringing China and the rest of the world closer together is the ultimate inspiration for our work.

We alone, however, are responsible for the contents of this study. It is truly a collaborative effort between a student of international organizations and a student of contemporary China. Cooperative work between an area specialist and a generalist does not occur as frequently as it should in American universities, and we hope this study will encourage others to embark on similar endeavors.

July, 1989

Contents

Tables

Acronyms

CASS	Chinese Academy of Social Sciences	ITO	International Trade Organization
CCP	Chinese Communist party	KIEO	keystone international economic organization
CIA	Central Intelligence Agency, United States of America	KMT	Kuomintang
		MFA	Multifibre Arrangement, GATT
CMEA	Council for Mutual Economic Assistance	MFN	most-favored-nation
		MOE	Ministry of Education, China
EDI	Economic Development Institute	MOF	Ministry of Finance, China
EEC	European Economic Community	MOFERT	Ministry of Foreign Economic Relations and Trade, China
GATT	General Agreement on Tariffs and Trade	NIEO	New International Economic Order, UN
GDP	gross domestic product		
GNP	gross national product	NMP	net material product
GSP	Generalized System of (Tariff) Preferences	OECD	Organization for Economic Cooperation and Development
IBRD	International Bank for Reconstruction and Development—World Bank	PRC	People's Republic of China
		RMB	*renminbi*, China's currency
ICITO	Interim Commission of the International Trade Organization	SAL	Structural Adjustment Loan, World Bank
IDA	International Development Association	SDR	Special Drawing Right, IMF
		SEC	State Economic Commission, China
IFC	International Finance Corporation	SIIEM	Shanghai Institute of International Economic Management, China
IMF	International Monetary Fund		

SPC	State Planning Commission, China	UNCTAD	United Nations Conference on Trade and Development
TSB	Textile Surveillance Body, MFA, GATT	UNSG	United Nations Small Group, China
UN	United Nations		

CHAPTER 1

China and the KIEOs:
The Historical Significance

What are the implications of the People's Republic of China's (PRC) membership in the International Monetary Fund (IMF) and the International Bank for Reconstruction and Development (IBRD or World Bank) and its possible full participation in the General Agreement on Tariffs and Trade (GATT)? The PRC assumed its seat in the International Monetary Fund and the World Bank in 1980, and it became a party to GATT's Multifibre Arrangement (MFA) in 1984. In July, 1986, China gave formal notice of its desire to participate fully in the GATT.

What has been the impact of China's membership upon the structure, functioning, and activities of the IMF and the World Bank? What would the likely consequences be of China's full participation in GATT? What are the consequences for China and its development policies of membership in these influential international economic organizations? What are the lessons to be derived from the experiences to date that might help smooth the way? These are the principal questions probed in this study.

The Issues at Stake

The IMF, World Bank, and GATT are the keystone international economic organizations (KIEOs) of the contemporary international political economy; they are the principal multilateral institutions providing coherence and stability to the international monetary, financial, and commercial systems. They have been a major factor in establishing and maintaining the conditions that have made possible the relatively free flow internationally of goods and capital that has characterized the post–World War II era and that has contributed to international economic growth. They are the pillars of the neoliberal international economic order.

Created at the Bretton Woods Conference in 1944, the IMF provides a forum for multilateral consideration of international monetary issues and is a source of funds to enable countries to deal with short-term balance of payments difficulties, thereby assisting them to maintain relatively stable exchange rates and keep or make their currencies convertible. The World Bank

group, more precisely the IBRD—which was also created at Bretton Woods—
and its affiliated agencies, the International Finance Corporation (IFC) and the
International Development Association (IDA—the Bank's soft loan window),
provides capital assistance to countries for the purpose of promoting economic growth and more broadly seeks to encourage the flow of capital from
the more prosperous to the less prosperous countries. GATT seeks to promote
trade liberalization through establishing a legal framework for the conduct of
international commerce.

All three multilateral institutions were designed to overcome problems
that had crippled the international economy in the period between the two
world wars. During the 1930s the volume and value of international trade fell
precipitously as countries erected tariffs and other barriers to protect domestic
industries and engaged in competitive "beggar thy neighbor" currency devaluations. Foreign investment dried up in the wake of debt repudiations. The
three institutions were designed to foster conditions that would promote expanding international trade and investment. Their mandates were based on
liberal principles, but were more complicated than the laissez faire prescriptions of classical liberalism. The mandates provided innovative frameworks
that would stimulate international trade and investment while at the same time
allowing the institutions' member states to pursue interventionist economic
policies aimed at achieving domestic welfare goals. It is in this sense that the
term "neoliberal" is an apt description of the international economic order that
they sustained.[1]

In contrast to the United Nations (UN) and most of the agencies of the
UN system in which each member state has one vote, member states' votes in
the International Monetary Fund and the World Bank are weighted in accordance with their financial contributions to the institutions. Under this arrangement, members of the Organization for Economic Cooperation and Development (OECD)—the industrialized states of North America, Western Europe,
and Australasia and Japan—have consistently held more than 55 percent of
the voting power. Furthermore, as this structural arrangement reflects, these
states control the financial resources that are essential to the Fund and the
Bank. In GATT, though there is formal voting equality among the contracting
parties, bargaining strength is based on market size, giving the United States,

---

1. Our term *neoliberal* closely corresponds with John Gerrard Ruggie's term *embedded*
liberalism. See his article "International Regimes, Transactions, and Change: Embedded Liberalism in the Postwar Economic Order," in *International Regimes*, ed. Stephen D. Krasner (Ithaca,
N.Y.: Cornell University Press, 1983), 195–232. We prefer *neoliberal* because it seems to us to
be a more accurate description and also because it is the term that many officials of the KIEOs
use.

the European Community, and Japan an enormous voice. For these reasons, the influence of the Western industrialized states is much stronger in the KIEOs than it is in the UN and like bodies.[2]

Until the 1970s, the KIEOs were comprised almost exclusively of states with market economies even though at the time of their creation, their founders envisaged that they would have universal membership. The Soviet Union refused to join them. In the late 1960s and 1970s a few of the Eastern European states joined one or more of the KIEOs, but because of the relatively small size of their economies their inclusion had little impact on the institutions. China's case was different. It raised key questions for both theory and practice as well as the prospect that the neoliberal international economic order might expand to include the two largest economies that had stood outside the order—China and the Soviet Union—and hence become a global economic order.

China's involvement in the KIEOs posed policy issues for the relevant international organizations, their member states, and China. The negotiations over China's full participation in GATT involved such thorny substantive issues as the transparency of the Chinese economic system, China's nontariff barriers, and its pricing and tariff policies. Knowledgeable officials in Geneva, Beijing, and the capitals of GATT's member states viewed the negotiations as difficult, complex, and likely to be protracted. At the World Bank, a major concern was the future scale of the Bank's activities in China, which would partly depend on the Bank's total lending capacity and on the periodic appropriations for the replenishment for the International Development Association, to be provided by the United States, the European Economic Community (EEC) countries, Japan, and other donors.[3] At the IMF, Fund officials continued to monitor China's monetary and trade position and make suggestions to remedy China's balance of payments problems. Any negotiations over the drawing of credits posed the issue of the conditions, if any, necessary to ensure that Chinese trade deficits would not become chronic.

China's entry marks a new stage in the history of the KIEOs. Those whom we interviewed were sharply aware that they were participating in a crucial historical process. Virtually unanimously our respondents shared the

---

2. See Robert W. Cox, Harold K. Jacobson, et al. *"The Anatomy of Influence: Decision Making in International Organization* (New Haven, Conn.: Yale University Press, 1973).

3. In 1987, the U.S. administration requested that Congress appropriate a total of $2.875 billion in three equal installments of $958.3 million starting with fiscal year 1988. The administration request would fulfill the U.S. obligation to provide 25 percent of the $12 billion target for the Eighth Replenishment of IDA (IDA VIII). Congress ultimately appropriated $915 million for IDA for fiscal year 1988.

view of academic observers that China's entry into the KIEOs was an "important development."[4]

In the post–World War II period, until the late 1960s, countries in Western Europe, North America, and Japan accounted for the predominant share of global economic activity. Starting the 1970s, several new nations, particularly those in East Asia, entered an era of rapid growth. This, coupled with the continuing rapid growth of Japan, widened the focal point of global economic activity to include the Pacific basin. In the 1980s, China entered a similar era of rapid economic modernization and steadily expanded its international economic activities.[5]

The patterns of economic interaction between China and the outside world that were being established in the late 1980s were likely to persist for many years. Precedents were being set that likely would govern China's external economic relations for the foreseeable future. But the incorporation of China into the KIEOs—on terms that preserve and advance the neoliberal international economic order—at this early stage in China's growth will not be easy. In a very broad sense, China's involvement in the keystone international economic organizations tests the capacity of these institutions to adjust to a changing environment. The KIEOs were designed to facilitate cooperation among states with market economies. Until the early 1980s, China had an overwhelmingly nonmarket, command economy and administered prices, and even with the economic reforms that have been adopted, China's economy was far from being predominantly based on market principles.

The underlying rules of international economic conduct grew out of the European and American experience. After having joined the KIEOs, developing countries have not succeeded in mounting a successful onslaught against the basic practices and procedures of these institutions. Rather, on balance, most developed countries have effectively utilized the KIEOs as instruments for ameliorating tensions between developed and developing countries. Deep conflicts of interest have existed among contributors to and beneficiaries of the KIEOs, and North-South polemics and demands have arisen inside, though more frequently outside, the KIEOs. Nonetheless, prior to China's participation, an uneasy pattern of interaction had gradually developed within the KIEOs that roughly accommodated the diverse values, interests, and styles of the participants.[6]

---

4. Both of the Chinese respondents ($n = 2$) strongly agreed with the statement that the entry of China into the KIEOs "is an important development"; 27.8 percent of the others agreed and 61.1 percent strongly agreed ($n = 18$).

5. See A. Doak Barnett, *China's Economy in Global Perspective* (Washington, D.C.: Brookings Institution, 1981).

6. See, for instance, Robert L. Ayres, *Banking on the Poor: The World Bank and Poverty* (Cambridge, Mass.: MIT Press, 1983).

What has been and will be the process of accommodation involved in China's entry? At least four major possibilities could be envisaged: (1) China's membership in the international economic order could so strengthen the forces demanding fundamental change in the KIEOs that existing arrangements would come under severe challenge and be transformed into a system more favorable to developing country interests; (2) China could seek to make incremental changes in the rules of the KIEOs so that Chinese traditions and practices would be incorporated into the operations of the KIEOs everywhere; (3) China could wish to be treated as a "special case," seeking exemption from the rules that are applied to other states; or (4) China could abide by the same rules that other large developing countries accept. How has the process of accommodation so far proceeded? Has one of the four possibilities been dominant or have they been realized to differing extents in different circumstances?

Implications for International Political Economy

Beyond these issues, the analysis of China's participation in the IMF, the World Bank, and GATT can be used as a case study to illuminate the interaction between international institutions and their member states and to scrutinize contemporary perspectives on—or theories of—international political economy. The Chinese case reveals how involvement in international economic institutions affects a developing country.

Many developing countries became KIEO members soon after they acquired independence and embarked upon their own development strategies. It is, therefore, difficult to identify precisely how membership in the KIEOs affected their national political and economic structures, processes, and policies since these were originally shaped to facilitate KIEO involvement. In contrast, from the mid-1960s until the mid-1970s China pursued autarkic economic policies; thus it is possible to trace the internal ramifications of China's late entry into the KIEOs. And it is possible to reconstruct how the process of entry occurred.

Hence our case study is pertinent to two broad issues in international relations theory that deal particularly with international political economy, issues that can be posed as questions. First, what are the consequences for states of membership in international organizations? Specifically, is membership in the KIEOs on balance beneficial or harmful for developing countries? Second and relatedly, what are the relationships between international organizations and trends in the international system? More pointedly, can the international organizations that were created at the end of World War II pursue their assigned purposes despite the relative decline in American power and the entry into the institutions of new members with economic and political systems that differ substantially from those of the founding states?

Turning to the first issue, several findings flow from previous studies about the interaction between international organizations and member states. These studies show that involvement in the activities of the KIEOs can noticeably affect the structures and policies of member states.[7] First, requirements for compliance with policies of international organizations may affect the participating governments. Governments may modify their policies to obtain benefits or avoid penalties; the extent of modification depends on a government's broad assessment of the domestic and international costs and benefits. Second, they may adjust domestic administrative structures to facilitate interaction with international organizations, with consequences for domestic processes and policies. For example, governments frequently create new agencies to manage their relations with an international organization and the officials in this bureau secure access to policy-making councils. This increases the chances that the norms and rules of the international organization are at least considered as governmental policy is made. Third, according to previous research, interchanges of personnel between international organizations and states are another source of influence. Through processes of socialization, individuals who serve in international organizations become more aware of the concerns, norms, and rules of international organizations. When they return home, whether or not they continue to manage relations between their government and international organization, they tend to bring this awareness to their government's consideration of its national and international policies. Examining China's participation in the IMF, the World Bank, and GATT enables us to modify and amplify these analyses and illuminate the conditions under which such changes occur.

These findings prompt a more abstract theoretical proposition: one major function of international organizations is to create and maintain networks that can gather information—data and concepts—and transmit it to and among member states and in this way facilitate international cooperation.[8] The contemporary world system is based on sovereignty; states acknowledge no

---

7. See Robin Broad, *Unequal Alliance: The World Bank, the International Monetary Fund, and the Philippines* (Berkeley: University of California Press, 1988); William T. R. Fox and Annette Baker Fox, *NATO and the Range of American Choice* (New York: Columbia University Press, 1967); L. K. Hyde, Jr., *The United States and the United Nations: Promoting the Public Welfare, Examples of American Cooperation* (New York: Carnegie Endowment for International Peace, 1960); Leon Gordenker, *International Aid and Development Decisions: Development Programs in Malawi, Tanzania and Zambia* (Princeton: Princeton University Press, 1976); Winsome J. Leslie, *The World Bank and Structural Transformation in Developing Countries: The Case of Zaire* (Boulder, Colo.: Lynne Rienner, 1987); and Stanley Please, *The Hobbled Giant: Essays on the World Bank* (Boulder, Colo.: Westview Press, 1984).

8. See Harold K. Jacobson, *Networks of Interdependence: International Organizations and the Global Political System*, 2d. ed. (New York: Alfred A. Knopf, 1984).

higher authority. Yet interdependence is high in the contemporary era due to the progress of science and technology; avoiding harmful and destructive actions and achieving mutually beneficial goals require that states adjust and coordinate their policies. Such adjustment and coordination can be achieved through coercion only at great cost; striving for consensus is much more attractive. By gathering and transmitting information, international organizations can provide a basis for achieving consensus; indeed, information can have a compelling quality, and even lead to a convergence of values. Analytical concepts—such as the notion of "gross national product"—provide uniform measures so that states can compare their behavior with that of others and learn from the experience of others. By so doing they can avoid ineffective and costly courses and choose those that have had high success rates. The transmission of information also facilitates states's anticipation of the likely reactions of other states to policies that they may adopt. It enables states to frame their policies in the context of knowledge about what other states have done in the past and are likely to do in the future. Such information may help gradually to force an international consensus on norms of behavior. Governments can become convinced that if certain practices are observed the benefits that all states involved obtain will exceed the costs that they incur.

Research about international regimes, especially by Robert O. Keohane, has suggested that participation in international institutions affects national policies by helping to overcome what he terms "political market failure."[9] By facilitating the transmission of information, international organizations reduce uncertainties and asymmetries of access to information. By providing a setting for regular meetings of members, international institutions affect transaction costs by "making it easier for governments to get together to negotiate agreements."[10] Once agreements are in place, acts that violate them have more serious implications than would have been the case in the absence of these agreements. Retaliation may be justified, and violation of an agreement with respect to one issue may call into question the sanctity of agreements concerning other issues. According to Keohane, regimes promote compliance with their rules by affecting "the calculations of self-interest in which rational, egoistic governments engage."[11] Once a regime is in place, acts that threaten it have serious costs, involving not only the issue at stake, but others as well. Regimes transform unique acts into acts that form part of a series, thus increasing their significance. A state's failure to comply with one rule may

---

9. See Robert O. Keohane, *After Hegemony: Cooperation and Discord in the World Political Economy* (Princeton: Princeton University Press, 1984); and Stephen D. Krasner, ed., *International Regimes* (Ithaca, N.Y.: Cornell University Press, 1983).

10. Robert O. Keohane, *After Hegemony*, 90.

11. Robert O. Keohane, *After Hegemony*, 100.

affect the future willingness of other states to follow this and other rules.

The optimistic perspective we have just outlined views the interaction between international organizations and member states as reciprocal and beneficial for all member countries and for the creation of a more peaceful, stable, and equitable world. Other analysts describe the same process of interaction—at least as it involves the KIEOs—in very different, pessimistic terms. Dependency, neo-Marxist, and many world systems theorists regard these international institutions as instruments of capitalist—and often specifically of United States—domination. Writing about the World Bank, Cheryl Payer put the issue clearly:

> . . . the World Bank is perhaps the most important instrument of the developed capitalist countries for prying state control of its Third World member countries out of the hands of nationalists and socialists who would regulate international capital's inroads, and turning that power to the service of international capital.[12]

As this quotation underscores, those holding these views see the three institutions as instruments for bringing developing countries into the capitalist, or U.S.-dominated, order and ensuring that they pursue policies appropriate to this order. They believe that the United States and other developed capitalist countries dictate the policies of the KIEOs. They argue that the three institutions' policies and programs have the consequence of blocking possibilities for indigenous economic growth within developing countries and preventing social transformation. They maintain that compliance with the KIEOs' policies puts unfair and disproportionate burdens on the poor and disadvantaged within developing countries, or as Cheryl Payer put it, the World Bank promotes "malignant growth." From this perspective, China's absence from the KIEOs was desirable, and its involvement in them could only have harmful consequences for China and by extension for other developing countries. Has China's initial experience with the KIEOs tended to support the optimistic or pessimistic view of the role of the KIEOs in today's world? We return to this question in our conclusion.

Our case study also sheds light on how international organizations are affected by the nature of the international system. Hegemonic stability theorists see the United States as playing an essential role in the keystone international economic organizations.[13] In their view, the KIEOs resulted from U.S.

---

12. Cheryl Payer, *The World Bank: A Critical Analysis* (New York: Monthly Review Press, 1982), 20.

13. See particularly Charles P. Kindelberger, "Dominance and Leadership in the International Economy," *International Studies Quarterly* 25, no. 3 (1981): 242–54. Kindelberger's theory of hegemonic stability was first expounded in his now classic work, *The World in Depression, 1929–1939* (Berkeley: University of California Press, 1973).

hegemony in the post–World War II era; they were established and functioned smoothly as a consequence of U.S. hegemony. The relative power of the United States, stemming from the preponderance of material resources under its control, was so compelling that other countries were naturally inclined to follow U.S. wishes, and U.S. strength and wealth were so great that it was easy for the United States to bear a disproportionate share of the costs of establishing and maintaining the collective goods that the KIEOs represented. Theorists of this persuasion argue that a hegemonic power—Great Britain in the nineteenth century and the United States in the mid-twentieth century—is necessary for the creation and maintenance of a liberal or neoliberal international economic order. In the late 1980s, hegemonic stability theorists were divided as to whether or not the United States retained a hegemonic position in the global system. Those who believed that the United States retained hegemonic power would expect that as long as China's involvement with the KIEOs suited the United States and was supported by the United States, it would proceed smoothly. Those who doubted that the United States retained hegemonic power would be more skeptical, and could see China's involvement raising difficulties or contributing to the further decline of the KIEOs and erosion of their rules.

A variant of hegemonic stability theory, espoused particularly by Robert O. Keohane in his theorizing about international regimes, maintains that although a hegemonic power may have been necessary for the establishment of the international institutions and rules essential to the post–World War II neoliberal international economic order, these institutions and rules can now be maintained without a hegemon.[14] According to this view, the consequences of China's involvement with the KIEOs would depend upon how well the institutions and rules of the neoliberal international economic order had been established and on the policies pursued by the more powerful members. If the institutions and rules were firmly rooted, and the more powerful members pursued constructive cooperative policies, China could become involved with minimum disruption; otherwise the issue would be more problematic.

Classical liberalism provides yet another perspective on China's involvement with the KIEOs. Those who ground their understanding of the contemporary world on classical liberal principles are critical of the KIEOs to the extent that they promote procedures and rules that deviate from pure market principles.[15] In this perspective, the involvement of China—an immense country that despite the reform that has occurred still adheres in substantial measure to governmental planning and state ownership of the means of

---

14. See Robert O. Keohane, *After Hegemony.*

15. See, for example, Peter T. Bauer, *Reality and Rhetoric: Studies in the Economics of Development* (Cambridge, Mass.: Harvard University Press, 1984).

production—with the KIEOs is likely to lead these institutions into further departures from market principles. Has China's involvement warranted their foreboding?

Another set of observers, who might be called "neomercantilists," believe that the world economy is inescapably heading toward increased protectionism and state intervention in international economic affairs. Their plea is for the United States to develop its own industrial policy and to gear itself for effective competition with other neomercantilist states. They would argue that the desire to incorporate China into the neoliberal international monetary, financial, and trade regimes is either misplaced or dangerous; misplaced because China will adopt the protective coloration of a market economy while retaining the essence of a neomercantilist state. Under those circumstances, the United States would be allowing a dangerous fox into the chicken coop it should be constructing. Does the analysis of China's involvement with the KIEOs through mid-1989 support these arguments?

Undergirding all these questions—immediate and long-term, specific and general—are more fundamental issues. What sort of challenge does the incorporation of China pose to the international economy? Phrased simply in terms of the magnitude of the challenge, is China's emergence likely to be highly contentious and disruptive? Phrased in more sophisticated terms, what factors affect the manner in which China's involvement takes place?

The Implications for China

Thus far we have focused on the significance of our topic for the KIEOs. Equally interesting and important are the implications for China. What sort of challenge do its moves toward the international economy pose for China? Can China still pursue the values it chooses and play a larger role in the international economy? Its political leaders and mass media until the late 1970s regularly flailed the KIEOs as mechanisms which facilitated imperialist exploitation and domination of the world. The same leaders rejected the notion of global interdependence and the theory of comparative advantage; they proclaimed policies of extreme self-reliance, sought balanced trade with each trading partner, avoided foreign borrowing and indebtedness, and sought to build a totally self-sufficient or comprehensive national economy. The entire political and economic system of China for nearly two decades was rooted in these principles, and over time, sprawling bureaucracies developed whose missions were derived from these principles.

In the 1980s China's leaders enunciated somewhat different principles. Still committed to a planned economy and basic self-reliance, their policies tacitly accepted the validity of such Western economic concepts as comparative advantage, an international economic division of labor, global interdependence, the usefulness of the marketplace, and prudent foreign indebtedness.[16] Policies derived from these ideas, however, challenged interests and viewpoints rooted in the previous order, and potentially threatened such fundamental socialist beliefs as the importance of ensuring an equitable distribution of the country's product, maintaining stable prices, and preventing unemployment. Bureaucracies tend to resist alterations, especially those that could result in diminutions of their authority, and thus perhaps adjustments necessary to facilitate cooperation with the KIEOs and involvement in the neoliberal international system. Many citizens, accustomed to an extremely stable personal economic environment, tend to be reluctant to face the challenges of differential incomes, fluctuating prices, and possible unemployment. Our topic therefore sheds light on a central issue: the capacity of nonmarket economies in their search for greater efficiency to transform themselves into planned market or even market economies and the role that the KIEOs can play in easing the transition.

A comprehensive assessment of China's entry into the international economy requires examining the size of its overall exports and imports, the composition of its trade, the direction of its trade, the size of its internal markets, its economic growth rates, its foreign capital requirements, its foreign currency reserves, external debt, and so on, and to chart the trends in light of global economic trends. The analysis would explore whether and how the world could absorb an economy of this sort, with the inquiry informed by comparisons with such previous entrants as Japan, South Korea, or Taiwan.

Such an assessment would be extremely complicated.[17] In lieu of such a detailed analysis, which is currently unavailable in the scholarly literature, one can sketch the broad dimensions of the issue. In the late twentieth century, China's gross national product has consistently ranked among the ten largest, and was eighth in 1980. China's exports have grown rapidly throughout the 1980s, roughly doubling in value from 1979 to 1986. Even so, its share of world exports in 1986 amounted to only 1.8 percent.[18] Since most world trade occurs between developed countries, more significant statistics concern China's ranking among the developing countries. In 1986 Chinese exports totaled roughly 5.6 percent of all exports from the developing countries, in contrast to its 3.4 percent share in 1980. In 1980, China ranked eighth among developing country exporters, while in 1986, China had become the fourth leading exporter among developing countries, and was on the verge of

---

16. This shift is described and analyzed in Harry Harding, *China's Second Revolution: Reform after Mao* (Washington, D.C.: Brookings Institution, 1987).

17. Harry Harding provides an overview in *China's Second Revolution*, chap. 6.

18. IMF, *Direction of Trade Statistics Yearbook, 1987* (Washington, D.C.: IMF, 1987), 2–7.

surpassing the Soviet Union in total exports. Chinese export performance in 1987 continued to be impressive. Total exports climbed to $39,464 million, 6.8 percent of all exports from developing countries.[19] China's export performance in 1987 among developing countries continued to rank only behind that of Taiwan, Hong Kong, and the Republic of Korea.[20] In 1987 China ranked sixteenth among all exporting countries. Its exports exceeded those of such developed countries as Spain, the German Democratic Republic, Austria, Australia, Denmark, Czechoslovakia, and Norway.

This rapid increase in Chinese exports has not caused great anxiety among its major trading partners, except in textiles and in a few other select commodities. These figures suggest that China has been increasing its market share at the cost of the market share of other developing countries, and that this is happening rapidly. One non-American governmental study projects that China could well have captured 20 to 30 percent of worldwide cotton fabric exports by the early 1990s. In certain other select markets—such as East Asian raw cotton and coal markets—China promises to give stiff competition to traditional suppliers.

In contrast, China's imports have developed unsteadily, reflecting the fluctuations in the domestic economy. Nevertheless, the growth has been substantial. By 1986, China's purchases abroad accounted for 8.2 percent of total imports by developing countries, which placed China as the largest market among developing countries. As it sought to rein in its economy, in 1987 China's imports remained more or less constant in absolute terms, but declined relatively, accounting for only 7.2 percent of those of developing countries, and Hong Kong assumed the place of the largest developing country market. Japan has become China's largest supplier by far, regularly capturing from a quarter to a third of the China market. China jumped from being Japan's fifth largest customer in 1980 to second place in 1985, but then dropped back to fifth in 1987.

China's absorption of foreign capital has also grown rapidly. Given the heavy debt burden of other developing countries (which discourages further capital inflows) and China's eagerness for foreign investment, the People's Republic became one of the leading recipients of foreign investments among developing nations in the mid-1980s. A high portion of the incoming funds is Overseas Chinese in origin and is devoted to upgrading tourist facilities. Foreign investment in China in 1988 exceeded $7 billion. Including obliga-

---

19. IMF, *Direction of Trade Statistics Yearbook, 1988* (Washington, D.C.: IMF, 1988), 2–7.

20. GATT, *International Trade: 87–88* (Geneva: GATT, 1988), 2:7.

tions arising from these investments and various forms of borrowing, China's external debt as of 1986 totaled over $44 billion.[21] This was well within the limits of a prudent debt load. Experts both in and outside China expected that the PRC's external debt would continue to grow as such agencies as the Ministry of Finance, the Bank of China, and the China International Trust and Investment Corporation entered the world money markets.

These statistics reveal the swiftness with which China has become a significant actor in the world economy. In less than a decade, China has become a factor to be reckoned with. Its surge in world economic affairs stems from its robust domestic economy—China's gross domestic product (GDP) grew at an average annual rate of 10.5 percent during the period 1980–86—making it one of the most rapidly expanding economies in the world.[22] On top of this, the portion of the national economy devoted to foreign trade has grown rapidly. According to World Bank data, exports constituted 6.4 percent of China's gross national product in 1980, but in 1986 the figure was 10.0 percent, and imports, which had been 6.9 percent of GNP in 1980 were 13.7 percent six years later.[23] These proportions were relatively high for a country as large as China. Many American economists believe that the methods of calculating this figure are misleading and exaggerate the percentage of GNP in the foreign trade domain. Nonetheless these experts agree with the conclusion that foreign trade has grown rapidly absolutely and as a percentage of GNP.

A more extensive assessment of such data would probably yield the following conclusion: the absorption of China into the world economy should not involve an insurmountable challenge. Neither the increments in its exports nor its thirst for foreign capital necessarily poses a major burden to an *expanding* world economy, while China's large appetite for foreign goods—largely constrained by its shortage of foreign exchange—can be a minor stimulus for world economic growth. However, China could prove quite disruptive if its expansion occurred without concern for established trading patterns, or the process could be derailed if fears in the developed world brought on rampant protectionism. Thus, the ability to absorb China into the world economy will be substantially shaped by the perceptions and expectations of the Chinese and their trading partners concerning global economic trends and the consequences of Chinese behavior in international affairs.

---

21. IBRD, *World Tables, 1987*, 4th ed. (Washington, D.C.: IBRD, 1987), 99.
22. IBRD, *World Development Report 1987* (Washington, D.C.: IBRD, 1988), 224.
23. IBRD, *World Tables, 1987*, 4th ed. (Washington, D.C.: IBRD, 1988).

A Historical Perspective

China's participation in the KIEOs, the United Nations system, and the world economy more generally followed a protracted period of separation from the West since 1949 and involvement with the Soviet bloc in the 1950s. But it is worth remembering that this is not the first time in modern times that the leaders of China have sought to become involved in international organizations and play an integral role in world affairs. Since China's policies of hostility toward and isolation from the West persisted for three decades, many outside observers concluded these policies were deeply embedded in Chinese tradition and reflected indigenous strands of intellectual thought. These observations were correct, but historians such as Paul Cohen, John Fairbank, Joseph Levenson, and Mark Mancall always stressed that the antiforeign and nativistic traditions that flourished in the Maoist era and that indeed could be traced far back in Chinese history coexisted in uneasy tension with more cosmopolitan traditions.[24] Historians have labeled these the traditions of coastal China and the interior: the former outward looking and trade oriented, the latter closedminded and bureaucratic. The Western aggression against China in the nineteenth century generated an intense debate between the inheritors of the two traditions.

In reality, the range of views cannot be easily classified into two categories.[25] Rather, a spectrum existed. At one pole stood the bearers of the "coastal tradition," who advocated an energetic Chinese involvement in world affairs as the best way to respond to the West. At the other extreme were the representatives of orthodoxy, who championed keeping the foreigners at arm's length. While the two poles have defined the terms of the debate for over a century, the majority of leaders fell at intermediate points along the continuum. Many individuals exhibited considerable ambivalence over the issues at stake and appeared to embrace both poles simultaneously. Moreover, leaders such as Chiang Kai-shek, Mao Zedong, and Deng Xiaoping changed their views over time.

The attraction and strength of these various positions along the spectrum varied through time. On several occasions, as in the 1980s, advocates of engagement in world affairs dominated the apex of the political system. Such

---

24. See Paul A. Cohen, *China and Christianity: The Missionary Movement and the Growth of Chinese Anti Foreignism, 1860–1870* (Cambridge, Mass.: Harvard University Press, 1963); Joseph R. Levenson, *Liang Ch'i-ch'ao and the Mind of Modern China* (Berkeley: University of California Press, 1970); and Mark Mancall, *China at the Center: Three Hundred Years of Foreign Policy* (New York: Free Press, 1984).

25. See Michel Oksenberg and Steven Goldstein, "The Chinese Political Spectrum," *Problems of Communism* 23, no. 2 (March–April, 1974): 1-13.

moments also had occurred in the mid-1800s, in the era after World War I, and in the aftermath of World War II.[26] The ascendancy of the cosmopolitans accompanied institutional changes to give the central government the organizational capability to deal with the outside world. Students were dispatched abroad to learn foreign cultures and languages, international law, military science, and foreign technology. And China participated in international conferences and organizations, dispatching diplomats such as Wellington Koo to Paris to attend the Versailles peace conference in 1919, or vigorously enjoining the League of Nations to respond to the Japanese invasion of Manchuria in 1931, or through the skilled efforts of T. V. Soong and H. H. Kung entreating the United States to heed vital Chinese interests during the silver debacle in 1934.[27] In these and other instances, Chinese diplomats and negotiators earned the admiration of their foreign counterparts for their skill, tenacity, and dedication to internationalist principles.

However, civil war, foreign aggression, or domestic political intrigue terminated the previous eras of cosmopolitanism. It is worth briefly mentioning the previous instances during which Chinese hopes were dashed in international arenas, for the policy failures in international arenas led the cosmopolitans to be perceived within China as lackeys of foreigners. For example, for all their diplomatic skill, neither Koo nor Soong was able to attain major triumphs. And in any case, the cosmopolitans frequently became disillusioned with their internationalist cause, for their reception in the international community did not meet their expectations. They believed that they represented a great and large civilization, but despite their personal diplomatic skills, they received the treatment accorded to representatives of weak and divided nations. Most disappointingly, during the 1930s the League of Nations completely failed to protect China against Japan's aggression, offering at most only moral support.

To the historian and to many Chinese, mainland China's participation in the United Nations system since 1971 contains an element of déjà vu. Lurking in the background are the questions prompted by the past record: Will the

---

26. See especially Masa taka Banno, *China and the West, Eighteen Fifty-Eight to Eighteen Sixty-One: The Origins of the Tsungli Yamen* (Cambridge, Mass.: Harvard University Press, 1964); Immanuel C. Y. Hsu, *The Rise of Modern China* (Oxford: Oxford University Press, 1982); James C. Thomson, Jr., *While China Faced West: American Reformers in Nationalist China, 1928–1937* (Cambridge, Mass.: Harvard University Press, 1974); Wang Yi Chu, *Chinese Intellectuals and the West, 1872–1949* (Chapel Hill: University of North Carolina Press, 1966).

27. Accounts of these instances can be found in Werner Levi, *Modern China's Foreign Policy* (Minneapolis: University of Minnesota Press, 1953); Dorothy Borg, *The United States and the Far Eastern Crisis of 1933–1938* (Cambridge, Mass.: Harvard University Press, 1964); and Arthur Young, *China and the Helping Hand, 1937-1945* (Cambridge, Mass.: Harvard University Press, 1963).

cosmopolitans prevail and endure this time? Will the international community accord China the stature it seeks? Or will Chinese expectations in the international arena again go unmet, to the political detriment of the cosmopolitans?

History suggests that an element of caution is warranted, as does the resurgence of antiforeign sentiment among the leaders following the Beijing tragedy of June 4, 1989, and this cautionary note surfaces at several points in this account. Yet viewing contemporary events against the historical record also provides some basis for cautious optimism, if not immediately, then in the longer run. First, in contrast to the previous instances, this Chinese entry into the international community occurs when mainland China is unified and has acquired military might. The basis exists for a relationship based on respect for Chinese strength. Second, the community of Western nations has changed; it is more prepared to welcome China on equitable terms than on previous occasions. Finally, there is a legacy of the previous cosmopolitanism upon which to build. All of these factors came into play during Beijing's involvement with the KIEOs from 1980 to 1989. Nonetheless, it is also worth stressing that the Western attitude toward China's inclusion in the international community also depends upon the rulers of China governing their country effectively and in increasingly humane fashion.

Our Chinese colleagues have stressed that, while the spectrum we have described above is valid, important changes have occurred within it over the decades. Today's "nativists" are much more aware of China's need for foreign technology than the nativists of the late nineteenth century. The Cultural Revolution and its aftermath, coupled with the rapid development of Japan, South Korea, Taiwan, and Hong Kong, underscored to all Chinese the high cost of isolation from world affairs.

Most of the Chinese with whom we spoke also emphasized that the "cosmopolitan-nativist" spectrum is not the only or even the most important dimension along which political debate occurred in the China of the 1980s. Rather, they suggested, another critical divide was between those who enthusiastically supported the domestic economic reforms and those who were skeptical of reform, either out of long- or short-term considerations. According to these colleagues, cosmopolitans could be found on both sides of the divide, with some arguing for and others against such internal changes as rapid expansion of the market, bureaucratic decentralization, or extensive liberalization in the economic and political realms. Moreover, our sources claimed that one should not assume that exposure to the West necessarily predisposes Chinese to be cosmopolitan. One senior American-trained economist, for example, was well known to be deeply troubled about China's entry into the international economy but also was quite supportive of reforms intended to produce a more efficient, better managed economy.

Cosmopolitan advocates of additional, rapid reform believed such change is necessary to facilitate entry into the world, while cosmopolitan opponents of reform believed further domestic changes—at least at this point—would risk loss of control over the process of entry. Similarly, some nativists supported limited domestic reforms as the necessary route to enable China more effectively to resist the outside world, while other nativists opposed the domestic reforms due to their perceived linkage to the outside world.

This important qualification to our argument has two significant implications. First, not every setback for reform should be interpreted as a triumph of the nativists. It may represent a victory of cosmopolitans who seek a careful and controlled entry into the world. Second, one should not assume the domestic reforms and the involvement in the world economy are integrally intertwined in all Chinese minds. Clearly, some Chinese sought an entry in which the domestic reforms remain circumscribed, but many outside observers believe this position is unrealistic. Involvement in the international economy, they contend, necessarily introduces the need for economic and political reform.

Principal Findings

At least in the first decade of its unfolding, the initial inclusion of China into the KIEOs was successful, judged by the standards of both sides. By and large, China abided by the rules that other large developing countries accepted. Moreover, China made discernible contributions to the operations of the KIEOs, particularly by helping to ameliorate tensions between the developed and developing countries. The hesitancy about Chinese membership, not openly voiced but frequently acknowledged in private interviews with officials from all quarters, came not from developed but developing countries, especially India, who competed with China for the resources that the KIEOs distribute.

The involvement of the World Bank and IMF in China grew rapidly. These organizations came to play significant roles, most importantly in reinforcing the reform program and the opening to the outside world that the leaders of China have pursued since 1978. Membership prompted changes in policies, policy processes, and institutions in China. Perhaps more significantly, the contacts between China's leaders and Fund and Bank officials, coupled with the influence of other Western economists, altered the perceptions of many Chinese leaders about both the world economy and their own economic performance. Standards of evaluation derived from Western economic theory, in the minds of many, replaced concepts imported from the Soviet Union in the 1950s.

At the same time, greater openness in the release of statistics and greater attention to accuracy in their accumulation meant China acquired a larger role in shaping Western evaluations of its performance. Before 1980, the U.S. Central Intelligence Agency (CIA) assembled the data on which the Fund, Bank, and third-country analyses were based. Since 1980, the responsibility has resided in Beijing.

The record of accomplishment was both impeded and facilitated by the Chinese sense of pride, greatness, and self-confidence. These qualities led the Chinese swiftly to reject *demands* by outside agencies to undertake changes but also enabled them to accept outside *advice* when the advice seemed appropriate. Both the KIEOs and the Chinese were circumspect about the tough bargaining that has gone on behind the scenes. Neither the Chinese nor the KIEOs were reticent in expressing their views, but the differences were settled through quiet diplomacy rather than through public posturing. Even the discussions on full Chinese participation in GATT largely escaped the glare of publicity. As a result, a measure of flexibility and mutual confidence was sustained in negotiations.

Success was not easily attained, however. On the Chinese side, its participation in the KIEOs and more generally the acceptance, albeit gradual, incomplete, and grudging, of the notion of global interdependence raised politically difficult domestic issues and encountered considerable opposition in Beijing. The hard-core supporters of isolationist economic policies—the cultural revolutionists—suffered setbacks in the early 1970s and were eliminated from the political arena following Mao's death in 1976. The opponents of releasing data to the KIEOs and of employing Western economic concepts for analyzing Chinese economic performance were by the early 1980s pushed to the sidelines, where they remained eager to reenter the political playing field. These conservative Marxist economists remained committed to a centralized, planned economic system, and they rejected the policy implications resulting from use of Western yardsticks of evaluation. Finally, the bureaucracies whose interests were harmed by KIEO membership were still active opponents. Thus, the possibility always existed for a reversal of course, should the domestic reform program that accompanied the economic opening to the outside world encounter severe difficulties. And there were limits to the pace of adjustments that ordinary Chinese were willing to accept.

Three broad factors explained the initial successes: a propitious international setting; wise leadership, careful planning, and patience on the part of both China and the KIEOs; and sensitivity on both sides to the political needs of the other. The international strategic setting was an essential factor—perhaps even a prerequisite—propelling the KIEOs to welcome China's interest. Since President Nixon's opening to Beijing in 1971, the United States, Japan, and the European Community countries believed that the inclusion of China in the international systems they led would draw China out of its dangerous isolation. The Cultural Revolution of 1966–69 had underscored the problems that an isolated and weak China would pose to stability in Asia. Thus, the principal member states of the KIEOs perceived strategic benefits to be gained from the incorporation of China. Similarly, in the 1970s and early 1980s Chinese leaders perceived a wide range of benefits to be derived from inclusion in the international system from which they had been excluded, especially as they then were under considerable pressure from the Soviet Union. The importance of the shift in the American posture, as an explanatory factor, of course, tends to support the validity of hegemonic stability theorists.

But the international setting itself was not sufficient. After all, the record clearly shows that the receptivity of the Fund and Bank to Chinese membership in 1980 came against the expressed though not unyielding opposition of the U.S. secretary of the treasury. Reference must also be made to the leaders of the KIEOs and China. Robert McNamara and A. W. Clausen at the World Bank, Jacques de Larosiere at the IMF, Arthur Dunkel at the GATT, and their staffs were important, independent actors in the drama. Due to their initiatives, the Bank, the IMF, and the GATT helped to create and then responded with alacrity to the opportunity to work with China. They acted upon their visions of a global neoliberal economic order. This part of the story tends to confirm Robert Keohane's argument that the institutions and rules of the neoliberal international economic order can be maintained without a hegemon.

China's leaders also played an indispensable part. China's preeminent leader, Deng Xiaoping, Communist party General Secretary and Premier Zhao Ziyang, and other reform-minded leaders proclaimed the policies that permitted membership in the KIEOs. They encouraged Chinese bureaucrats to cooperate with the Fund and the Bank. In addition, a number of sophisticated and farsighted Chinese economists, mostly over sixty years of age in the early 1980s, guided China's approach to the KIEOs. Communities of senior and middle-level economists in such key agencies as the Bank of China, the People's Bank, and the ministries of finance, foreign economic relations and trade, and foreign affairs; researchers in the Chinese Academy of Social Sciences; and academics in universities were able to act on their visions of China's playing an integral role in the creation of a more equitable international economic system. These communities, enjoying access to and the backing of top leaders, played a decisive role in forging the contacts with the outside world. Both they and the top leaders were indispensable to the process; neither could have done the job alone.

Finally, the KIEOs and the Chinese approached each other with foresight, maturity, and sensitivity. In particular, our research unearthed new information about China's careful and methodical preparation for membership in the IMF and the World Bank, dating to the PRC's acquisition of its United Nations seat in 1971. They approached negotiations about GATT in similar fashion. This care on both sides meant that each was keenly aware of the issues and trends confronting its potential partner. Each side sought to take these changes into account and to meet the needs of its potential partner. For instance, the Chinese repeatedly demonstrated keen sensitivity to the domestic politics of KIEO members, and they timed their moves accordingly. For example, they applied for IMF and World Bank membership only after the Sino-American trade agreement of 1979 had received congressional blessing in early 1980. Beijing did not wish prematurely to risk its dealings with Congress by demanding Taiwan's expulsion from the IMF while the trade agreement was still pending on the Hill. As another example, it understood the World Bank's need not to reallocate funds available under IDA's Sixth Replenishment to China so as to avoid antagonizing other developing countries. China sought ways to assist President Ronald Reagan in rebuffing congressional protectionist pressures by appearing to be reasonable in its overall trade posture. Its approach to GATT grows partly out of that strategy. The Fund, Bank, and GATT exhibited similar sensitivity to Chinese concerns.

The politics behind KIEO-Chinese cooperation illuminate the contingent or problematic quality of the process. This dimension is sometimes neglected by or is inaccessible to scholars of international affairs. We seek to unearth this dimension in the following, empirical chapters. We posit that the process of China's participation in the KIEOs entails discernible stages, and each chapter analyzes a separate stage. Chapter 2 sets the stage by describing the trends within the KIEOs and China as they initiated contact with each other. Chapter 3, on the process of engagement, traces the negotiations and the internal preparations that the IMF and World Bank and China undertook as their paths came together. Chapter 4 continues this story for GATT. Chapter 5, on the process of initial participation, describes the cooperation that ensued. Chapter 6, on the process of mutual adjustment, analyzes the consequences of China's membership for the KIEOs and China.

Our concluding chapter looks to the future and, drawing upon our findings, stipulates conditions for the continued, successful inclusion of China in the KIEOs and for the possible inclusion of the Soviet Union; in other words, for the creation of a global economic order. Our conclusion, though optimistic for the long run, is cautious and guarded. While the underlying strategic setting conducive to China's inclusion in the international economy and hence the KIEOs attitude is likely to persist, the signs of protectionism in China, vexation with China's economic practices, or its turn away from economic and political reform could change Western attitudes toward China. But even if the future is a more complicated one, the record of the past offers some clues as to what might go wrong and how to ameliorate the difficulties.

CHAPTER 2

Two Moving Targets
of Undetermined Trajectories

China's participation in the KIEOs entails the inclusion of a nation in the midst of change in international governmental organizations also in the midst of change. The process of integration involves neither the forging of links between stationary objects nor the move of one (either China or the KIEOs) toward the other. Moreover, the developmental paths of China and the KIEOs do not primarily result from some strong magnetic attraction between them. Rather, their trajectories are largely determined by their responses to the broad challenges and opportunities that their respective leaders and institutions confront. The changes in the KIEOs are not occurring primarily in order to facilitate China's membership, nor is China transforming itself just so it can be involved in the KIEOs. Thus, the process we describe in subsequent chapters occurred in no small measure because the *separate* developmental paths of China and the KIEOs converged. Nonetheless, as our account also makes clear, the serendipitous convergence was not enough. As China and the KIEOs approached one another, efforts were necessary on both sides to ensure that the institutional linkages occurred. Here is where the leaders, bureaucrats, and intellectuals in China, the KIEOs, and their member states played their political roles.

To capture this complex process, our analysis must be multifaceted. We must explore both the independent developments of China and the KIEOs and the forging of links between them. We must trace the organizational consequences of those links upon China and the KIEOs, and we must assess in turn the ramifications of these internal changes upon the external ties. We begin our analysis with separate treatments of the KIEOs and China.

The Origins and Purposes of the KIEOs

To understand trends in the KIEOs at the time of China's involvement in them, it is essential to review their origins and evolution. The IMF and the World Bank were created at the Bretton Woods Conference in 1944. Both were designed to correct problems that had plagued the international economy during the 1930s: the competitive devaluation and nonconvertibility of currencies and the drying up of international investment.[1] Both problems had contributed to the disastrous slump in international trade and the prolonged economic depression. Efforts to solve these problems in the 1930s, including those undertaken by the League of Nations, had achieved very little.

The IMF and the World Bank were innovative efforts to tackle these problems anew. They drew on studies conducted by universities, research institutes, national governments, and the League of Nations of the catastrophes of the 1930s. Utilizing the framework of Keynesian economics, these studies proposed ways to avoid repeating the catastrophes.

The IMF's purpose was ". . . to promote exchange stability, to maintain orderly exchange arrangements among members, and to avoid competitive exchange depreciation."[2] Especially after the failure of the London Economic Conference of 1933, as countries faced increasingly severe balance of payments problems, a growing number made their currencies nonconvertible in order to control and limit their imports. This contributed to the downward spiral of international trade. Countries also engaged in competitive devaluations, hoping to discourage imports and encourage exports, in effect seeking to solve their unemployment problems at the expense of other countries.

Under the IMF's Articles of Agreement, member countries were assigned quotas; the size of a country's quota was roughly based on its share in international trade. Countries' voting rights were based on their quotas. Each country was obliged to give 25 percent of its quota to the Fund in gold and the remainder in its national currency. The IMF uses the monetary resources placed at its disposal to make short-term loans to countries that suffer temporary balance of payments difficulties. These loans—or in IMF terminology, drawings—enable member countries to cover balance of payments deficits so that they would not have to devalue their currencies or make them nonconvertible. In effect, the IMF manages a pool of shared resources that increases the reserve funds of member countries. If a member country has a balance of payments need, it is entitled to draw its reserve tranche, which is equivalent to the amount of gold that it deposited with the Fund—or one quarter of its quota, without challenge from the Fund. Drawings in the four credit tranches, each equal to one quarter of the country's quota—the sum equaling the country's total quota, require justification in terms of balance of

---

1. Charles Kindelberger describes this collapse of the international economic order and attributes it to the decline of British hegemony in his *The World in Depression, 1929–1939* (Berkeley: University of California Press, 1973).

2. Article I, Section (iii) of IMF's Articles of Agreement. For a good, brief, broad overview of IMF see Margaret Garritsen de Vries, *The IMF in a Changing World, 1945–1985* (Washington, D.C.: IMF, 1986). Kenneth W. Dam has written an excellent longer account, *The Rules of the Game: Reform and Evolution in the International Monetary System* (Chicago: University of Chicago Press, 1982).

payments needs and a commitment by the country to the IMF to pursue policies designed to ameliorate the balance of payments deficits. Undertaking the commitment is a condition for obtaining permission from the Fund to make the drawing. Over the years, the Fund has developed various supplementary facilities that have enabled countries to draw amounts that equal from three to four times their quotas. The Fund imposes progressively stiffer conditions for drawings in the higher credit tranches and in the supplementary facilities.[3] Since the purpose of Fund drawings is to enable countries to surmount temporary balance of payments difficulties, and the loans are for short periods, the conditionality of the loans is virtually axiomatic, but because the IMF's conditions often require implementing domestic policies that involve cutting back imports, public employment, and subsidies, they are often, if not always, the subject of domestic political controversy.[4]

As a corollary to the Fund's oversight of member's exchange rate policies and its lending activities, the Fund requires members to collect and publish economic statistics according to Fund determined standards.[5] The Fund also provides technical assistance in the areas of its competence to member states.

The purpose of the International Bank for Reconstruction and Development was to reinvigorate private foreign investment. Because of the large number of defaults on foreign loans that occurred during the 1920s and 1930s, the confidence of investors plummeted, and private foreign investment had virtually evaporated by the time World War II began. IBRD was to become the "lender of last resort."[6] At the time of Bretton Woods, postwar reconstruction was seen as the primary need for international investment and development as a secondary purpose. Reconstruction needs, however, exceeded the Bank's capacity, or the willingness of the United States to fund that capacity, and development soon became the Bank's primary purpose.

Under IBRD's Articles of Agreement, member countries subscribe to capital shares. These shares are related to countries' quotas in IMF, and membership in the Bank is open only to members of the International Mone-

---

3. The process of member countries drawing Fund resources is described in "How Countries Use Resources through Tranches, Facilities," IMF, *Survey*, January 5, 1976, 2–3.

4. For a discussion of the economic and noneconomic issues raised by conditionality see John Williamson, ed., *IMF Conditionality* (Washington, D.C.: Institute for International Economics, 1983). An IMF view of conditionality is presented in Manuel Guitian, *Fund Conditionality: Evolution of Principles and Practices*, IMF Pamphlet Series, no. 38 (Washington D.C.: IMF, 1981).

5. Article VIII, Section (v), IMF Articles of Agreement.

6. See Article I, Section (ii) of IBRD's Articles of Agreement. For a good history of the first two decades of the World Bank see Edward S. Mason and Robert E. Asher, *The World Bank since Bretton Woods* (Washington, D.C.: Brookings Institution, 1973).

tary Fund. Countries' voting rights are proportional to their voting shares. Twenty percent of members' subscriptions are subject to call as needed by the Bank for its operations, and the remaining 80 percent are subject to call by the Bank to meet obligations arising out of its lending operations. Countries have to provide the Bank with only 1 percent of their subscription in convertible funds, and 9 percent in non-interest-bearing letters of credit in their own currency, although most developed countries make most or all of the full amount of their paid-in capital available for Bank purposes. IBRD makes loans to members from its unimpaired paid-in capital and surplus. In addition, it raises funds on private capital markets, which it then relends to members; the Bank's authorized capital is assurance that it will repay its loans. Finally, the Bank can use its authorized capital to guarantee loans that private individuals make through normal investment channels.

In practice, most IBRD loans are from pooled resources that the Bank has raised on the capital markets of the major Western countries and, after the 1970s, those of the petroleum-producing countries of the Middle East. IBRD relends these funds at a slightly higher interest rate than it had to pay to borrow the funds. IBRD loans typically have a grace period of three to five years and a maturity period of fifteen to twenty years. IBRD loans are made to governments, government agencies, and private enterprises that can obtain government guarantees for the loan. As mentioned in chapter 1, and as will be described in detail shortly, the World Bank also established a soft loan window, the International Development Association.

The General Agreement on Tariffs and Trade was drafted at the Havana Conference in 1947, and the treaty came into effect on January 1, 1948.[7] As were IMF and IBRD, GATT was designed to ameliorate a problem that had stymied the international economy in the 1930s, the growth of almost insurmountable obstacles to trade resulting from protective tariffs, such as the U.S. Smoot-Hawley Tariff, and nontariff barriers. GATT promotes trade liberalization primarily by insisting that its members—referred to as contracting parties, reflecting the General Agreement's character as a treaty that imposes obligations and confers privileges—observe three basic principles: (1) reciprocity; (2) nondiscrimination; and (3) transparency. According to these principles, obstacles to trade should be reduced through the reciprocal exchange of concessions, all contracting parties should be treated equally and so should receive the benefit of any concessions by any one contracting party to

---

7. Olivier Long, a former director-general of GATT has written an excellent broad overview of the organization, Law and Its Limitations in the GATT Multilateral Trade System (Dordrecht, The Netherlands: Martinus Nijhoff Publishers, 1985). The most authoritative legal study of GATT is John H. Jackson, World Trade and the Law of GATT (Indianapolis: Bobbs-Merrill, 1969).

another, and all obstacles to trade should be readily apparent—thus tariffs are the preferred form of protection. The General Agreement's purpose is to promote the liberalization of international trade, or put in other terms, the conduct of international trade according to market principles.

GATT was created to be a negotiating forum in which countries would agree to reciprocally reduce their tariffs, and then these reductions would be extended to all contracting parties to the General Agreement on the basis of the most-favored-nation (MFN) principle. The third introductory paragraph of the General Agreement on Tariffs and Trade commits contracting parties to enter ". . . into reciprocal and mutually advantageous arrangements directed to the substantial reduction of tariffs and other barriers to trade and to the elimination of discriminatory treatment in international commerce. . . ." It is the process of reciprocally negotiating concessions that ties countries' influence in GATT to the size of their markets: the larger a country's market the greater its bargaining power. Throughout the post–World War II period, the United States has been the largest single-country market; thus GATT's tariff-cutting negotiating rounds have in practice been tied to U.S. legislation authorizing trade concessions.

Article I of the General Agreement establishes the principle of non-discrimination among contracting parties, or most-favored-nation treatment. It requires that ". . . any advantage, favour, privilege or immunity granted by any contracting party to any product originating in or destined for any other country shall be accorded immediately and unconditionally to the like product originating in or destined for the territories of all other contracting parties."

The General Agreement insists that all obstacles to trade be transparent. The requirement of transparency is specified in Article X. According to this article,

> Laws, regulations, judicial decisions and administrative rulings of general application, made effective by any contracting party, pertaining to the classification or the valuation of products for customs purposes, or to rates of duty, taxes or other charges, or to requirements, restrictions or prohibitions on imports or exports or on the transfer of payments therefor, or affecting their sale, distribution, transportation, insurance, warehousing, inspection, exhibition, processing, mixing or other use, shall be published in such a manner as to enable governments and trades to become acquainted with them.

Under most circumstances, the General Agreement forbids quantitative restrictions to trade. Article XI of the General Agreement specifies that: "No prohibition or restrictions other than duties, taxes or other charges, whether made effective through quotas, import or export licenses or other measures, shall be instituted or maintained by any contracting party on the importation of any product of the territory of any other contracting party or on the exportation or sale for export of any product destined for the territory of any other contracting party."

A contracting party that feels that another contracting party has violated these or other obligations specified in the General Agreement or in treaties negotiated within the GATT framework can bring the matter before the contracting parties. If its accusation is upheld, it can be authorized to take retaliatory action. The General Agreement, however, encourages contracting parties to engage in negotiations rather than initiate a potential spiral of mutually damaging retaliatory steps.

Its founders conceived the General Agreement on Tariffs and Trade to be part of the then contemplated International Trade Organization (ITO), which was to have functions beyond GATT's mandate to bring about trade liberalization. It was to deal, for instance, with problems concerning trade in primary commodities and other more development-oriented issues. ITO, however, never came into being because of opposition within the U.S. Congress to its proposed functions.[8] In these circumstances, GATT eventually took on the attributes and characteristics of an international governmental organization. Rather than remaining merely an international agreement, it became the sole agency within the UN system for the conduct of trade negotiations.

The Evolution of the KIEOs

Just as GATT became something different than had originally been intended, neither the IMF nor the Bank functioned exactly as it had been conceived at the Bretton Woods Conference. Post–World War II reconstruction needs were far beyond the financial resources of either institution; instead these needs were met by the United States European Recovery Program (more commonly known as the Marshall Plan), and the Fund and the Bank had only modest programs in the late 1940s and early 1950s. By the mid 1950s, though, both became more active, and by then GATT's activities were in full swing too.

Although it had been intended that each institution would be open to all countries, the countries with centrally planned economies either chose not to join, or withdrew, or were expelled.[9] The Soviet Union had participated in the

---

8. See Kenneth W. Dam, *The GATT: Law and the International Economic Organization* (Chicago: University of Chicago Press, 1970), 149.

9. The relationship of the USSR and the other countries of Eastern Europe with centrally planned economies to the IMF and the World Bank is described in Valerie J. Assetto, *The Soviet Bloc in the IMF and the IBRD* (Boulder, Colo.: Westview Press, 1988).

Bretton Woods Conference, but it chose not to join the IMF and the World Bank.[10] Poland was an original member of both the Fund and the Bank, but voluntarily withdrew in 1950; Czechoslovakia, also an original member, was expelled from the two institutions in 1954. For most of the 1950s and all of the 1960s, Yugoslavia was the only Eastern European country with a centrally planned economy to remain in the IMF and the World Bank. It was an original member of the two institutions and stayed with them. The Soviet Union refused to attend the conferences at which the General Agreement on Tariffs and Trade was negotiated and used the UN as a forum to criticize the principles on which the Agreement was based.[11] Poland, Czechoslovakia, and Yugoslavia, however, did attend the conferences. During the 1950s and most of the 1960s, Czechoslovakia and Yugoslavia were the only countries with centrally planned economies to be members of GATT. Czechoslovakia was one of GATT's original contracting parties. The Agreement was signed before the Communist party assumed full control in the country, but it was ratified after this had occurred.[12] Yugoslavia gained observer status in GATT in 1950, provisionally acceded to the General Agreement in 1962, and fully acceded in 1966. Yugoslavia's expulsion from the Cominforn in 1948 was undoubtedly a factor explaining its membership in the KIEOs during this period.

In the first two decades of their existence, the KIEOs in effect organized an international economic order for countries with market economies. This situation would not begin to change until the late 1960s when some of the Eastern European countries with communist governments entered one or more of the KIEOs. Poland acceded to the General Agreement on Tariffs and Trade in 1967, Romania acceded in 1971, and Hungary in 1973. Romania joined IMF and IBRD in 1972. As of 1980, when China took its seat in the Fund and World Bank, Yugoslavia and Romania were members of these two institutions and Czechoslovakia, Hungary, Poland, Romania, and Yugoslavia were members of GATT.

The Eastern European countries with centrally planned economies received relatively favorable treatment in the KIEOs, especially in the Fund and the World Bank, obtaining access to more than what could be considered a proportionate share of the institutions' resources, given their economic and

---

10. For an analysis of Soviet policy toward these institutions during this era see Harold K. Jacobson, *The USSR and the UN's Economic and Social Activities* (Notre Dame: University of Notre Dame Press, 1963).

11. See Harold K. Jacobson, "The Soviet Union, the UN, and World Trade," *Western Political Quarterly* 11, no. 3 (September, 1958): 310–14.

12. See M. M. Kostecki, *East-West Trade and the GATT System* (London: Macmillan, 1979).

political characteristics.[13] They were not, however, completely diligent in fulfilling the obligations that they assumed when they decided to participate in the institutions. Romania did not provide the requisite statistics for IMF and maintained a multiple exchange rate system, which the Fund forbids. Other GATT contracting parties were disappointed with the trade performance of the countries with centrally planned economies; their imports from GATT members did not increase as had been expected. The Eastern European countries may also have been disappointed, for their exports to other GATT contracting parties similarly failed to increase sharply.

An early but important scholarly appraisal by M. M. Kostecki of the experience of Hungary, Poland, and Romania in GATT concluded that the removal of conventional barriers to East-West trade ". . . was certainly more modest than expected—both in the East and in the West."[14] Kostecki concluded that because the protocols of accession required so little, and thus gave so little to the contracting parties, Hungary, Poland, and Romania in turn had little bargaining power to use in opening Western markets. The Eastern European countries gained status by joining GATT, status that helped them to borrow funds from Western banks in the 1970s, but they did not gain an ability to expand their exports so that they could service these debts.

There were also several other significant aspects of the evolution of the KIEOs, which can more easily be analyzed by first examining each of the institutions separately and then returning to a broader focus to describe the general attack that developing countries mounted against the KIEOs in the 1970s.

The International Monetary Fund

In 1958, the major Western European governments made their currencies convertible, at least for current account, or trade purposes, and the IMF began fully to play the role for which it had been designed. During the 1960s the IMF made many loans to both developed and developing countries that helped to tide them over temporary balance of payments difficulties.

Under the fixed exchange rate system, the currencies of the major trading countries other than the United States were set in terms of U.S. dollars, they were convertible into all other major currencies including the U.S. dollar, and the U.S. dollar was denominated in terms of and convertible into gold. Thus, directly or indirectly, the value of the currencies of all of the major trading countries was based on gold. Two problems arose in connection with this system.

---

13. See Valerie J. Assetto, *The Soviet Bloc in the IMF and the IBRD*, 184.
14. See M. M. Kostecki, *East-West Trade and the GATT System*, 130.

First, the supply of gold placed constraints on the creation of international liquidity. It was broadly feared that international liquidity could not be increased rapidly enough to keep pace with the expansion of international trade. This issue also had political overtones because the Soviet Union and South Africa were the principal sources of new gold and consequently could reap considerable benefits from efforts to substantially increase gold reserves. In response to this problem, in July, 1969, after several years of negotiation, the First Amendment to the Articles of Agreement entered force and the International Monetary Fund created Special Drawing Rights (SDRs). SDRs are essentially a paper reserve asset; their creation increased the resources that the Fund could lend to member governments. The Special Drawing Rights were allocated among IMF's members in accordance with their preexisting quotas. The First Amendment specified that a special majority of 85 percent of the voting strength would be required for decisions concerning adjustments in quotas or increases in quotas. This requirement gave the United States, or the members of the European Community acting collectively, veto authority over such decisions. With the establishment of the Special Drawing Rights Department, the International Monetary Fund gained the capacity to create international liquidity and thus began to take on the attributes of an international central bank. Special Drawing Rights form part of member countries' international reserves. They can be used among official holders for a wide range of transactions and operations, including obtaining foreign exchange. Their use is not subject to Fund conditionality.

The ultimate solution to a second problem that had been festering for some time and came to a head in 1971, however, greatly diminished the significance of the creation of the Special Drawing Rights Department. In August, 1971, a crisis occurred in the international monetary system because the United States was no longer willing to allow dollars to be converted into gold. The United States had been running persistent balance of payments deficits throughout the 1960s, which were covered in effect by non-Americans simply holding dollars. Eventually the quantity of dollars held abroad came to far exceed the U.S. supply of gold. France's threat to convert some of its dollars into gold provoked the United States to end the convertibility of the dollar into gold, and this U.S. action ultimately ended the system of having par values or fixed exchange rates for the currencies of the major trading countries.

The U.S. government was convinced that the U.S. balance of payments difficulties stemmed at least in part from what it felt was the overvaluation of the dollar. Two of the United States' major trading partners, the Federal Republic of Germany and Japan, refused to appreciate their currency as much as the United States felt would be necessary to correct the deficit in the U.S. balance of payments. On the other hand, the fact that the dollar was such an important component of so many countries' foreign exchange reserves inhibited the United States' ability to devalue the dollar. Furthermore, under the pre-1971 international monetary system, any devaluation of the dollar would be general, not simply against currencies of the countries with which the United States had trade deficits. Thus, it might exacerbate the situation of countries that already had a trade deficit with the United States. Precluded from responding to balance of payments difficulties by exchange rate manipulations, the only other course for the United States would have been to adopt contractionary domestic policies, a course the U.S. government was unwilling to follow. In the end, the Nixon administration chose to abandon the convertibility of the dollar into gold to avoid having its domestic policies tied to its external trade position.[15]

Efforts were made to restore the pre-1971 international monetary system, but these foundered, and in 1974 the IMF began to seek consensus among its major members on the outlines of a new system, a process that took four years. Thus, the 1971 U.S. decision effectively ended the system of fixed exchange rates among the currencies of the world's major trading countries, although it did not affect their convertibility. Since the early 1970s, the international monetary regime for the currencies of the major trading countries has been a managed floating system. Although the value of the major trading countries' currencies have been basically determined by market forces, governments have intervened in currency markets to ward off abrupt changes. This system was accorded full legal status when the Second Amendment to IMF's Articles of Agreement came into effect in April, 1978. In addition to allowing member countries to choose their own exchange rate regime, the amendment provided for the gradual elimination of the role of gold in the international monetary system. As early as 1977, the IMF had begun to resell to member states the gold that they had deposited, a process completed in February, 1980.

The adoption of the Second Amendment, and the major trading countries' abandonment of par values for their currencies, altered the role of the International Monetary Fund. IMF loans became much less important for the major trading countries, which simultaneously are the more developed member states of the OECD. IMF's contribution to the monetary relations among these major Western states dropped significantly.

The focus of IMF lending shifted sharply toward developing countries, whose share of IMF loans had in any event been steadily increasing. Other changes in the global economy further contributed to altering the IMF's role.

---

15. For a detailed account of the U.S. decision see Joanne Gowa, *Closing the Gold Window: Domestic Politics and the End of Bretton Woods* (Ithaca, N.Y.: Cornell University Press, 1983).

During the 1970s, private lending by the banks of the developed countries to the governments, private corporations, and individuals in developing countries increased dramatically. The increase in bank lending to the Third World was associated with the sharp rise in the price of petroleum caused by the "oil shocks" of 1973 and 1979. Oil-exporting developing countries invested much of their surplus earnings in Western banks, and their so-called petrodollars greatly enlarged the lending capacity of these institutions. Confident that their capacity for substantial export earnings would last, some oil-exporting developing countries borrowed heavily. Oil-importing developing countries were forced to borrow to cover the increased costs of the petroleum they needed.

As these loans fell due in the less expansionary international economic climate of the 1980s, when the price of petroleum was substantially lower than it had been immediately after the two "oil shocks," many developing countries found it extremely difficult to make the required payments. Some had to strain even to pay the interest to service their debts, and a few came close to defaulting. Many developing country debts had to be rescheduled.

In these circumstances, the IMF assumed a new role. Developing countries facing debt crises found that they had to obtain IMF backing in the form of a loan before Western private banks would agree to reschedule their debts or lend new money. IMF's policy of insisting on progressively stiffer conditionality for upper tranche drawings was the reason for this; to obtain substantial funds from IMF—and during the 1970s the Fund had greatly enlarged developing countries' access to its resources—member states had to agree to implement policies that would lessen their balance of payments deficits. The banks could not impose these conditions themselves, since to do so could be seen as an unacceptable intrusion of private entities into a state's sovereign affairs. In contrast, IMF conditionality, because it was imposed by an international governmental organization of which the country itself was a member, had greater legitimacy.

IMF's conditionality policies had always been debated, but in the late 1970s and early 1980s, they became highly controversial.[16] Because the adandonment of par values for their currencies lessened the burden of supporting their currencies, no developed country has drawn funds from IMF since Italy's drawing in 1977. As a result, IMF conditionality has subsequently been applied only to developing countries. Because obtaining an IMF standby agreement to draw funds became a prerequisite to rescheduling private bank

---

16. For a sample of the attack on Fund conditionality policies see Cheryl Payer, *The Debt Trap: The IMF and the Third World* (New York: Monthly Review Press, 1975). For a more moderate and balanced critique see Stephan Haggard, "The Politics of Adjustment: Lessons from the IMF's Extended Facility," in Miles Kahler, ed., *The Politics of International Debt* (Ithaca, N.Y.: Cornell University Press, 1986), 157–86.

loans or to obtaining new loans from private banks, IMF was placed more and more in the position of appearing to guarantee private capital.

When the People's Republic of China entered the International Monetary Fund in 1980, controversies about the Fund's conditionality policies were roiling, and they would become even more turbulent. China's past attacks on the Fund, had it chosen to continue them, might have found an even more receptive audience throughout the world. In joining the Fund, however, China assumed the institution's ninth largest quota, the largest of any developing country. China thus became a major holder of the Fund's resources and inevitably had to be concerned about the prudent management of these funds. In addition to the controversy about the Fund's conditionality, there was a broad sense that the Fund should regain some role with respect to monetary relations among the major Western countries, however difficult it might be to define this role. In joining the Fund, China assumed a place in the Fund's policy process just at a time when the Fund was in transition and when some of its core policies were under severe attack. China could not help becoming involved in the debates, and its participation in them would inevitably affect the outcome.

The World Bank

The International Bank for Reconstruction and Development was also in the midst of controversies in the late 1970s and early 1980s. As IBRD's operations moved to full swing in the 1950s, its primary function became providing financial and technical assistance to developing countries. The Bank's technical assistance was an outgrowth of its lending operations. Since its loans had to be repaid, the Bank wanted to ensure that they would be used constructively and for purposes that would facilitate repayment, and thus they—or at least a large proportion of them—had to generate foreign exchange. According to its Articles of Agreement, the bulk of the Bank's loans must be for projects.[17] Consequently, Bank staff had to develop microanalytical methodologies and techniques for evaluating the costs and benefits of projects. To understand how projects fitted into the larger framework of a country's economic growth, the Bank staff had to develop expertise on economic development strategies, or macroanalysis.

The requirement that Bank loans had to be repaid exerted strong pressures on the Bank staff to favor export-promotion rather than import-

---

17. Article III, Section (vii) of IBRD's Articles of Agreement. An authoritative, retrospective defense of the project lending approach can be found in Warren C. Baum and Stokes M. Tolbert, *Investing in Development: Lessons of World Bank Experience* (Washington, D.C.: IBRD, 1985).

substitution strategies of economic development, but rather than being a separate force, these pressures merely reinforced the staff's natural inclinations derived from the tenets of orthodox neoliberal economic analyses. Historical studies of economic growth have consistently stressed the leading role that foreign trade could play.[18]

As the Bank's lending increased, the world provided a laboratory to test its ideas about project evaluation and economic development strategies, and transmitting the Bank's expertise in project evaluation and development strategies to its borrowers became a major aspect of its activities. Conditions attached to project loans came to be a form for passing on the Bank's wisdom gained through microanalyses; loan agreements specify that to receive funds for the project the recipient country must adopt certain policy measures. These conditions manifested the World Bank's policy of conditionality. In discussions about the Bank's project activities, they are usually referred to as leverage. Actually, the Bank's exercise of leverage has seldom been very forceful and has virtually never been coercive; some countries have blatantly ignored the Bank's conditions and still have received funding.[19] Bank staff also tender advice gained from microanalyses in the process of their oversight of projects. The Bank's macrolevel advice has been transmitted in book-length studies of member countries' economies and in dialogues between Bank staff and high-level national officials.

Early in its history it was clear that funds that could be lent on easier terms than those relent by the IBRD would be extremely useful to promote development in the less developed countries. To respond to this need, in 1960 the Bank created the International Development Association. IDA's capital is raised by subscriptions from all member states. Subscriptions of developed countries (in the language of IDA's Articles of Agreement, Part I countries) must be paid in convertible currencies, while subscriptions of developing countries (Part II) are paid in their national currencies. IDA loans do not involve interest but carry a 0.5 percent annual commitment charge on undisbursed funds and a service charge of 0.75 percent on disbursed amounts of the loan. IDA loans have a grace period of ten years and an average maturity period of fifty years. Because of the long maturity period for its loans, IDA's capital must periodically be replenished. Without periodic replenishment, IDA would not have money to lend. IDA's funds can be lent only to its poorer members, which are identified in terms of their per capita gross national

---

18. See Simon Kuznets, *Modern Economic Growth: Rate, Structure, and Spread* (New Haven, Conn.: Yale University Press, 1966), and Lloyd G. Reynolds, *Economic Growth in the Third World, 1850–1980* (New Haven, Conn.: Yale University Press, 1985).

19. See especially Winsome J. Leslie, *The World Bank and Structural Transformation in Developing Countries: The Case of Zaire* (Boulder, Colo.: Lynne Rienner, 1987).

product. A ceiling is set in terms of per capita GNP that is periodically adjusted upward. Only the very poorest countries receive loans that are comprised exclusively of IDA funds. Most countries receive loans that are a blend of IDA and IBRD funds.

When Robert McNamara became president of the World Bank in 1968, he sought to vastly expand the volume of IBRD and IDA lending and also to reorient the Bank so that loans for social purposes such as education and health would be easier to make and would constitute a larger share of the Bank's portfolio.[20] World Bank lending increased dramatically under McNamara's leadership, and a significant portion of this increase was devoted to projects in the new social fields that McNamara stressed.

Another innovation that McNamara spurred was the introduction in 1980 of the Bank's program of structural adjustment lending and Structural Adjustment Loans (SALs). This program was introduced in response to the grave problems that many developing countries faced in the late 1970s. Structural Adjustment Loans are not tied to specific projects, but rather to a recipient country's plans for restructuring a sector of its economy, and they are intended to ease the costs of an institutional transition. A major criterion for such loans is whether such a transition will help address causes of persistent balance of payments deficits. Countries frequently use SALs to ease balance of payments problems, and in this sense are like IMF drawings. The World Bank attaches conditions to its SALs and, unlike those involved in project loans, these are macrolevel and relate to a broad sector of the recipient's economy such as agriculture or energy. Structural Adjustment Loans cannot comprise more than 25 percent of the Bank's lending to any one country. With the Bank's adoption of structural adjustment lending, the sharp distinction that had been drawn at Bretton Woods between the functions of the IMF and the World Bank began to erode.

By the end of 1980, IBRD had made 1,875 loans for a total of $59,341.5 million and IDA had awarded 973 credits worth $20,569.8 million.[21] No World Bank loan had ever been refinanced, and there had never been a default on a World Bank loan.

On the surface, the World Bank's record presented a success story. Underneath, however, there were several problems. These problems spawned debates about the Bank's record and its future direction. As economic growth in the international economy slowed during the late 1970s and early 1980s, so

---

20. McNamara's strategy and its implementation by the Bank are analyzed in Robert L. Ayres, *Banking on the Poor: The World Bank and Poverty* (Cambridge, Mass.: MIT Press, 1983).

21. IBRD, *World Bank Annual Report, 1981* (Washington, D.C.: IBRD, 1981), 188.

did economic growth in the developing countries, and this added urgency to the debates.

The adoption of the structural adjustment lending program had been a response to some of the problems that the developing countries faced. Yet it had its critics. The program had the potentiality of bringing the Bank into conflict with the International Monetary Fund; what if the two institutions had different ideas about the macroeconomic actions that a borrowing country should take? The World Bank and the Fund tend to emphasize different criteria in assessing borrowers' macroeconomic performance. The Fund's mandate requires it to stress the status of the borrowers' balance of payments, the Bank is more inclined to emphasize aggregate growth figures. Even before the adoption of structural adustment lending, some Bank staff worried that the conditions imposed by the International Monetary Fund were harmful to Bank-funded projects.[22] Fund conditions frequently required reducing government budgets, and this could jeopardize the local funds required for the support of Bank projects. Furthermore, if the Bank seriously sought to impose macroeconomic conditions, its reputation for being gentle with developing countries, because of its refusal to forcefully exercise leverage, could be at risk. It could find itself subject to criticism similar to that levied at the International Monetary Fund. The SAL program was controversial. Some thought it should be expanded and others wanted it cut back or eliminated.

Many members of the Bank's staff had questioned McNamara's emphasis on social projects, and this questioning continued. They and others worried that since these projects were not directly tied to the promotion of exports it was not clear how funds would be generated to repay the Bank's loans for them. Others saw the social projects as the Bank's only way of reaching the poor, felt funds for these projects should be increased, and condemned the Bank staff for not wholeheartedly embracing McNamara's vision.

Some outside observers of the Bank's operations sharply attacked the Bank's continuing emphasis on export-promotion strategies of economic development.[23] Although their attack echoed a longstanding disagreement between those who favored import-substitution over export-promotion strategies, the argument gained renewed force as growth in the world economy slowed after 1973 and the Western industrialized countries, the primary markets for exports from developing countries, became less able and less willing to absorb a steadily increasing volume of goods from abroad.

---

22. See Stanley Please, *The Hobbled Giant: Essays on the World Bank* (Boulder, Colo.: Westview Press, 1984), 20–23.

23. See Robin Broad, *Unequal Alliance: The World Bank, the International Monetary Fund, and the Philippines* (Berkeley: University of California Press, 1988).

Faced with severe problems in their own economies in the late 1970s and early 1980s, donor countries were becoming reluctant to contribute funds either to expand the Bank's capital or to replenish IDA. As the per capita GNP of some developing countries neared and surpassed those of poorer European countries, donor countries began to argue that developing countries must "mature" and "graduate"; that as their per capita GNPs increased they should accept loans in which the proportion of IBRD funds increased relative to IDA funds, and that ultimately they should become ineligible first for IDA and then for IBRD funds. Developing countries resisted the arguments for their "maturation" and "graduation."

Within the United States, the World Bank's largest shareholder and contributor, there was considerable controversy about the Bank. Conservatives alleged that the Bank did not serve U.S. interests, and argued that the U.S. contribution should be cut. They argued that the Bank did not favor development of the private sector, and they complained about loans for projects that were creditworthy and capable of financing at commercial interest rates or by multinational corporations. Loans for petroleum development were an example the critics cited. The conservatives therefore saw the World Bank as an agent of socialist development paths. Ronald Reagan's victory in the 1980 U.S. presidential election brought conservatives into the administration and meant that these criticisms would be heard. In the spring of 1981, shortly after its inauguration, the new administration launched an interagency review, chaired by the Department of the Treasury, of the Multilateral Development Banks, including the World Bank. This review would not be completed until February, 1982.[24] In the interim, the U.S. financial and political commitment to the World Bank was uncertain, and a debate raged in the United States about the Bank.[25]

When China entered the World Bank in 1980, it joined and became part of a widespread and far-reaching debate on the role and future of the organization.

The General Agreement on Tariffs and Trade

The General Agreement on Tariffs and Trade conducted its first multilateral trade negotiation in Geneva in 1947. Between then and 1986, when China sought full participation, GATT had conducted six additional rounds of trade negotiations, the last being the Tokyo Round that started in 1973 and con-

---

24. U.S. Department of the Treasury, *United States Participation in the Multilateral Development Banks in the 1980s* (Washington, D.C.: GPO, 1982).
25. See Edward R. Fried and Henry D. Owen, eds., *The Future Role of the World Bank* (Washington, D.C.: Brookings Institution, 1982).

cluded six years later in 1979. As a consequence of these seven rounds of trade negotiations, tariffs had been cut so that they were an insignificant factor in trade in manufactured items among industrialized countries.[26]

GATT's work, however, was by no means completed as of 1979. Trade in agricultural products had largely been excluded from GATT's multilateral trade negotiations, first because of United States insistence, and then because of the insistence of the European Community, Japan, Switzerland, and other developed countries that also maintained restrictions on agricultural trade. By the early 1980s, however, because of the costs of subsidizing agricultural production in the developed countries and the conflicts that had arisen as a consequence of the restrictions on agricultural trade, there was growing sentiment that GATT's contracting parties should try to liberalize trade in this sector.

Developing countries were slow to join GATT. Many of them argued that GATT did not adequately represent their interests; that it was biased in favor of the developed countries. The Charter for the International Trade Organization contained several provisions that were of particular interest to developing countries, but only one of these provisions, that concerning governmental assistance for economic development, was included in the original version of the General Agreement. This article, Article XVIII, though, provides quite a broad exemption. It allows governments of developing countries under certain conditions to enact protective tariffs to facilitate the establishment of particular industries, to apply quantitative restrictions on imports to protect their balance of payments position, and to deviate from the application of other provisions of the Agreement. An additional factor explaining the hesitancy of many developing countries toward GATT beyond their disappointment that ITO was not created was the fact that many of them pursued import-substitution strategies of economic development. They sought to discourage imports and to develop local industry behind high, protective tariffs. Countries pursuing such strategies were not eager to join GATT and assume an obligation to progressively liberalize their trade even if this were only a very weak obligation.

In 1964, at the insistence of the developing countries, the United Nations convened the first United Nations Conference on Trade and Development (UNCTAD). Within a few years these countries succeeded in transforming the conference into a full-fledged semiautonomous agency within the UN system. In contrast to GATT's emphasis on nondiscrimination and re-

---

26. See Stephen D. Krasner, "The Tokyo Round: Particularistic Interests and Prospects for Stability in the Global Trading System," *International Studies Quarterly* 23, no. 4 (December, 1979), 1–22; and Gilbert R. Winham, *International Trade and the Tokyo Round Negotiations* (Princeton: Princeton University Press, 1986).

ciprocity, UNCTAD stressed preferential treatment for developing countries. And in contrast to the IMF and the World Bank, UNCTAD espoused import-substitution rather than export-promotion strategies of economic development. Some developing country officials and sympathizers nourished the hope that UNCTAD would eventually supplant GATT as the main forum for trade negotiations. Even such a nonradical scholar as Ernst B. Haas at one time argued that UNCTAD must ". . . become the centerpiece of a coordinated and rationalized approach to aid and trade."[27] In his proposed reorganization of the UN system, GATT would have been eliminated and IMF and the Bank subordinated to UNCTAD. The preference that many held for UNCTAD reflected both a strong commitment to rapidly accelerating economic growth in developing countries and a faith that governmental intervention in economic affairs based on rationalistic planning could yield significantly better outcomes than relying primarily on market forces.

In 1964, in an obvious effort to make GATT more appealing to developing countries and thereby dampen their enthusiasm for UNCTAD, the contracting parties added Part IV to the General Agreement, which was devoted to the problems of developing countries. One article in Part IV absolves the developing countries of the obligation of reciprocity. It states that " . . . the developed contracting parties do not expect reciprocity for commitments made by them in trade negotiations to reduce or remove tariffs and other barriers to the trade of less-developed contracting parties."[28] Part IV also provided for the establishment of the Committee on Trade and Development, thereby providing a designated forum for the discussion of development issues. In 1971, the contracting parties granted a waiver from the obligation of nondiscrimination so as to allow preferential treatment for developing countries. However, this was not given formal legal status until the conclusion of the Tokyo Round in November, 1979.[29]

These moves had an effect. So did the growing stake of developing countries in international trade and the prosperity of developed countries—their major market. With this enlarged stake, the importance of the protection for access to markets that GATT offered loomed larger. More and more developing countries acceded to GATT, so that by 1986 there were more than ninety members including all of the large developing countries except China. Many developing countries, however, continued to be critical of GATT and to drag their feet in GATT proceedings. Developed countries, on the other hand,

---

27. Ernst B. Haas, *Tangle of Hopes: American Commitments and World Order* (Englewood Cliffs, N.J.: Prentice-Hall, 1969), 290.

28. Article XXXVI, Section 8, General Agreement on Tariffs and Trade.

29. See Olivier Long, *Law and Its Limitations in the GATT Multilateral Trade System*, 100–101.

feared that the special treatment accorded to the developing countries diluted the trade regime, and they argued that preferential trade treatment granted to developing countries could not be permanent. Just as in the World Bank, developed countries argued that the concept of "graduation" should be applied. In sum, fully integrating developing countries into the GATT system remained unfinished business.

Another item before GATT was the numerous quantitative restrictions inaugurated by the developed countries starting in the 1960s. Developed countries used their bargaining strength to force developing countries—and in some cases other developed countries—to establish restrictions on their exports. Since GATT dealt with restrictions on imports, not exports, many of these so-called Voluntary Export Restrictions, for instance on automobiles, footwear, and steel, escaped its jurisdiction. Those on textiles, products of particular importance to developing countries, however, did not. In 1961, a short-term agreement on cotton textiles was negotiated within GATT. This was renewed. Then, in 1974, it was replaced with the Multifibre Arrangement. In effect, the MFA allowed textile-importing countries to establish restrictions, but committed them to progressively enlarge these and established a mechanism, the Textile Surveillance Body (TSB), for monitoring the restrictions.[30] The quantitative restrictions on exports were worrisome deviations from the movement toward trade liberalization, and the MFA was controversial from its inception.

The question of how those economies that were referred to in GATT parlance as nonmarket economies should be dealt with was also among GATT's unfinished business in the 1980s. Hardly any knowledgeable official or observer claimed that the arrangements that had been made for the participation of Eastern European countries with communist governments in GATT had proved satisfactory, and the issue of how to bring into this category the countries with the largest economies, China and the USSR, had not yet been addressed.

In a sense, by the end of the Tokyo Round, GATT had finished the relatively easy tasks involved in dismantling and prohibiting the most visible obstacles to trade. If it were to do more—and many argued that it had to do more, that trade liberalization, like a bicycle, had to move forward or it would topple—the tasks would be harder. Agricultural trade, the treatment and practices of developing countries, and export restraints were all difficult and politically sensitive issues.

In addition, GATT had just begun to deal with nontariff barriers to trade

---

30. For a description of the MFA and an analysis of its functioning, see Vinod Aggarwal, *Liberal Protectionism: The International Politics of Organized Textile Trade* (Berkeley: University of California Press, 1985).

in the Tokyo Round. As customs duties declined as a consequence of GATT negotiations, the importance of nontariff barriers to trade increased. Several agreements, or codes, covering areas other than customs duties were negotiated during the Tokyo Round.[31] These included: a code on subsidies and countervailing duties; an agreement on customs valuation; a revised anti-dumping code; an agreement on import licensing procedures; an agreement on government procurement; an agreement on technical barriers to trade or standards applied for health or safety reasons; and agreements on trade of civil aircraft and component parts and their repairs, on dairy products, and on bovine meat. The first four of these elaborated and developed provisions of the General Agreement, the last five dealt with issues that were not covered in the Agreement. Not all contracting parties were willing to sign these codes, and developing countries especially were reluctant. All contracting parties were anxious to evaluate their implementation and effectiveness.

From the point of view of developing countries, the failure of the Tokyo negotiations to produce a code on safeguards that would refine Article XIX of the General Agreement dealing with the right of importing countries to limit imports when serious market disruption occurred was a serious disappointment. The key obstacle to obtaining an agreement during the Tokyo Round was the insistence of the European Community negotiators that a safeguards agreement would have to include a provision for applying restrictions selectively against the exporter causing the market disruption, and the equally strong insistence of the United States and many developing countries that restrictions imposed under the terms of a safeguards agreement would have to be applied in a nondiscriminatory manner. Obtaining an agreement on safeguards became one of the developing countries' principal objectives.

Finally, as of the end of the Tokyo Round, GATT had yet to confront the problems involved in liberalizing the growing trade in services. Services include such traditional sectors as banking, insurance, and construction, and also the newer sectors of engineering and management consulting and data and information transmission. According to one estimate, trade in services grew by 20 percent in the 1970s, as rapidly as merchandise trade, and in 1980 accounted for 20 percent of global trade.[32] Services were coming to constitute a larger share of the developed countries' economies, and the developed countries—especially the United States—wanted GATT to liberalize trade in them. The developing countries were reluctant, fearing that liberalization might stunt the development of their domestic service industries.

31. For the texts of these codes see GATT, *The Texts of the Tokyo Round Agreements* (Geneva: GATT, 1986).

32. Gary Clyde Hufbauer and Jeffrey J. Schott, *Trading for Growth: The Next Round of Trade Negotiations* (Washington, D.C.: Institute for International Economics, 1985), 66.

Then came China. As China began to participate in GATT, the organization was just beginning to face many of the most difficult tasks it would undertake. Because of the difficulties of these tasks, some observers even felt that the organization's future was in question.

The Demand for a New International Economic Order

Not only did the three keystone international economic organizations each face serious issues when China began its participation in them, but they had also collectively been under severe attack in the United Nations and elsewhere by the developing countries, aided and abetted by the Soviet Union. At the Sixth Special Session of the UN General Assembly in May, 1974, heady with the success of OPEC in quadrupling the price of petroleum, the developing countries pushed through the Declaration on the Establishment of a New International Economic Order (NIEO).[33] This resolution touched off a confrontation that would last through the early 1980s.

The developing countries demanded that the neoliberal international economic order should be sharply revised in their favor.[34] They wanted the trading system to emphasize preferential treatment for developing countries rather than nondiscrimination and reciprocity, and they wanted the preferential treatment to be permanent. They wanted the flow of resources to developing countries to be enlarged and made automatic. They wanted an increased role and greater influence in the International Monetary Fund and the World Bank and also in GATT, if it were not supplanted by UNCTAD. The developing countries demanded that the developed countries open negotiations on these issues. An impasse soon resulted. Although the developed countries were willing to make some concessions, they adamantly refused to substantially alter the KIEOs and their rules.

The attack on the KIEOs was orchestrated by the Group of Seventy-seven, the developing country caucus in the UN. The caucus was formed by 77 developing country participants in the first UNCTAD meeting. By the 1980s, the caucus included more than 120 members. UNCTAD studies and discussions provided the intellectual inspiration and the blueprint for the alternative world economic order envisaged in the demand for NIEO. Import-substitution economic development strategies were at the core of this vision. The Soviet Union and its Eastern European allies enthusiastically supported the Group of Seventy-seven attack on the KIEOs. The Soviet Union had criticized the KIEOs since the late 1940s. Its own economic development

---

33. General Assembly Resolution 3201, S VI.

34. See Stephen Krasner, *Structural Conflict: The Third World Against Global Liberalism* (Berkeley: University of California Press, 1985).

strategy, because of its own inclinations and trade restrictions imposed by Western governments, had emphasized import substitution, almost to the point of autarky.

China's move toward the KIEOs occurred in the context of the North-South confrontation about NIEO and had major implications for this confrontation. In the UN and UNCTAD, China had joined the other developing countries in their attack on the KIEOs even though it was not a formal member of the Group of Seventy-seven. Would it continue the attack with the KIEOs? Was China's move toward the KIEOs an effort to fight from within for NIEO? Or should China's participation in the KIEOs be regarded as an adandonment of NIEO and a triumph for neoliberalism?

Put in broader terms, did China's move toward the KIEOs represent a significant step toward expanding the geographical scope of the neoliberal international economic order that these institutions served, pushing it in the direction of becoming a global neoliberal economic order? Or would China's move contribute to transforming these institutions and their policies so that the order that they sustained could no longer appropriately be described as neoliberal?

China's Successive National Security and Development Strategies[35]

At the founding of the People's Republic of China on October 1, 1949, Mao Zedong proclaimed that the Chinese people had stood up. They would no longer be humiliated in world affairs. The new chairman of the People's Republic and his associates were determined to eliminate the special influence that Western Europeans, Americans, and Japanese had exercised in China. From the 1840s through the early 1940s foreigners enjoyed positions of privilege gained through a series of unequal treaties and concessions that such military and economically superior powers as Britain, France, Germany, the United States, Russia, and Japan had extracted from successive Chinese governments. From 1927 on, Chiang Kai-shek's Nationalist government gradually terminated many of the formal privileges, such as the system of extra-

---

35. This section is based primarily on recent Chinese historiography; cf. Hao Mengbi and Duan Haoran, eds., *Zhongquo gongchandang liushinian* (Sixty years of the Chinese Communist party) (Beijing: People's Liberation Army Press, 1984); Fang Weizhong, ed., *Zhonghua Renmin Gongheguo jingji dashiji* (1949–1980) (Chronicle of the Economy of the People's Republic of China) (Beijing: Chinese Social Science Press, 1984); Chinese Communist Party, Central Committee Party History Research Office, *Zhonggong dangshi dashi nianbiao* (Chronology of major events in the history of the Chinese Communist Party) (Beijing: People's Press, 1987).

territoriality under which foreigners governed themselves in settlements under their jurisdiction, but the influence and status of foreign residents remained great. China remained more acted upon than an actor in world affairs.

Mao and his colleagues had achieved power, in part, because of their effective nationalistic appeals. Due largely to Chiang's delayed and ineffective response to the Japanese invasion of the 1930s, many Chinese, especially among the intellectuals, had concluded that the communists were more likely than the Nationalist party to restore China's national honor and domestic tranquility. The Communist party had pledged to terminate China's century of perceived humiliation at the hands of the outside world. The communist triumph over Chiang Kai-shek's Nationalist China government in part resulted from Mao's having successfully wrested away from Chiang the banner of Chinese nationalism. The galloping hyperinflation in China from 1937 through 1949 also contributed to discrediting the Nationalist government.[36] Not only did the inflation have serious economic and social consequences, it was also viewed in historical terms as an indication of governmental weakness.

Rising to power under such circumstances, the new leaders were hardly predisposed to adopt national security and development strategies that entailed a continued, extensive Western presence in China.[37] They were also deeply committed to gaining and maintaining monetary and fiscal stability.

But the appropriate route to national wealth and power has been no more evident to China's communist rulers than it was to their predecessors. In the broadest terms, Mao and his associates pursued two somewhat different security and development strategies in their first two decades of rule. Neither proved to be as successful as the top leaders wished, and in the 1970s, during Mao's waning years, some of his associates were groping toward the formulation of a third strategy that would allot a role to Japan and the West in facilitating economic growth and enhancing national security. China made contact with the KIEOs at the precise moment in 1979–80 when thoughts about the third strategy were beginning to crystallize. The leaders' evaluation of their previous development and security strategies shaped their approach to the KIEOs and, for that reason, it is important to understand the path that these leaders had traveled.

---

36. See Alexander Eckstein, *China's Economic Revolution* (Cambridge: Cambridge University Press, 1977), 159–66.

37. For a more elaborate discussion of this view, see Steven Goldstein, "Chinese Communist Policy toward the United States, 1944–1949: Opportunities and Constraints," in *Uncertain Years: Chinese-American Relations, 1947–1950*, ed. Dorothy Borg and Waldo Heinrichs (New York: Columbia University Press, 1980).

The First Strategy:
Emulate the Soviet Union, 1950–60

For a period in 1944–45, Mao and his associates had hoped to elicit American support or at least neutrality in their struggle with Chiang's forces, but by 1946 that hope had begun to fade. In the spring of 1949, with victory over Chiang in sight, they recognized that the birth of the new communist regime would occur in the international context of the Soviet-American Cold War. They announced that in their foreign policy, the communist government would "lean to one side"—that of the Soviet Union. Mao and his lieutenants saw little chance that their new regime could adopt a neutralist stance between the United States and the Soviet Union. Driven both by necessity and a sense of affinity with fellow Marxist-Leninists, they chose to align themselves with the Soviet Union.

From 1950 to 1953, the Korean War and the inexorable excesses of revolution—attacks on Western-trained Chinese intellectuals, the seizure of Western corporate assets, the imprisonment of remaining Westerners in China—almost totally severed the remaining links between China and the West, and a period of intense hostility between China and the West followed. The United States proclaimed and enforced an economic embargo on China that kept China's trade with Japan and America's European allies to a minimum.

This international setting helped shape China's security and development strategy of the 1950s. It entailed a reliance upon the Soviet Union for military assistance and an emulation of Stalin's development strategy. The new government developed the organizational capacity to administer a centrally planned economy, and in 1953 it launched the First Five-Year Plan (1953–57). In the process it smothered the marketplace as the locus for exchanging commodities, labor, and capital. The state assumed the responsibility for setting prices through bureaucratic means. Agriculture was collectivized and all of the nonagricultural sectors were nationalized. Foreign trade was conducted by centralized foreign trade corporations organized along product lines, operating under the direction of the Ministry of Foreign Trade. With the state in control of the economy, the leaders gave priority to rapid development of heavy industry—especially steel—through high rates of savings and capital accumulation. Foreign trade was used to supplement shortfalls in production, primarily in food, raw materials, and capital goods.

As part of the Soviet bloc, Chinese trade was oriented toward the USSR and Eastern Europe, and the Soviet Union became the major source for foreign development assistance. During the 1950s, the Soviet Union provided China with $1.4 to $2.2 billion in credits and assisted in the construction of

256 major industrial projects.[38] Perhaps more important, the leaders of China sought to structure their entire economic system of the 1950s along Soviet lines. The economic doctrine on which the leaders based their policies was Soviet or more precisely Marxist-Leninist-Stalinist in origins. Soviet economic advisers flocked to China. Over ten thousand Chinese students were sent to the Soviet Union for advanced training, especially in engineering and the natural sciences. And Soviet influence in the social sciences—especially in economics—penetrated such key academic bodies as the Institute of Economics, part of the Division of Philosophy and Social Sciences of the Chinese Academy of Sciences, and People's University, a rapidly expanding institution in northwest Beijing, where many of the bureaucrats were being trained to staff such pivotal agencies as the State Planning Commission, the Ministry of Finance, the Party Organization and Propaganda departments, and the state judicial and security system.

Even during the height of Soviet influence, however, the Chinese leaders rebuffed Soviet overtures to join the Council for Mutual Economic Assistance (CMEA).[39] Mao and his associates did not wish to be part of a Soviet-orchestrated international division of labor. As Zhou Enlai stated in 1954,

> The fundamental aim of our great people's revolution is to free the productive forces of our country . . . so as to enable our national economy to advance rapidly and according to plan along the road to socialism in this way raising the level of the people's material well-being and cultural life and strengthening the independence and security of our country. . . . Unless we establish a powerful modern industry, modern agriculture, modern communication and transport services and modern national defense we shall be able neither to shake off backwardness and poverty, nor attain the goal of our revolution.[40]

Thus, the Chinese leaders sought to retain their national independence and to reject becoming totally enmeshed in the Soviet-led international economic system of the 1950s.

---

38. A. Doak Barnett, *China's Economy in Global Perspective* (Washington, D.C.: Brookings Institution, 1981), 213–14, offers a range of estimates depending on the ruble-yuan conversion rate, among other factors. The number of major construction projects is in Samuel Ho and Ralph Huenemann, *China's Open Door Policy: The Quest for Foreign Technology and Capital* (Vancouver: University of British Columia Press, 1984), 14–15.

39. Alexander Eckstein, *China's Economic Revolution*, 121–22.

40. From Zhou Enlai's report on the work of the government, delivered to the First Session of the First National People's Congress, September 23, 1954, in *People's China*, October 16, 1954, 3.

By the mid- and late 1950s, however, China's leaders increasingly questioned the applicability of this strategy and of the Soviet model to their condition. As early as 1956, they began to resent Soviet efforts to dominate them and take advantage of their dependency upon Soviet assistance. They also became aware that certain features of the Soviet model, such as its legal institutions or its industrial management system, were incompatible with Chinese cultural predispositions. Further, the Soviet development strategy was ill-suited to an overwhelmingly rural, agriculturally based economy. China's Second Five-Year Plan (1958–62) gave greater emphasis to agriculture.

In addition, the highly centralized, bureaucratic nature of the Soviet system began to frustrate Mao and some, but by no means all, of his associates. Also, even as China imported the Soviet model, Nikita Khrushchev began to jettison parts of it. Finally, tensions between the Soviet Union and China arose in their foreign policies. Mao and his colleagues felt that in a series of foreign policy initiatives toward his allies, the United States, India, and the Middle East, Khrushchev had not taken adequate account of the interests and views of his junior ally. The growing discord within the Soviet-led bloc from 1956 to 1960 prompted Mao and his colleagues to be more skeptical of the Soviet economic development strategy and to be willing to risk Soviet displeasure by charting their own course toward modernity. In short, by the late 1950s, a combination of factors had propelled China's leaders to search for a second, altered strategy for the attainment of wealth and power.

In 1958, the Chinese Communist party (CCP) launched the "Great Leap Forward" and the "People's Commune Movement," and this effectively terminated the Second Five-Year Plan, which was never published. These poorly thought through and rashly implemented programs aimed at rapidly expanding agricultural production, factory output, and small-scale production resulted in economic chaos. During the period of the Second Five-Year Plan, agricultural production fell by 4.3 percent.[41] There was a severe famine in 1960 and subsequent years in which, according to one Western estimate, as many as 30 million people may have died.[42]

The Second Strategy: Self-Reliance, 1961–71

The Sino-Soviet dispute of the late 1950s and early 1960s left China essentially isolated in world economic and political affairs, and the disaster of the

41. Ma Hong, *New Strategy for China's Economy*, trans. Yang Lin (Beijing: New World Press, 1983), 20.

42. James T. H. Tsao, *China's Development Strategies and Foreign Trade* (Lexington, Mass.: Lexington Books, 1987), 23.

"Great Leap Forward" left the Chinese economy ruinously disordered. Making a virtue of necessity, Mao and his associates trumpeted the value of "self-reliance" (*zili gengsheng*), and their ideologues developed a rather appealing and coherent rationale for the benefits the nation would obtain from "relying on its own efforts" and "maintaining initiative in its own hands."[43] The concept of self-reliance was applied not only to China in relation to the rest of the world, but also to regions within China in relation to each other. The emphasis on self-reliance committed China to an import-substitution development strategy.

After a period of adjustment, the second, integrated economic development and national security strategy gradually took shape and was embodied in the Third Five-Year Plan (1966–70). Drafted in 1964–65, it involved high rates of capital accumulation, construction of local, small-scale industries, mobilization of labor, dispersal of heavy industries to the interior, and war preparedness. At the core of the new strategy was a militant defiance of both the Soviet Union and the United States but also a willingness to import from abroad.

In spite of the rhetoric and strategy, many of the Chinese leaders realized the potentially high cost of their isolation, and they made efforts in the early and mid-1960s to establish diplomatic and commercial contacts with Japan and Western Europe. In the period 1963–65, in fact, China went on a brief buying spree, especially seeking equipment and technology in the petroleum and metallurgy areas.[44] America's and China's growing involvement in the conflict within Vietnam, however, intensified Washington's vigilance in enforcing its controls over allied exports to China, and China's external overtures of the mid-1960s encountered difficulties.

The Third Five-Year Plan, however, was never implemented, due primarily to major political struggles over power and policy among the top leaders that soon engulfed the entire governmental apparatus and the bulk of the populace. The "soft" self-reliance strategy of that plan was abandoned in favor of the intense autarky of the Cultural Revolution (1966–69). From August, 1966, through late 1968, Mao and a newly gathered coterie of domestic allies sought to remove from the ranks of the top leaders and the bureaucracy people whom Mao thought would abandon his utopian vision after his death. Mao's power and influence were so great that he was able to

43. For analyses of the policy of self-reliance, see Michel Oksenberg and Steven Goldstein, "*Tzu-li Keng-Sheng:* China's Developmental Principle" (manuscript); Friedrich W. Wu, "Socialist Self-Reliant Development within the Capitalist World-Economy: The Chinese View in the Post-Mao Era," *Global Perspectives* 1, no. 1 (Spring 1983): 8–34.

44. The 1960s' turn outward is in Samuel P. S. Ho and Ralph Huenemann, *China's Open Door Policy.*

compel the entire nation to turn its attention inward. In his desire to commit Chinese society to the pursuit of his vision, in the summer of 1966 Mao harnessed the energies of discontented elements in the urban areas—portions of the students, workers, and even bureaucrats—to attack the "establishment" in the Party government, cultural, and educational hierarchies. The effort, however, soon escaped Mao's control, and the mobilized groups broke into warring factions, attacking one another and vulnerable citizens. From 1966 to 1968, wave after wave of terror swept the urban populace—especially intellectuals and civil servants—and the nation hurtled toward the precipice of civil war.[45]

Beginning in late 1968, somewhat aware of the damage he had wrought and increasingly cognizant of the growing military threat that the Soviet Union posed, Mao sought to reimpose order on the land. For the next three years, Mao and his associates were consumed with three challenges: how to reinstill discipline and rebuild the organizations shattered during the previous few years, how to cope with the growing Soviet military challenge against China, and what strategy to adopt to enable China to develop economically. The responses to these problems could not entail an explicit rejection of the Cultural Revolution, for Mao's prestige was so intertwined with the policies of 1966–68 that any repudiation of the Cultural Revolution would generate a challenge to his authority.

The Politics over the Initial Opening to the Outside, 1970–71

Not surprisingly, Mao's supporters were deeply divided over the appropriate response to this set of issues. Mao's heir apparent at the time and the head of the military, Lin Biao, was a principal architect and advocate of the self-reliance strategy of the 1960s, and his preference through mid-1970 was for increased defense expenditures, continued defiance of both the United States and the Soviet Union, and a continued, high level of popular mobilization for economic construction purposes. He also deployed the armed forces into factories, farms, universities, and government bureaucracies in order to quell domestic strife.

By mid-1970, for reasons that are unclear and may have been as much due to personal and power considerations as to policy preferences, Mao had become openly disenchanted with Lin Biao. Instead, he turned to Zhou Enlai to be his chief lieutenant. From late summer 1970 through the summer of

---

45. Two accounts of the era are captured in Yue Daiyun with Carolyn Wakeman, *To the Storm: The Odyssey of a Revolutionary Chinese Woman* (Berkeley: University of California Press, 1985); Nien Cheng, *Life and Death in Shanghai* (New York: Grove Press, 1987).

1971, Mao embarked on a series of measures to weaken Lin. The designated heir apparent was unwilling to acquiesce to his fate, as the earlier associates subjected to Mao's scorn had been. In events still shrouded in mystery, Lin Biao apparently encouraged his son (or so his son thought) to organize an assassination attempt against the Chairman. Mao had discovered the plot, and on September 13, 1971, Lin died while attempting to flee. Premier Zhou Enlai then became the leader in charge of day-to-day affairs at the headquarters of the Chinese Communist party, and long-time associates of the premier were placed in charge of the military and government apparatus.

The Emergence of a Third Strategy:
Turn to the Outside, 1971–76

The ascent of Zhou Enlai and the demise of Lin Biao involved much more than intrigue at the apex of the political system. The chaos of the Cultural Revolution and the Lin Biao affair signaled the bankruptcy of the economic development and national security strategies adopted in the wake of the Sino-Soviet dispute. The policies of self-reliance, high defense budgets, popular mobilization, simultaneous defiance of the Soviet Union and the United States, and intense ideological indoctrination of the populace had yielded a deeply divided leadership, a tension-ridden populace, and a nation facing a grave external threat from the Soviet Union. Moreover, although some portions of the economy continued to perform well (particularly the petroleum sector), high overall quantitative growth rates were sustained through neglect of quality and through high rates of capital accumulation. In effect, growth was obtained at an ever-increasing price. Due to such shortcomings as inefficiencies in management, problems in the work force, and bottlenecks in transportation and communications facilities, more and more had to be invested in order to sustain the same high level of growth. Clearly, this pattern could not be sustained indefinitely. The populace had been forced to forgo increases in living standards since the mid-1950s, but the economic and national security strategies adopted in the mid-1960s had brought neither prosperity nor tranquillity.

Deng Xiaoping joined the leadership group of Zhou and his entourage in 1973. Mao brought Deng back to Beijing from rural Jiangxi province in south China, where the Chairman had banished the former CCP general secretary for being a "capitalist roader" and a "revisionist." Mao evidently looked upon Deng as a potential replacement for Zhou, who had been diagnosed as suffering from cancer in May, 1972, and whose health deteriorated rapidly in 1973–74. Zhou and Deng were the leaders of networks of officials scattered throughout the country who owed their allegiance to them, who constituted part of their base of political power, and whom they sought to protect. (The

Chinese call this network a *guanxi hu*.) The ascent of Zhou and the return of Deng therefore had profound political consequences, for it prompted the return to office of experienced bureaucrats who had been disgraced or under attack during the Cultural Revolution and the heyday of Lin Biao.

Beginning in 1970–71, Zhou Enlai and his entourage, joined by Deng Xiaoping and his associates after 1973, began to shape an alternative economic development and national security strategy. They had to tread carefully, lest they raise Mao's ire. Mao had nurtured alternative leaders to Zhou and Deng, especially a group centering on his wife Jiang Qing and several ideologues and activists from Shanghai. This cluster, later known as the Gang of Four, had encouraged Mao to launch the Cultural Revolution, believed in many of its objectives, and had gained from it. Zhou and Deng dared not risk challenging the Chairman directly; he might cast them aside in favor of the cultural revolutionaries. By his own account, however, Deng was somewhat more willing to risk alienating Mao than was the ever tactful Zhou. Thus, as Zhou and Deng forged a new development and national security strategy for China, the initial elements of which were evident in the Fourth Five-Year Plan (1971–75), they sought the Chairman's support, and they tended to avoid directly attacking his bedrock policies and slogans.

Nonetheless, by the mid-1970s, they had succeeded—with Mao's blessings and sometimes at his initiative—in departing significantly from the national strategy of the early 1960s to the early 1970s, and the Fifth Five-Year Plan (1976–80) even more clearly reflected their priorities. Thus, many of the changes that became particularly visible in post-Mao China can be traced to the early and mid-1970s. Foremost among these developments was the opening to the outside world, which began with the quiet contacts between the Nixon administration and the Mao-Zhou team in 1970 and blossomed in 1971–72 with the Kissinger visit, the seating in the United Nations, the Nixon handshake with Mao Zedong, and the establishment of governmental relations with Japan. The diplomatic initiative under Mao and Zhou's aegis resulted in forty-three countries establishing full diplomatic relations with the Beijing government from October, 1970, through December, 1972.[46]

The Ending of Intellectual Isolation

The diplomatic breakthroughs facilitated the resumption of scholarly exchanges with the outside world as well. Scientists, engineers, medical personnel, social scientists, and humanists from the United States, Western Europe,

---

46. The number includes the resumption of diplomatic relations with Tunisia, Burundi, and Ghana after their suspension during the 1960s, and the elevation of relations with the Netherlands and Great Britain from consulate to embassy status.

and Japan began to develop contacts with their Chinese colleagues. To be sure, the exchanges were limited in duration and depth, and Chinese intellectuals who dealt with foreigners remained under the intense scrutiny of security officials. Nonetheless, ideas began to flow across China's boundaries. This was a significant development against the background of the rupture of the nation's educational and research institutes during the 1966–69 period.

In some respects, China's intellectual isolation was even more serious than its diplomatic isolation during the Cultural Revolution era. There literally was no broad-based source of ideas to which policy analysts could safely refer in the early 1970s. China's deep past was suspect for its feudalism; the Soviet and Eastern European experiences in applying Marxism were taboo for their revisionism; Western thought was forbidden for its liberalism and bourgeois or capitalist traditions. The distorted diatribes against the concepts and contributions of the key architects of the Chinese Communist party (particularly Liu Shaoqi, Chen Yun, and Peng Zhen) had effectively cut policymakers off from their own past. They could not even examine their guerrilla experience with honesty. And Lin Biao's reduction of Mao Zedong's thought into the aphorisms in the *Little Red Book* had even deprived Chinese officials of applying the Chairman's guidance in an appropriately complex way. The limited opening to the outside world, especially to the United States, Japan, and Western Europe, had immediate consequences in the realm of ideas. The external contact provided impetus to reopen the universities and to restore the scientific research institutes. The contacts also underscored China's intellectual poverty, and through Mao and Zhou's meetings with Overseas Chinese, they became aware that China was falling behind the rest of East Asia not only materially but in most realms of knowledge and scientific endeavor. For leaders who achieved power in part through the promise of restoring China's greatness, this evidently was an unsettling finding.

An additional, sobering note came from Deng Xiaoping and his associates. The time they spent in the countryside in disgrace had exposed them to many of the inadequacies of communist rule: the continued, grinding poverty; the dogmatism and oppressiveness of local officials; and the inapplicability at the grass roots of policies that somehow seemed logical or ideologically appropriate in Beijing. In short, Deng and many other early purgees of the Cultural Revolution returned to power in the mid-1970s convinced that many policies and institutions of the late Mao era required adjustment.

Thus, the initial opening to the outside world from 1971 on, coupled with the impulses of returned top officials who had spent extended periods in disgrace at lower levels, induced a desire among many Chinese leaders to search for appropriate sources of inspiration to solve their problems. After the Chairman's death in 1976 and the subsequent incarceration of the cultural revolutionaries, Mao's successors debated the applicability and relative merits of various experiences: China's own policies of the 1950s and early 1960s; the reforms of various East European countries within a Marxist framework; the economic systems of the developed countries rooted in Western economic theories; and the development of Japan, Taiwan, South Korea, and Hong Kong. The diplomatic gains of the early 1970s helped to stimulate a receptivity to reexamine old issues.

Increasing Foreign Trade

In addition to the diplomatic opening to the outside and the conceptual and policy developments, the third departure encouraged by Zhou and Deng came in the area of international trade. Foreign trade grew rapidly from 1971 to 1975, totaling $4.8 billion in 1971, $6 billion in 1972, $10.3 billion in 1973, $14.1 billion in 1974, and $14.6 billion in 1975.[47] Moreover, the direction of trade was reoriented toward the OECD countries. The share of the OECD countries' trade with China accounted for 46.6 percent of China's total foreign trade in 1971 and grew to 55.6 percent by 1975.[48] Perhaps more significant than the changes in volume and direction of trade were the tacit indications that China was prepared for a long-term commercial involvement with the outside world. In 1973, China and Japan agreed upon the outlines for a sustained trade relationship involving Chinese exports of fossil fuels—coal and oil—in exchange for Japanese metals and technology for modernizing its own metallurgy industry. Since Chinese export capability would lag behind its import capacity, the financing arrangements would be carried by the Japanese. The Chinese would defer their payments, a disguised form of indebtedness. These two measures were the surface manifestation of an internal decision, reached in early 1973 at Zhou's recommendation and with Mao's explicit approval, substantially to increase Chinese imports of whole plants from abroad. Called the "4-3 program," it was a plan to import $4.3 billion worth of equipment and whole plants over a four-year period.[49]

---

47. Richard E. Batsavage and John L. Davie, "China's International Trade and Finance," in *Chinese Economy Post-Mao*, U.S. Congress, Joint Economic Committee, 95th Cong., 2d sess. (Washington, D.C.: GPO, 1978), 734.

48. See Richard E. Batsavage and John L. Davie, "China's International Trade and Finance," 734–35.

49. For further discussion, see Samuel P. S. Ho and Ralph Huenemann, *China's Open Door Policy*, 15-17; Kenneth Lieberthal and Michel Oksenberg, *Policy Making in China: Leaders, Structures, and Processes* (Princeton: Princeton University Press, 1988), 179–80; Hao Mengbi and Duan Haoran, eds., *Zhoughua Renmin Gongheguo jingji dashiji* (1949–1980), 505.

Domestic Political Developments, 1975–78

The changes from 1971 to 1975 in China's external relations, whether diplomatic, intellectual, or economic, were not matched by similar developments in domestic policy. The military's involvement in administering the economy was curbed, and the political influence of regional commanders was eroded. The universities and scientific research institutes began to function again. Discipline began to be restored in the nation's factories. But these steps were taken haltingly, against political opposition.

As Mao's and Zhou's health waned in 1975, the cultural revolutionaries launched their last bid to retain political power in the post-Mao-and-Zhou era. Their nemesis clearly was the acerbic and potentially vengeful Deng Xiaoping, as well as the senior figures in the military. The period from mid-1975 to mid-1977 is probably best seen as an interregnum during which: (1) Zhou died (January, 1976); (2) the campaign of the cultural revolutionaries to remove Deng from power won Mao's favor (April, 1976); (3) another group of possible successors (variously called "neo-Maoists," "restorationists," or "mobilizers" by Western scholars) emerged with Mao's backing who were enamored neither with the Cultural Revolution nor with Deng's 1975 program (summer, 1976); (4) Mao died (September, 1976); (5) a coalition of the new successor group and Deng's supporters imprisoned Mao's wife and her cultural revolutionary supporters (October, 1976); (6) Deng Xiaoping returned to power in a carefully negotiated agreement with the "neo-Maoists" (spring, 1977); and (7) Deng Xiaoping and his associates engineered the full return of many additional, prestigious Party leaders who had been in eclipse or in total disgrace, and in alliance with them, the Deng-led coalition established its dominance in the Party, government, and army, prevailing over the neo-Maoists (the second half of 1978).

The political stage had been set to elaborate a new integrated economic development and national security strategy, drawing in part upon the pieces that Zhou and Deng had begun to assemble in the early and mid-1970s but which Mao's mercurial disposition, their own political vulnerabilities, and factional strife had precluded them from elaborating.

Deng and his allies perceived that they confronted a number of serious problems. Growth rates in agriculture were lagging, and the number of mouths to feed in the countryside continued to increase. During the bureaucratic chaos of the mid-1970s, the family planning program ceased to be vigorously implemented, and birthrates began to climb. Per capita grain consumption and caloric intake in the mid-1970s was no higher than the mid-1950s. The rural wage system offered insufficient incentive for peasants to increase their labor. The urban populace was exhausted from and disenchanted with the ceaseless political campaigns to which they had been sub-jected in the Mao era. A decade of neglect in the training of scientists, engineers, managers, and technicians had created huge shortages of skilled manpower, but at the same time poorly educated urban youths found in-adequate employment opportunities in the large coastal cities. Such cities as Beijing, Shanghai, Tianjin, Wuhan, and Guangzhou had large pools of unemployed youths who were reluctant to accept job assignments in the interior of China. The industrial sector, while exhibiting high growth rates, was plagued by bottlenecks in the transportation, communication, and energy sectors. Inefficiency, waste, and low quality of production were endemic problems.

Reviewing China's progress through 1978, Ma Hong, a noted Chinese economist and then President of the Chinese Academy of Social Sciences (CASS), offered a semiofficial critique of the development strategies that had been pursued through the first five-year plans,

— First, we one-sidedly sought high targets in production and construc-tion and neglected economic results.
— Second, we placed undue emphasis on the development of heavy industry at the expense of agriculture and light industry.
— Third, we only depended on new capital construction projects for expanded production and neglected to give full play to the role of already existing enterprises.
— Fourth, we overemphasized the output of primary and intermediate products in such industries as iron and steel and neglected the produc-tion of final consumer goods.
— Fifth, we placed a one-sided emphasis on high accumulation at the expense of people's necessary consumption.
— Sixth, we failed to control population growth as a result of our undue emphasis that with more people, things would be easier to handle.
— Seventh, we closed the country to international contacts due to our narrow interpretation of the theory of self-reliance, resulting in waste that could have been avoided.
— Eighth, we became too impatient in carrying out the transformation of the relations of production and unrealistically stepped up the pace of transfer to public ownership.[50]

Despite the evident progress that China had made, the defects of the develop-ment strategies that had been pursued were evident.

In addition to the economic and social difficulties, there were the politi-

---

50. Ma Hong, *New Strategy for China's Economy*, 26–27.

cal and ideological problems. A decade of factional strife at the top had induced a good deal of cynicism about the leaders of the country. The banner of Mao Zedong's thought, which so many had rallied to defend when the Chairman proclaimed it to be endangered in 1966, had become tarnished in the ensuing decade. What appeals could rally the populace to support their new leaders? How could Deng and his associates legitimate themselves in the eyes of their populace? Nor were relations between the political system and the populace the only difficulty Deng perceived. He confronted problems within national ministries and provincial and lower level units. The factional struggles at the top were echoed in the bureaucracies, and many agencies were plagued by divisions, mistrust, and strife. There was a need to reinstill discipline and common purpose and to reorient bureaucrats from inward struggles over past behavior toward public activities for the future.

Finally, Deng and his associates faced an epistemological issue. On what evidence were policy issues to be resolved? To Deng especially, who was inclined toward pragmatic and empirical thought, the Cultural Revolution represented a flight from reality. Instead of examining philosophical tracts or referring to Mao's writings when confronting problems—as the neo-Maoists supposedly advocated—Deng gave prominence to an old Chinese slogan, "seek truth from facts." Seeking to break away from dogmatism, he called for the Chinese to "dare to explore forbidden zones."

The economic, social, political, and philosophical challenges confronting Deng and his associates propelled them to assign primacy to economic growth and to search for solutions to China's problems in an open-minded fashion. This broad determination, however, set a general orientation; it did not precisely specify the policies that should be followed. At the time of China's move toward the KIEOs, these were matters of debate, and they have continued to be matters of debate throughout the 1980s, a debate that after 1980 has been affected in some measure by China's relationship with the KIEOs.

Conclusion

We have examined the trajectories of China and the KIEOs. In the 1970s, their paths of development were largely self-determined in the case of China and determined by the dynamics and needs of each institution and its participating states in the case of KIEOs. These trajectories brought Beijing and the KIEOs close together by the late 1970s. As we will note in our concluding chapters, their trajectories could pull them apart. For example, internal political changes in China such as occurred in June, 1989, could lead Beijing to adopt a new set of economic development and national security strategies. Or, efforts to cope with problems stemming from global debt and trade imbalances could push the KIEOs into paths that would diminish their attractiveness to China.

No one authority—a supposedly hegemonic United States, an international regime enforcing its norms, or the petitioning state—is in control of this process. Further, there is nothing inevitable about the process. In the next chapter, we will see how purposeful political action is necessary actually to forge links between two institutions whose paths are converging.

CHAPTER 3

The Process of Engagement with IMF and IBRD

The People's Republic of China entered the International Monetary Fund and the World Bank in 1980 and gave notice of its desire for full participation in GATT in 1986. How did this process of engagement come about? How successful was it, and what accounts for the extent of success? This chapter chronicles early contacts with the KIEOs and the process of China's entrance into IMF and the World Bank.[1] Chapter 4 deals with the negotiations about China's full participation in GATT.

A Successful Engagement

We must first establish criteria by which the process of engagement can be judged. What would a successful process of engagement involve? What standards should be met? These criteria relate primarily to the stage of engagement, though they unavoidably touch upon the process of participation and adjustment and the impact of engagement upon the Chinese political-economic system, the KIEOs, and the neoliberal international economic order that these institutions serve. Was the engagement a step toward the creation of a global economic order, and if it were, what kind of order would be likely to result? These broader issues are more easily addressed holistically, after all aspects of China's relationships with the KIEOs have been analyzed.

For purposes of this and the following chapter, the criteria for a successful process of engagement can be drawn fairly narrowly. A process can be regarded as successful if it prepares the international organization and its new member to pursue a fruitful interaction. For this to be the result, several developments have to occur.

— First, the process of engagement should resolve whatever contentious issues might exist between the aspiring entrant on one side and the organization and its members on the other. Disputes, whether nascent

---

1. For an early account of China's entering and initial participation in the IMF and World Bank see William Feeney, "Chinese Policy in Multilateral Financial Institutions," in *China and the World*, ed. Samuel S. Kim (Boulder, Colo.: Westview Press, 1984), 266–92.

or manifest, should not be left to linger and poison the interaction after entrance. This would involve the entrant having a clear understanding of the obligations and privileges of membership, and the organization and the entrant reaching mutual agreement if any derogations from full compliance were to be allowed. Such understanding and agreement should cover both the organization's decision-making processes and its substantive activities.

— Second, the process of engagement should not significantly disrupt the ongoing activities of the organization, and provision should have been made to bring the new entrant into these activities. If the ongoing activities were interrupted, it could undermine support for the organization among those states that already were members. And if the new entrant could not soon be included in these activities, at least some of the aspirations it had for participation in the organization would be blocked, and its enthusiasm for membership could wane. This criterion has special importance in this instance because of China's size and because of the character and importance of the KIEOs' activities. The IMF and the World Bank play crucial roles in providing financial and technical assistance. GATT's role in formulating and supervising rules for the conduct of international trade may be even more important.

— Third, the two sides should take the necessary steps to ensure that a mutually beneficial relationship can be supported administratively. This means that bureaucratic structures should be established on both sides to facilitate regular contact and interaction, and each side should know something about the other, enough to avoid egregious mistakes and to begin to develop mutually rewarding programs. Relationships between member states and international organizations that consist only of transfers of resources or episodic participation in conferences are unlikely to make much difference either to the state or to the organization. International organizations can serve as effective networks for the transmission of information only if meaningful information is developed and received, which normally requires bureaucratic structures on both sides.

— Finally, the relationship should be institutionalized; it should not depend primarily on individual personalities on either side. Instead, the process of engagement should result in a relationship that is deeply and firmly rooted on each side and can survive the political reversals of particular leaders and administrators. This is particularly important if the entrant is a state without a well-established pattern for the transfer of authority.

Both the aspiring entrant and the international organization need to take appropriate actions for these criteria to be met. The state needs to prepare carefully for its bid, and the international organization needs to react to the state's overtures responsively and with sympathy. An unprepared bid and a harsh and misunderstanding response would surely guarantee an unsuccessful outcome.

Judged by these standards, China's approach to the KIEOs was impressive. It came after a lengthy period of careful preparation, and its requests were welcomed by the KIEOs. Let us now turn to the story.

To the Mid-1970s

The Period of Isolation from the KIEOs, 1950–71

In spite of the rhetoric of the Mao era, several Chinese leaders, a number of middle-level officials, and various institutions had retained a keen interest in reclaiming China's seat in the World Bank, IMF, and GATT. Sino-American animosity, the Taiwan presence in the KIEOs, and denial of PRC membership in the United Nations had precluded serious consideration by Beijing of membership in UN-affiliated organizations until 1971. To be sure, in 1950 the new government in Beijing sought to be recognized as the successor government and to have its representatives seated as the delegates of China in the UN and many of its affiliated bodies, but the UN continued to accept the credentials of the nominees put forward by the authorities on Taiwan as delegates from the Republic of China.

The KIEOs were among the organizations from which the PRC was excluded. In February, 1950, the issue of Chinese representation on the IMF board of directors was raised by Czechoslovakia and Poland, but the board resolved that this was a matter that the board of governors should decide.[2] In August, 1950, Zhou Enlai dispatched a cable to Camille Gutt, the managing director of the IMF, claiming that the People's Republic of China was the sole legal government of China and seeking expulsion from the annual meeting of the Fund's board of governors of the representatives who were appointed by the Taipei authorities. During the annual meeting in September, 1950, Czechoslovakia, supported by Yugoslavia and India, proposed a resolution that would have excluded the Taiwan-designated Chinese governors, executive directors, and their alternates from the Fund and the Bank, but the resolution

---

2. These events are described in J. Keith Horsefield, *The International Monetary Fund, 1945–1965: Twenty Years of International Monetary Cooperation* (Washington, D.C.: IMF, 1969), 1:258.

was defeated on a hand vote after the Philippines suggested that it was out of order because it dealt with a political issue then under consideration by the United Nations. Thus began the protracted period of the People's Republic of China's noninvolvement in the KIEOs. Czechoslovakia introduced proposals like the one that it had offered in September, 1950, at the annual meetings of the boards of governors of the Fund and the Bank from 1951 through 1954, but the results were always the same.[3] After Czechslovakia's expulsion from the two organizations in December, 1954, the matter was dropped. The issue of Chinese representation was, however, raised annually in the UN and several specialized agencies. Until 1971, the result was always the same: the delegates designated by Taiwan retained China's seats.

Nonetheless, several Chinese-Americans and international civil servants of Chinese ethnicity who were familiar with the work of the KIEOs sustained contact with PRC organizations throughout the 1950s and 1960s, providing detailed information about the IMF, the World Bank, and GATT. Because GATT's headquarters were in Geneva, Switzerland, and Beijing had had formal diplomatic relations with Switzerland since 1950, the PRC was in a position to observe GATT activities firsthand, unlike the situation that prevailed with respect to the IMF and the World Bank, where China's absence from Washington precluded close observation. Bank of China branches in Hong Kong and London were especially active in informing Chinese leaders about the world financial situation, in which Zhou Enlai apparently took a keen interest. Leading Chinese economists—many of whom had been trained in Western universities in the late 1940s and then returned to China to serve in the new government—and some in the foreign community in Beijing (such as former U.S. Treasury and IMF official Frank Coe) also sought to remain abreast of developments in international financial institutions. Thus, even during the period of PRC absence from the UN system, threads existed that provided some connection to the KIEOs. A community of specialists on the subject existed in Beijing that was quietly interested in and somewhat informed about the issue and that guided the policymakers when the appropriate opportunity arose.

Admission to the United Nations

All this information and informal contact did not mean Beijing was prepared rapidly to assert itself in international organizations immediately following the UN General Assembly vote in October, 1971, to seat the PRC delegation.

---

3. See Joseph Gold, *Membership and Nonmembership in the International Monetary Fund: A Study in International Law and Organization* (Washington, D.C.: IMF, 1974). After the PRC entered the war in Korea, its support declined, *New York Times*, September 11, 1951.

To the contrary, the Chinese Foreign Ministry in particular and the foreign policy community more generally—including the specialists on the KIEOs—were ill equipped for the event. Above all, the previous five years of the Cultural Revolution had severely shaken this community, and in October, 1971, a significant portion of the most qualified bureaucrats were in the countryside engaging in manual labor. In addition, the Chinese government did not expect to win the UN vote that fall. Its leading analysts, heeding the Nixon administration's pleas to be patient and watching the energetic efforts of its new American friends in 1971 to lobby on behalf of Taiwan, had concluded that 1972 would be the year the PRC would gain the China seat.

During his October, 1971, visit to Beijing, Henry Kissinger had requested Chinese understanding of the American position on this issue. As Kissinger's plane taxied away from the Beijing airport to begin the long return journey to Washington, one of the officials from the Ministry of Foreign Affairs pulled out his portable radio to listen to the morning news. Straining to hear the broadcast above the roar of the U.S. Air Force Boeing 707 as it sped down the runway, the foreign affairs officials suddenly learned that their government had been awarded the China seat in the United Nations. The joyous Chinese waved a warm farewell to Kissinger, knowing something the president's emissary had not yet learned.

The next day, Zhou Enlai gathered a large number of his aides to discuss when China should dispatch a delegation to New York. A substantial number of officials at the meeting, perhaps a majority, were inclined not to send a delegation immediately, but rather to do the necessary internal work first. The experts told the premier that they were unprepared. No papers had been written in anticipation of the event. The Ministry of Foreign Affairs did not have a sufficient staff assigned to deal with international organizations. But the premier disagreed with his advisors. It would be best, he concluded, to show the flag quickly, particularly in order to demonstrate to all parties that China was going to behave in a dignified, careful, and responsible manner.

The October, 1971, vote had a catalytic effect. It necessitated strengthening the international organization staff in the MFA. Qualified diplomats and bureaucrats had to be recalled from the countryside to plan for China's participation in UN-affiliated organizations. It also had ripple effects throughout the agencies of the UN system.

The United Nations Small Group

Soon after the PRC entered the UN, several of China's contacts abroad recommended strategies for its entry into the KIEOs. Even more important, a United Nations Small Group (UNSG) was set up in 1972 within the Bank of China to analyze membership in all UN financial agencies, including the

World Bank and the IMF. This group worked closely with the Ministry of Foreign Affairs and other related agencies. Before Premier Zhou Enlai was weakened by cancer, criticisms from Mao, and attacks from the cultural revolutionaries in 1973–74, he encouraged the group's work.[4] As Zhou's strength ebbed, Vice-Premier Li Xiannian assumed the portfolio as the top leader in charge of planning for China's relations with the KIEOs.

The United Nations Small Group was located within the Institute of International Finance, a subordinate unit of the Bank of China. At the time, the Bank of China, as it was known to the external world, was listed on "internal" (nei-bu) organizational charts as the Bureau of International Affairs of the People's Bank of China. It continued to be subordinate to the People's Bank until the mid-1980s. The head of the UN Small Group was a senior banking official, and its members all came from the Bank of China. Officials from other agencies, such as the Ministry of Finance, the Ministry of Foreign Affairs, and the State Statistical Bureau attended its meetings.

The group began to follow developments in the IMF and World Bank with close attention. It did so, it should be recalled, in a general political environment in which the radical supporters of Mao Zedong were capable of subjecting people they suspected of harboring "capitalist" tendencies to harsh criticism, imprisonment, and torture. Involved Chinese officials differ over whether this unsettled situation penetrated to the Small Group. According to some of its participants, even though the Small Group enjoyed the protection of Zhou Enlai and the leaders of the finance and economics sector, courage, conviction, and confidence that the radical era would pass were necessary for some of its members to consider China's eventual membership in organizations their potential tormentors abhorred. Other participants, however, firmly reject the claim that the Small Group worked in a dangerous or uncertain environment. But in any case, the group submitted its views to the top leaders in a carefully considered fashion.

Unpursued Openings, 1971–75

Thus, China's membership in the UN stimulated its interest in the KIEOs, but the domestic political environments in China and the United States precluded pursuit of opportunities to establish direct contact.

The first opportunity came soon after the October, 1971, vote to seat the PRC. The People's Republic did not pursue a 1971 opening to have formal contact with the GATT. China was a founding member of the General Agree-

---

4. For reference to Mao's criticism of Zhou see Hao Mengbi and Duan Haoran, eds., *Zhongquo gongchandang liushinian* (Sixty years of the Chinese Communist party) (Beijing: People's Liberation Army Press, 1984), 632.

ment on Tariffs and Trade. In March, 1950, the authorities on Taiwan formally notified the secretary-general of the UN (the official depository for the General Agreement) of their intention to withdraw from GATT, effective May 5, 1950. In 1965, Taipei requested observer status in GATT, which was granted, despite the statement by several countries that the People's Republic was the only legal government of China. On November 16, 1971, after the PRC's accession to the UN, the contracting parties agreed that Taiwan should no longer have this observer status.

Through this decision, GATT in effect invited China to initiate direct contact, but the Chinese government did not act upon this opening.[5] The opportunity came at a particularly difficult time in Beijing as China was then consumed with the aftermath of the Lin Biao affair, and the Minister of Foreign Trade was not deeply conversant with the subtleties of international relations. While the GATT opportunity received high-level attention, Chinese officialdom was simply not prepared to pursue intelligently its new opportunities in international organizations.

Beijing chose instead to use its newly established permanent mission to the United Nations office at Geneva to monitor GATT activities. This same office managed Chinese participation in the United Nations Conference on Trade and Development. In addition, Chinese nationals served in the UNCTAD secretariat in capacities that brought them in contact with GATT.

Opportunities also presented themselves at the Fund and IBRD. Taiwan's presence in the IMF and the World Bank had been reduced by its own actions and those of other member states. From 1972 on, Taiwan was not represented on the executive board of either institution. Taiwan had lost the right to appoint executive directors in 1960 because of the decline in the relative size of its quota and subscription. Starting in 1972, Taiwan was not included in the constituency of any elected executive director.

In September, 1973, just before the annual meetings of the boards of governors of the IMF and the World Bank, Minister of Foreign Affairs Ji Pengfei telegraphed the managing director of the Fund and the president of the Bank claiming that Taiwan had seized the seat in these organizations that rightfully belonged to the People's Republic and requesting that the "KMT [Kuomintang] counterrevolutionary clique" should be expelled. Mao Zedong personally approved this cable, thereby indicating that he countenanced Chinese participation in the IMF. Later, this tacit endorsement helped quell the opposition of conservatives when the top leaders considered the IMF issue in the post-Mao era.

Although the political climate in the United States did not permit a more forthcoming response, World Bank President Robert McNamara did acknowl-

---

5. *Beijing Review*, November 5, 1971.

edge this signal on November 2, 1973, by sending a telegram to Beijing stating that an application from China to join the World Bank would be welcomed. McNamara was strongly interested in having China participate in the Bank. He felt that the Bank's function was to be a development assistance organization, and he believed China needed assistance for its development programs. Because of China's size and importance, McNamara felt that the World Bank did not truly deserve its name without Chinese participation. He also felt that China's membership and obvious needs would be a lever for increasing the Bank's resources. The main question for him was how to bring about China's participation without creating a controversy that would deeply divide the Bank's membership. He was particularly concerned about the United States, the Bank's largest contributor and Taiwan's most devoted and powerful advocate. In spite of its opening to China, the Nixon administration was reluctant to advance the new relations at Taiwan's expense; the administration was reluctant to raise the ire of Taiwan's strong supporters in the Congress. U.S. opposition effectively blocked McNamara for several years from opening negotiations with China or attempting to bring the matter of Chinese representation to a vote.

The Chinese never responded to McNamara's November cable, although the matter was considered internally. In June, 1974, a report was prepared by the Ministry of Finance (MOF) and the Ministry of Foreign Affairs that recommended against joining the International Monetary Fund and the World Bank for two reasons.

First, the two ministries were concerned that, because of the weighted-voting formula in the IMF and World Bank, the two institutions would not provide China with a suitable platform from which to pursue its broader foreign policy objectives. Already displaying sensitivity to the issue of Chinese voting power, the two ministries noted that were the People's Republic to inherit Taiwan's existing position, Beijing would have only 1.68 percent of the total votes in the IMF and 2.83 percent of those in the World Bank. Moreover, the main spearhead of Chinese foreign policy at that time was directed against the Soviet Union and secondarily but still vigorously against the United States. The degree of vehemence directed at each was carefully calibrated. Since the Soviet Union was not a member of either body, it would place China in the awkward position of having to criticize the United States while being deprived of the opportunity of lambasting the Soviet Union, the favorite target.

Second, the ministries of Finance and Foreign Affairs claimed that the Articles of Agreement of the IMF were contradictory to a socialist monetary system. They feared that China would face restrictions on the determination of its foreign exchange rate and control over the administration of its foreign exchange. This was considered unacceptable at a time when China's leaders adhered to a policy of extreme self-reliance in world affairs. The Chinese system for foreign trade was designed to insulate the Chinese economy from world market forces, which were regarded as irrational and harmful to Chinese national interests. The system in effect created an "air lock" between the Chinese and the international economies. Finally, the report noted that, in accordance with the then prevailing policy against external borrowing, China would not borrow money from the IMF, but it still would have to pay its quota. The top leaders agreed with this report.

Establishing Direct Contact with the KIEOs, 1976–79

Developments within the IMF finally forced the pace of decision in Beijing. At a meeting of the Interim Committee of the IMF in Jamaica in January, 1976, agreement was reached to sell a portion of the gold that member states had deposited with the Fund as backing for IMF credits.[6] Part of this gold would be sold to member states at the "official price" of $35 per ounce at which they first contributed gold, allowing them to reap the benefits of reselling the gold at the much higher market price. The Fund would sell the remaining part of the gold at the market price and use the proceeds to establish a trust fund for those Fund members that had developing country status.

This raised the issue of whether Taiwan would be considered the claimant for China's share of the gold and hence a beneficiary of the sale. The PRC's United Nations Small Group followed this development carefully, translating the IMF documents into Chinese and informing the top leadership. Upon the recommendation of the UNSG, the vice-president of the People's Bank, Chen Xiyu, sent a cable to the managing director of the IMF at the Jamaica meeting, asserting that the gold belonged to the PRC as the Chinese member of the IMF and should not go to the regime on Taiwan. This note was followed by a telegram from the president of the People's Bank to the IMF at its annual meeting, held in Manila in October, 1976, asserting that all properties and rights in the IMF belong to the Chinese people and that the IMF should expel the representatives of the "Chiang Kai-shek clique" from the IMF immediately.

These 1976 initiatives reveal that the Chinese government was able to galvanize itself on this deeply divisive issue during those tumultuous months of 1976 when Zhou Enlai died, Deng Xiaoping was purged under the radical onslaught, and Mao Zedong died. Indeed, the cable to Manila was sent in the brief interlude between Mao's death and the arrest of Mao's wife and her

---

6. For the details and implementation of this agreement see Margaret Garritsen de Vries, *The International Monetary Fund, 1972–1978: Cooperation on Trial* (Washington, D.C.: IMF, 1985), chaps. 31–34, 607–82.

Cultural Revolution associates, a period of national mourning, elite plotting, and supposed political paralysis. But when substantial resources and membership in international organizations were at stake, the leaders were able to focus on the issue.

Behind the scenes, the UNSG continued to be active in Beijing. The question of China's resuming its membership in the International Monetary Fund and the World Bank was placed on the State Council docket in 1976, but in the end, a decision was deferred. The issue, though, was clearly on the agenda, and once the 1977–78 uncertainty surrounding the succession to Chairman Mao was removed through the emergence of Deng Xiaoping as China's preeminent leader, the situation became propitious for State Council action.

The external environment was also beginning to stimulate forward movement. For example, in September, 1978, Chinese Minister of Finance Zhang Jingfu visited Romania. During his visit, the Romanian vice-president and minister of finance expressed the hope that China would participate in IMF. In October of the same year, the counselor of the Yugoslavian embassy in Beijing, acting on behalf of his government, called on the International Bureau of the Ministry of Finance and reported on the annual meeting of IMF's board of governors which took place in Washington in September. In the course of his report, he too recommended that China should participate in the Fund. At that time, other than the Indo-Chinese states, Romania and Yugoslavia were the only members of the Fund that had nonmarket economies.

The Decision for Participation in IMF and the World Bank, 1979 through Winter, 1980

Changes in the Domestic Setting

The Beijing decision to participate in the IMF and World Bank came in January–February 1979. As the preceding section detailed, this decision came after an extended period of considering and preparing for membership. Even more important, since 1971 the leaders of China gradually and haltingly had made a series of moves to increase their commercial contacts with Japan, the United States, and the EEC countries. The choice to seek involvement with the Bank and Fund followed, rather than preceded, a number of significant policy changes that, in turn, helped to ease the process of engagement with the World Bank and IMF.

Among the landmark, incremental adjustments to the policy of strict self-reliance were decisions in 1971–72 to initiate a large number of whole plant imports, the agreement with Japan in early 1973 to sell coal and crude petroleum to and import metals from Japan, the 1973 decision to purchase foreign commodities through deferred payments, the 1977 reaffirmation of these policies after a protracted internal struggle between those committed to autarky and those involved in acquisition of foreign technology and equipment, an early 1978 decision to expand scientific contacts with the outside world, a 1978 decision to invite foreign investment in China, and a 1978 decision to use foreign capital and vigorously enter foreign markets. In sum, these policy innovations prompted rapid increases in foreign trade through the 1970s and reoriented the direction of foreign trade toward Japan, the United States, and the EEC. Cumulatively, these policies propelled China toward entry into the international economy.

The dramatic change in China's relations with the United States and Japan in 1971 permitted the evolution in foreign trade policies. From 1949 to 1970, the United States sought to keep China poor, weak, and isolated in world affairs. But the Vietnam War and the Cultural Revolution underscored to Washington the high cost and risk of that policy, while increasing awareness of the Sino-Soviet dispute finally led the American government to understand the strategic benefits to be secured by an opening to China.[7] Japan's leaders from Prime Minister Yoshida's time forward all, to varying degrees, chafed under the trade constraints with China imposed by the United States; within Japan, a portion of the business community longed to resume the previous lucrative trade to China.[8] Thus, when the Nixon administration relaxed American constraints on trade with China, the Chinese were able to initiate trade policies that they previously were unable to pursue, while many Japanese in particular were quick to stimulate the Chinese appetite for their goods and capital. The January–February, 1979, decision to seek participation in the World Bank and the IMF was therefore the product of a seven-year evolution in Chinese foreign commercial policies that in no small measure was a response to fundamental changes in the American and Japanese orientation to China.

The January–February decision also was nested in sweeping changes in domestic politics and policies following Mao Zedong's death and the elimination of the pro–Cultural Revolution elements in the Chinese leadership.[9] The period from Mao's death in September, 1976, to Deng Xiaoping's consolida-

---

7. Henry Kissinger, *The White House Years* (Boston: Little, Brown, 1979); Richard Nixon, *RN: The Memoirs of Richard Nixon* (New York: Grosset and Dunlap, 1978).

8. Yoshihida Soeya, "Japan's Postwar Economic Diplomacy with China: Three Decades of Non-Governmental Experiences" (Ph.D. diss., University of Michigan, 1987).

9. See Jurgen Domes, *The Government and Politics of the PRC: A Time of Transition* (Boulder, Colo.: Westview Press, 1985), 137–72; A. Doak Barnett, *China's Economy in Global Perspective* (Washington, D.C.: Brookings Institution, 1981), 63–83.

tion of his position as the preeminent leader lasted over two years. During that period, the underlying purpose of rule shifted from the Maoist emphasis upon attainment of cultural and social change to Deng's emphasis upon modernization and economic development. The policy process itself began to be modified, so that decisions would be based upon empirical observation rather than through reference to ideological texts. Finally, policies began to be set in motion that signaled a retreat from the state's total control of the economy and society. Unlike the Maoist era of the 1960s and 1970s, a significant foreign involvement in China's development became conceivable.

Then came the watershed Third Plenary Session of the Eleventh Central Committee of the Chinese Communist party in December, 1978, when major decisions were taken to move forward with economic reform, to radically change the agricultural sector, to introduce market influences through the personal responsibility system, to open China's economy to the world, and to work decisively to expand exports and foreign exchange earnings.[10] The self-critique of the development strategies that China had pursued was previously summarized in chapter 2 (p. 54).

Table 3.1 shows the context in which the Chinese decisions were taken. China's economic growth in the 1960s and 1970s had been impressive, amazingly so in light of the political and economic turmoil that had consumed the country, but China's growth had not kept pace with the rate that had been achieved by a number of neighboring countries, several of which had substantial Overseas Chinese populations. Although the data in table 3.1 could not have been available to Chinese leaders, they were aware that China's progress had lagged behind that of important referent countries. They were also probably aware, as such scholars as Alexander Eckstein had signaled, that even sustaining past rates of growth would be more difficult because of the new stage that the Chinese economy had reached.[11]

The decisions of the Third Plenary Session were aimed at maintaining and accelerating China's development. These decisions were based on a careful analysis of the past and a broad vision of needed changes in development strategies. China abandoned the previous strategy of extensive development that had stressed the expansion of the means of production and the suppression of consumption with a program of readjustment, restructuring, consolidation, and improvement that stressed improved utilization of existing capacity and gave greater emphasis to consumption. The decisions of the

---

10. For a description by a leading Chinese economist of the context of these decisions, their broad nature, and implementation see Ma Hong, *New Strategy for China's Economy*, trans. Yang Lin (Beijing: New World Press, 1983).

11. Alexander Eckstein, *China's Economic Revolution* (Cambridge: Cambridge University Press, 1977).

**TABLE 3.1.   Average Annual Percentage
Growth in Gross Domestic Product in China and
Other Developing Countries, 1965–80**

Country	Growth Rate
China	6.4
All developing countries	6.1
Low income developing countries	
other than China and India	4.8
Hong Kong	8.5
India	3.7
Indonesia	7.9
Korea	9.5
Malaysia	7.4
Singapore	10.4
Taiwan	9.7

Source: IBRD, *World Development Report 1988* (Washington, D.C.: IBRD, 1988), 224–25. *Source for Taiwan:* Official Statistics of Taiwan.

Third Plenary Session shifted China's trade policy from what World Bank economists in a report published in 1988 termed autarky to a more outwardly oriented one, but one that they nevertheless characterized as modified import substitution.[12] The decisions of the Third Plenary Session set the stage for the decision to seek the China seat at the IMF and the Bank.

A Ministerial Recommendation, January, 1979

In January, 1979, seizing upon the new political environment of the Third Plenary Session, the People's Bank of China, the Ministry of Finance, and the Ministry of Foreign Affairs prepared and forwarded a report through channels to the State Council, in effect China's cabinet. The report drew upon the deliberations over the previous seven years by the UNSG and the community of KIEO specialists. It argued that the overall situation favored quick action. The acting general manager of the Bank of China, Feng Tianshun, elliptically referred to this report when he disclosed to a visiting U.S. congressional delegation that he had "officially recommended" that the PRC should join the IMF.[13] The report was detailed and analyzed the benefits of resuming China's seats in the IMF and the IBRD.

The report from the People's Bank, the Ministry of Finance, and the

---

12. IBRD, *China: External Trade and Capital* (Washington, D.C.: IBRD, 1988), 1–6..
13. *China Business Review*, January–February, 1980, 55.

Ministry of Foreign Affairs enumerated the factors in the overall world situation that made a move by China timely. Sixteen UN bodies other than the IMF and the IBRD and its affiliated bodies had already expelled Taiwan. The United States and the PRC had established formal diplomatic relations on January 1, 1979. The United States had simultaneously severed official diplomatic relations with Taipei, which meant that the Carter administration was not likely to pose obstacles to the expulsion of Taiwan from the IMF and the World Bank. The report stated that Third World governments wanted China to be in the Fund and the World Bank. The report also suggested that the disposition of Chinese assets in the Fund could be decided at the same time Chinese membership was decided, rather than be settled as a precondition to Chinese membership, which had been the Chinese position.

The report noted that its authors were prepared to investigate the experience of other countries and to submit more detailed recommendations. The State Council accepted the proposal, and a major mission with seven members went to Romania and Yugoslavia in the period from May 6 through June 7, 1979. Headed by Lin Jixing, the interagency delegation included officials from such agencies as the Ministry of Foreign Affairs, the Ministry of Finance, the Bank of China, and the State Statistical Bureau. By sending the delegation, the State Council had basically decided to seek participation in the two organizations. In fact, Deng Xiaoping had signaled this decision in his characteristically blunt fashion when he told the president of Kyodo News Service on February 26, 1979, that "there would be no hitch on China's part in joining the IMF if the Taiwan issue is settled."[14]

Evidently, over a period of time the Chinese leaders had carefully weighed the pros and cons of membership. The benefits that participation in the Fund and the Bank would bring were obvious. (1) It would entail withdrawal or expulsion of Taiwan, a major diplomatic victory for the People's Republic. (2) From a political vantage, having entered the United Nations, China should seek membership in all its affiliates, including the IMF and World Bank. It was a logical step. (3) Membership in these two bodies would reinforce the bilateral relations China was then seeking to build with most countries in the world. (4) Membership would yield China more information about international finance and economics, thereby assisting its development program. Moreover, it would reduce dependence upon intermediaries in obtaining information about the international economy. (5) China would be eligible for concessional interest rate loans and IMF drawing privileges, even though it did not plan to exercise its rights to such funds in large amounts. Our Chinese sources recall that the last consideration was clearly the least important one to the UNSG and the top leaders.

---

14. *China Business Review*, May–June, 1979, 31.

Several consequences were also foreseen that many Chinese considered onerous. (1) China would have to submit data that its leaders then considered highly confidential. In particular, its gold reserves and currency in circulation were "top secret" (*ji-mi*) and known only to a few top leaders. The top leaders would have to change these policies, a decision only they could make. (2) The IMF and World Bank would send frequent missions to their member countries, seeking information and visiting localities. (3) China would have to contribute financially to meet its quota in the IMF and subscription in the World Bank, and the sums entailed could be significant. In addition, Taiwan's representation in the two organizations posed an immediate obstacle to PRC membership.

Missions and Contacts Abroad, 1979

The mission to Romania and Yugoslavia, both of which had friendly relations with China and both of which had already urged China to participate in the IMF and IBRD, sought information on how these two nonmarket economies supplied data to the IMF and World Bank, what their procedures were to host visiting missions from these bodies, how much money—loans and credits— they obtained, and what specific projects they undertook. Both the Romanian minister of finance and the Yugoslavian State Bank president strongly suggested that China participate in these organizations.

After its return, the group wrote a lengthy report, which it submitted in August, 1979, suggesting that the PRC should take swift measures to participate in the IMF and World Bank. The first steps would be to invite the IMF to send an informal working group to be followed by one from the World Bank to explore issues surrounding Chinese membership. Compared to the January, 1979, recommendation, this report was more concrete and expressed confidence that the benefits outweighed the costs. The experience of Romania and Yugoslavia demonstrated that nations committed to planned economies and socialist principles could work within the framework of these organizations.

Meanwhile, informal contact had begun to develop in the United States and elsewhere between Chinese and IMF and World Bank officials. Soon after normalization, Secretary of State Cyrus Vance indicated to Robert McNamara that he thought China would soon be seeking World Bank membership, and with McNamara's blessing some World Bank personnel began to brief officials in the Chinese embassy in Washington about its procedures and activities. In February, 1979, Chinese-Americans in California helped to arrange a two-week private tour of China by twenty-one World Bank officials. The Bank officials covered their own expenses. McNamara insisted that the Bank should have nothing officially to do with the trip. The group was led by David Gordon, director of the Bank's International Development and Finance

Department. They did not have contact with Chinese officials dealing with the Fund or the Bank, but they did begin to familiarize themselves with China.

Also early in 1979, before the conclusion of the Tokyo Round of multilateral trade negotiations, officials from China's permanent mission in Geneva directed inquiries to the GATT secretariat about the likely results of the negotiations. They were given a briefing and relevant documents. In addition, it was arranged that in 1980 a Chinese official from the Ministry of Foreign Economic Relations and Trade, Liu Xianming, would enroll in one of the short courses in commercial policy that the GATT secretariat offered. From this point on, there was regular contact between the Chinese permanent mission in Geneva and the GATT secretariat, but China did not immediately take any steps beyond this to increase its contact with GATT.

In October, 1979, Zhao Mingde, who at that time was special assistant to the under-secretary general, Department of Technical Cooperation for Development of the United Nations, journeyed to Belgrade to attend the annual meeting of the boards of governors of the IMF and the World Bank as an observer. Zhao attended the meeting on behalf of Bi Jilong, the UN under-secretary general. Zhao met privately with a World Bank vice-president, and this was soon followed by another high-level contact in Hong Kong. China's participation in the Bank was discussed on both occasions. Personnel from the Chinese mission to the UN then visited Washington to obtain more information and secured considerable documentation on Bank activities. During the fall, the IMF's new China desk had several contacts with personnel in the Chinese embassy in Washington.

It therefore came as no surprise when, in February, 1980, the Chinese ambassador to Washington, Chai Zemin, asked to see Robert McNamara. The timing of the call was dictated by congressional ratification of the U.S. trade agreement with China, which extended most-favored-nation treatment to China. As noted earlier, the Chinese had decided not to risk arousing unfavorable congressional sentiment by simultaneously pressing for expulsion of Taiwan from the Bank and IMF. As soon as the trade agreement cleared congressional hurdles, the ambassador began to move on the IMF and World Bank. Chai invited McNamara to visit China within the next few weeks and indicated that the People's Republic wished to reacquire its seat in the following month. McNamara underscored what pertinent bureaucrats in Beijing already understood, namely that in accordance with the Articles of Agreement, entry into the IMF was the first step, a prerequisite to membership in the Bank.

Internal Preparation at the IMF and World Bank

The IMF and World Bank responded to these overtures internally and began to prepare themselves for Chinese membership. In June, 1979, the International Monetary Fund hired two individuals to work on China, Luc-Henry de Wulf and Françoise le Gall. Luc-Henry de Wulf was a broad-gauged economist, and Françoise le Gall had been trained as a specialist on the Chinese economy. Various papers had been prepared on China starting in 1977. Using these papers as a base, the newly created China desk set out to learn everything that would be relevant to the Fund about China's economy. Most of the data for analysis of the Chinese economy that was available to the Fund's staff, and to all other Western analysts, came from materials that were openly published by the U.S. Central Intelligence Agency, where an office had long and carefully charted China's economic performance. So the early analyses of the Chinese economy were based on unclassified CIA data.

Under McNamara's direction, the Bank also established a small working group in anticipation of Chinese membership. Led by Edwin Lim, it began to draft and commission briefing papers on the nature of the Chinese economy, to identify the specific issues that would have to be addressed as China acquired its seat, and to develop a broad strategy for incorporating China in the Bank's activities. Lim had worked on China previously only in the context of preparing materials for the Bank's annual *World Development Reports*. The estimates of China's gross national product and GNP per capita that were published in the *World Bank Atlas* were derived from unclassified CIA data. Using these data, the *World Bank Atlas 1979* estimated China's per capita GNP for 1977 and 1978 to be $410 and $460,[15] figures that were subsequently revised downward after China began supplying statistical data to the IMF and the World Bank. The *World Bank Atlas 1980* listed China's per capita GNP for 1978 as $230.[16]

At the time, only countries with a per capita income of less than $400 were eligible for IDA loans, and the downward revision placed China in the same range as India and Indonesia, which the *World Bank Atlas* listed as having per capita incomes of $180 and $340 respectively. The CIA estimate of China's per capita GNP had been based on the concept of purchasing power parity. It had calculated the Chinese per capita GNP in terms of dollars, setting the dollar value of Chinese currency on the basis of an estimate of the equivalent purchasing power of the two currencies within their own economies. The figures published in the *World Bank Atlas* for virtually all other countries were those provided by the countries themselves. These figures were normally transformed into dollars by using the official exchange rate or an average of the official exchange rate over time. Using the official exchange rate, Alexander Eckstein calculated China's 1974 per capita GDP as $190, a figure that would be consistent with the figure published in the *World Bank*

---

15. IBRD, *World Bank Atlas 1979* (Washington, D.C.: IBRD, 1979), 14.
16. IBRD, *World Bank Atlas 1980* (Washington, D.C.: IBRD, 1980), 14.

Atlas 1980.[17] Even though the change in China's per capita GNP was simply a consequence of using the same type of data for China as were used for most other countries, some commentators in Third World countries maintained that it was a device to make China eligible for IDA funds. Within the Bank's staff and governing bodies, however, no one argued that China was so well off that it should not receive IDA funds.

Negotiating the Terms for Membership in IMF and the World Bank, Spring–Summer, 1980

The next steps were two missions, one headed by Tun Thin, Director of IMF's Asian Department, in March, and another headed by McNamara in April. These trips were crucial.

The International Monetary Fund

The eight-member IMF delegation, led by Tun Thin, was deliberately staffed so as to contain representatives of all the departments in the Fund that would be necessary to handle all aspects of membership negotiations. Before leaving for China, Tun Thin and the delegation met with the Fund's managing director, Jacques de Larosière, who told them, "Do anything you can!" The IMF delegation was hosted by the Bank of China and during its stay in China it also had discussions with officials from the Ministry of Foreign Affairs, the Ministry of Finance, the People's Bank, and Vice-Premier Yao Yilin.

When the delegation was initially welcomed to China, they were asked if they were empowered to negotiate. Relying on de Larosière's general exhortation, Thin replied "yes." As soon as formal discussions opened, the Chinese asked a series of telling questions relating to the rights and obligations of membership in the Fund. The Chinese then asked the delegation to put the information that they had provided in writing, which the delegation did by working through the night, producing a document of about fourteen pages.

This document became the basis for the negotiations. Eventually it was boiled down to three or four pages that embodied the agreements that were reached. The entire mission lasted about two weeks. In the midst of the delegation's visit, the U.S. embassy in Beijing, acting at the behest of Secretary of the Treasury William Miller, sought to delay the negotiations. Tun Thin cabled de Larosière, who instructed him not to delay. Tun Thin told the U.S. embassy that he would not delay the negotiations and that the Chinese were pushing for a rapid conclusion.

The discussion between the IMF delegation and the Chinese centered on

17. See Alexander Eckstein, *China's Economic Revolution*, 227.

the rights and obligations of Fund members. The Fund's holdings of gold contributed by China were a central issue. The status of Taiwan and procedures for dealing with Taiwan were also discussed. In addition, the allocation of the increase in the Special Drawing Rights that would occur in January, 1981, the size of China's quota, and Chinese representation upon the Fund's executive board were touched upon, though they were in no way settled, for they could not be under the terms of IMF's Articles of Agreement. Quotas for the Fund's members are set by the board of governors, which acts on the basis of a recommendation of the executive board, which in turn bases its decision on a paper prepared by the IMF staff. Representation on the executive board is dependent upon the size of a country's quota, as are allocations of Special Drawing Rights.

The Chinese queried the Fund delegation about what China's quota would have been had the People's Republic held continuous membership and its quota been regularly and proportionately increased. The Fund delegation could not respond to this hypothetical question. They could only explain the procedure for determining Fund quotas and stress the fact that quotas were based on information supplied by countries concerning the size and character of their economies. China agreed to provide the relevant statistics and agreed that they could be included in the Fund's annual publication, *International Financial Statistics*. This would involve the Chinese releasing previously undisclosed data on trade and currency reserves.

Despite the inconclusiveness of the discussion concerning the size of China's quota, the Chinese nevertheless received the impression that once China became involved in the Fund, and the size of its quota was settled, it would have access to about $1 billion from the Fund without strict conditionality being imposed. This total could be gained by combining drawings from the Trust Fund and the first credit tranche.

Because the negotiations were so highly successful, on April 17, 1980, less than two weeks after Tun Thin's IMF delegation returned from China, the IMF Executive Board decided that henceforth the People's Republic would represent China in the Fund. Detailed negotiations about China's quota and the disposition of the gold reserves then followed.

The issue of the size of China's quota was important and complex. When the IMF was created, China's subscription was set at $550 million. A member country's subscription is equivalent to its quota and determines both the amount of funds that it can draw from the IMF and its voting power in the Fund. China's initial subscription gave it the third largest quota in the IMF and entitled China to appoint an executive director. Only five other countries had this, the other executive directors being elected by constituencies comprised of several countries. Over time, the IMF's resources were periodically expanded as a result of General Quota Reviews, but the authorities in Taiwan asked that China's subscription not be increased. Eventually, China's quota relative to that of other member countries fell to the point that in 1960 China lost the right to appoint an executive director.

Early in the negotiations between the PRC and Tun Thin's mission, an understanding was reached that China's subscription—by then expressed as 550 million Special Drawing Rights due to changes in the Fund and the international monetary system—would be renegotiated upward. IMF's quotas are set on the basis of one of several formulae that take into account a member's total GNP, per capita GNP, and role in international trade. Thus the data that China provided were crucial to determining the quota. Torn between a desire to keep its quota, and thus its potential liability, low, and a desire to attain a quota larger than India's and one that would enable it to elect an executive director with a single country constituency, the Chinese opted to become a major contributor. The details were worked out in subsequent negotiations.

In July, 1980, an IMF delegation collected data and further discussed this issue, with the result that in September, 1980, the board of governors decided that the PRC quota should be SDR 1.2 billion. The board of governors then retroactively authorized an increase in China's quota by up to 50 percent under the same terms and conditions as had been authorized for members in the Seventh General Review, conducted in 1978. Under the terms of this authorization, in November, 1980, China's quota was increased to SDR 1.8 billion. As a consequence of the Eighth General Review in 1983 China's quota was further increased to SDR 2.39 billion. Since 1980 India's quota has been just under that of China; as of the Eighth General Review it was set at SDR 2.2 billion.

China's renegotiated quota became the ninth largest in the IMF.[18] Because of the size of its quota, it was agreed that China would constitute a single constituency with respect to the Executive Board and thus be able to elect its own executive director. The size of the executive board would be expanded from twenty-one to twenty-two to accommodate this without the necessity of rearranging the existing constituencies and dropping one of the sitting executive directors. With its renegotiated quota, China had 18,250 votes, or 2.82 percent of the total. Since the Eighth General Review in 1983, it has had 24,159 votes, but because of the large size of the overall increase this comprised only 2.58 percent of the total.

All aspects of the decision to admit China were extremely important for both China and the Fund. For example, if the size of the executive board had

18. Those member states having quotas larger than China's were, in order of the size of their quotas: the United States of America, the United Kingdom, the Federal Republic of Germany, France, Japan, Saudi Arabia, Canada, and Italy.

not been increased, China's entrance into the Fund would have forced a rearrangement of constituencies for the board and the displacement of existing representation patterns. The French government was extremely interested to ensure that China's entrance did not disturb the tradition of having a francophone African on the board.

Finally, the IMF, after serious intervention by the United States, worked out a solution to dispose of the gold. During the visit to China of the Tun Thin–led IMF delegation, the Chinese believed that an agreement in principle was reached that the gold belonged to the People's Republic of China and that the reserve assets obligation would be paid by the PRC. Three days before the executive board decided that the PRC should represent China in the Fund, however, at the insistence of the United States it was announced that Taiwan would be allowed to purchase the gold at the official price using Taiwanese currency. Although the Chinese authorities protested this action, they could not prevent it, and the transaction was consummated on April 16, 1980. Taiwan repurchased SDR 124.1 million using U.S. dollars, thus restoring China's reserve tranche position, and giving the People's Republic of China a clear credit position with the Fund when it assumed China's membership the following day. China secured access to an unencumbered reserve tranche and to SDR 309 million in the Trust Fund, a source that had very generous terms of repayment. Taiwan had a profit even though it used part of the proceeds of the sale of the gold to clear China's reserve position. According to one IMF official who participated in the negotiations, "It was a Pareto optimal solution, everyone benefited." The People's Republic of China, however, did not see it this way, and the outcome continued to anger Chinese officials.

As a result of these arrangements, beyond having access to its reserve tranche and SDRs, China could obtain SDR 309 million from the special Trust Fund, and it would be able to submit a request for a standby credit arrangement in the first credit tranche, which with China's quota of SDR 1.8 billion would amount to SDR 450 million. At that time, the total of SDR 759 million amounted to roughly $1 billion. Conditionality hardly applied to drawings from the special Trust Fund, and with a drawing in the first credit tranche, conditionality would be less stiff than in the higher tranches.

The World Bank: Spring–Summer 1980

Upon its return to Washington, the Tun Thin delegation informed Robert McNamara prior to his departure for Beijing that the Chinese wished to arrange for full participation in the World Bank quickly, and hence the World Bank mission was prepared for the same message.

The discussions between the Chinese and the McNamara mission were not quite as specific as those involving the IMF mission, but the rough parameters of Chinese accession to membership were hammered out. The Chinese made clear that Taipei would have to depart in order for Beijing to fill the China seat, a step that the authorities on Taiwan subsequently took without the resistance they could have offered. The Bank would have to stop its work on Taiwan, abandoning among other things the study of a case that the Bank had found intriguing. In a 1979 publication, *Growth with Equity: The Taiwan Case*, the Bank had commended Taiwan as an example that demonstrated that it was possible to simultaneously achieve both rapid economic growth and greater equity in income distribution.[19] The study argued that the Taiwan case provided ground for optimism that other developing countries could avoid the conflict between the two objectives of growth and equity.

McNamara informed the Chinese that China would not have access to any of the Sixth Replenishment of the International Development Association (IDA VI), that its claim on the Seventh Replenishment would build slowly, and that not until the Eighth Replenishment would it reach a steady, targeted rate of borrowing from IDA at concessional terms. To get a World Bank program underway swiftly, however, efforts would be made to find uncommitted funds and to identify projects for which the usual feasibility study could be shortened. The Chinese expressed the hope that they could obtain not only project assistance but technical assistance and advice on broad, strategic issues concerning economic development. Bank officials responded positively to these suggestions, and the possibility of a comprehensive World Bank study of the Chinese economy was broached. As in the IMF, China would constitute a single-state constituency and be able to elect its own executive director to the board of the Bank. China would have: 12,250 votes in the IBRD or 2.84 percent of the total; 4,404 votes in IFC or 0.83 percent of the total; and 91,311 votes in IDA or 2.07 percent of the total. In 1988 there was a general increase of $74.8 billion in IBRD's authorized capital, bringing the total to $171.4 billion. China's share was increased to $3,032,764,000, giving it 25,390 votes or 3.19 percent of the total. At that time China's share of the voting power in IDA was 2.01 percent and in IFC was 0.85 percent. Table 3.2 compares China's voting power in 1988 in the Fund and the World Bank group of agencies with that of the 19 other industrialized and developing countries that had more than 1 percent of the total voting power in IMF. In IMF, IBRD, and IDA, China ranked among the most powerful of the 151 members.

In addition to World Bank issues, the McNamara mission included discussions between the Bank president and Chinese leaders concerning the

---

19. John C. H. Fei, Gustav Ranis, and Shirley W. Y. Kuo, *Growth with Equity: The Taiwan Case* (Washington, D.C.: IBRD, 1979).

TABLE 3.2.   China's Relative Voting Power in 1988 in IMF, IBRD, IDA, and IFC

Country	Rank in IMF	Percentage of Total			
		IMF	IBRD	IDA	IFC
United States	1	19.14	19.62	18.11	22.89
United Kingdom	2	6.63	5.14	6.14	6.39
Federal Republic of Germany	3	5.79	5.36	7.10	6.48
France	4	4.81	5.14	3.90	5.77
Japan	5	4.53	6.94	9.21	4.99
Saudi Arabia	6	3.44	3.32	2.66	1.66
Canada	7	3.16	3.32	3.31	4.11
Italy	8	3.13	2.62	2.40	3.73
CHINA	9	2.58	3.19	2.01	.84
Netherlands	10	2.44	2.29	2.09	2.84
India	11	2.38	3.14	3.26	3.87
Belgium	12	2.25	2.08	1.11	2.51
Australia	13	1.75	1.73	1.45	2.40
Brazil	14	1.59	1.56	1.58	2.00
Venezuela	15	1.49	1.47	—	.83
Spain	16	1.40	1.33	1.16	1.19
Mexico	17	1.27	1.23	0.58	1.19
Argentina	18	1.21	1.24	1.39	1.94
Sweden	19	1.16	1.11	2.21	1.37
Indonesia	20	1.10	1.10	1.07	1.26

Sources: IMF, *International Monetary Fund: Annual Report, 1988* (Washington, D.C.: IMF, 1988), 156–59; IBRD, *The World Bank: Annual Report, 1988* (Washington, D.C.: IBRD, 1988), 168–70, 187–89; and IFC, *International Finance Corporation: Annual Report* (Washington, D.C.: IFC, 1988), 53.

global strategic situation. These conversations, including a several hour *tour d'horizon* between McNamara and Deng Xiaoping, helped place China's impending membership in proper historical context and probably facilitated the entry process.

One month after McNamara's return, on May 15, 1980, the executive board of the World Bank formally decided to accord to the People's Republic representation in the organization. The decision came over objection from the U.S. Secretary of the Treasury William Miller. Some in the Carter administration feared that congressional reaction to Taiwan's withdrawal might make securing the Seventh IDA Replenishment more difficult, but McNamara persisted in believing that the strength of the Taiwan lobby on the Hill had ebbed. In fact, he calculated that given the enthusiasm in the United States for the China market, Chinese membership would enhance the ability of the Bank to attract congressional funding for IDA VII.

The stage of preparation for China's participation in the IMF and the World Bank ended in May with organizational steps on both sides. The World

Bank established a China Division, and McNamara's then assistant Caio Koch-Weser was named to head it, and Edwin Lim became the chief economist. A decision was made to staff this division not with China specialists but with competent functional specialists, and a talented staff was soon assembled. By mid-1986, the total bank staff devoted to China had grown to be the third largest in the bank after India and Brazil. Approximately seventy people were devoted to the China effort: seven economists and five loan officers in the China division, two to three people working on China in the fifteen functional divisions with China programs, and twenty person-years of consultants. When the Bank was reorganized in 1987, and nineteen country departments were created, China was one of three countries to have a country department exclusively devoted to its program; India and Brazil were the other two. The China Country Department, which was headed by Shahid Javid Burki, had a full-time staff of approximately seventy full time professional officers.

The Chinese named their first governor to the IMF, People's Bank President Li Baohua, and to the World Bank, Minister of Finance Wu Po. Zhang Zicun became China's first executive director in the International Monetary Fund, and Wang Liansheng became China's first executive director in the World Bank.

The Chinese executive directors were the first representatives of a Communist country to sit on the boards of executive directors of the International Monetary Fund and the World Bank.[20] The smaller Communist countries that were already in the two institutions were included in constituencies that always chose to be represented by officials from market economies. Several members of the boards wondered how their new colleagues would behave.

The appointment of Zhang Zicun did much to assuage their concerns. After completing his doctorate in economics from Cambridge University in the mid-1940s, Zhang had joined the staff of the International Monetary Fund. After a few years, he left the Fund to become a member of the secretariat of the United Nations. He spent his career in the UN, eventually retiring and settling in Larchmont, New York. He was recalled from retirement to assume the post of China's executive director. He brought exceptional credentials to the position. He was an excellent economist. He had worked as a staff member in the Fund. Because of his career in the UN, he was familiar with and practiced in the ways of international bureaucracies.

With these appointments, the Chinese began to settle the internal bureaucratic issues as to which agencies would be the Fund's and Bank's counterparts. The hosts for the IMF and World Bank missions had been the Bank of China, and it appeared to some World Bank officials that Vice-Premier Gu

---

20. For a brief period in the late 1940s, however, a Czechoslovakian national was on the board of the Fund.

Mu and the State Capital Construction Commission were making a bid to become the Bank's counterpart. But in the end, the baton was passed to the People's Bank for the IMF and the Ministry of Finance for the World Bank. While each had distinguished senior people to head the newly established bureaus, the resident capabilities and knowledge in these two organizations were thin.

Since China's move toward the KIEOs involved all three institutions, IMF, the World Bank, and GATT, an evaluation of the process of engagement according to the criteria that were established at the outset of this chapter should be deferred until the negotiations about China's full participation in GATT have been analyzed. To this we now turn.

CHAPTER 4

Negotiations about China's Application
for Full Participation in GATT

The Chinese approach to the General Agreement on Tariffs and Trade was more restrained than its approach to IMF and the World Bank.

Participating in the IMF and the World Bank gave China access to advice and funds, and the issues for China were both clear and relatively limited. First, China had to release data that previously had been held secret, and second, it had to provide the necessary reserves for the increased quotas it sought in IMF and for any increases that there might be in its subscription to the Bank. The extent of IMF's conditionality would depend on how much of the Fund's resources Beijing chose to use. Thus it would be to a large extent under Beijing's control. Full participation in GATT would give China certain privileges in international trade, but China in turn would have to make concessions in opening its markets to GATT members and would have to submit its trade regime to international scrutiny and surveillance. In addition, China would also have to undertake measures to liberalize its trade regime that would be commensurate with the actions taken by the contracting parties in the years since GATT began to loosen their own restrictions. From the outset, full participation in GATT had wider ramifications than participation in the IMF and the World Bank.

Early Contact, 1980–83

China's request for full participation in GATT came only after further decisions to reform and adjust the Chinese economy. Starting in 1983, additional reforms in the agricultural sector were adopted and reforms were inaugurated in the urban economy. These included reduction in the scope of mandatory planning, increases in the autonomy of state enterprises, changes in the wage system, and reforms in the state finance system. In addition, as will be described, the foreign trade regime was restructured and cities along the Chinese coast were given flexibility to attract foreign investment and trade. As this went on, China launched its bid to GATT.

Starting in 1980, China regularly sent its officials to participate in the commercial policy courses conducted by GATT. In April, 1980, China resumed its seat on the UN's Interim Commission for the International Trade

Organization (ICITO). Because GATT was originally designed to be part of a UN specialized agency with a broad mandate to deal with international trade, no provision was made in the General Agreement for a secretariat. When it became apparent that the broad trade organization was stillborn, the Interim Commission for the International Trade Organization appointed a secretariat for GATT. ICITO's sole function remains the appointment of the GATT secretariat, thereby creating the anomalous situation in which the GATT civil servants are not appointed solely by the contracting members. By resuming the China seat on ICITO in 1980, China signaled its interest in GATT and was able to participate in the election of Arthur Dunkel to be GATT's director-general.

In July, 1981, China requested and received authorization to be an observer at a GATT meeting dealing with the renewal of the Multifibre Arrangement, which sets rules for textile trade. China was rapidly becoming a major textile exporter. In November, 1982, China requested and was allowed to be an observer at the session of the GATT Contracting Parties at the ministerial level. This ministerial session set the work priorities for GATT for the 1980s.

In December, 1983, China applied for membership in GATT's Multifibre Arrangement, and its application was accepted. In January, 1984, China signed the Arrangement Regarding International Trade in Textiles. This arrangement permits industrialized countries to limit imports of textiles and related products from developing countries in cases where market disruption could occur, but also commits the industrialized countries gradually to decrease these limits. Agreements between participating industrialized and developing countries concerning these issues are subject to scrutiny by a specially created institution, the Textile Surveillance Body, which also attempts to resolve disputes stemming from these agreements. China had concluded agreements concerning trade in textiles with the European Economic Community in 1979 and with the United States in 1983. Because of China's adherence to the MFA, these agreements, subsequent amendments to them, and all other Chinese agreements covering trade in textiles would be subject to the scrutiny of the TSB. China decided to participate in MFA because it wanted the assurance that the arrangement provides that its growing textile exports would have access to markets in industrialized countries. In addition, participating in MFA would give China experience with GATT procedures.

Changes in China

In the meantime, several changes had occurred in China's foreign trade and its foreign trade regime.[1] The direction and magnitude of China's foreign trade

---

1. For more detail, see Michael Moser, ed. *Foreign Trade, Investment, and Law in the People's Republic of China* (Oxford: Oxford University Press, 1984).

TABLE 4.1.   China's Trade Strategy and Export Growth

Years	Export Strategy	Average Annual Percentage Growth in Export Earnings
1960–78	Autarky	7.8
1978–85	Modified import substitution	15.7

Source: IBRD, *China: External Trade and Capital* (Washington, D.C.: IBRD, 1988), 6.

had changed. Throughout the 1950s, China's trade had been predominantly with the Soviet Union and the communist countries of Eastern Europe, but starting in 1961 Sino-Soviet trade dropped sharply. At the same time, Chinese trade with Western countries began to grow, and this reorientation of Chinese foreign trade continued. In addition, from 1971 onward the total volume of Chinese foreign trade expanded significantly, and the rate of this expansion accelerated after the decisions of the Third Plenary Session of the Eleventh Central Committee of the Chinese Communist party. Table 4.1 shows the average annual percentage increase in China's export earnings before and after these decisions. The relatively high average annual growth in export earnings for the years prior to 1979 is primarily attributable to growth that occurred during the 1970s. From 1953 through 1970 the average annual rate of growth of export earnings was 4.8 percent.[2] Prior to 1979, China's foreign trade was "import-driven"; that is, the first step in the planning process was to draw up a list of imports regarded as necessary and then exports would be projected sufficient to cover the costs of these imports. Starting in 1979, the first step became establishing an export target; then this would be used to determine the level of imports that could be afforded. This shifted the focus of foreign trade planning, giving greater emphasis to the expansion of exports.

In 1953, 70 percent of China's trade was with centrally planned economies. By 1966, when China's debt to the Soviet Union had been fully repaid, China's trade with the Soviet Union had virtually ceased, and only 22 percent of the total was with centrally planned economies. The share of the centrally planned economies fell to 12 percent by 1979.[3] During the 1980s, about 85 percent of China's exports were to the contracting parties of GATT and more

2. IBRD, *China: Socialist Economic Development*, vol. 2, *The Economic Sectors: Agriculture, Industry, Energy, Transport, and External Trade and Finance* (Washington, D.C.: IBRD, 1983), 413.

3. IBRD, *China: Socialist Economic Development*, 2:426.

than 90 percent of its imports were from these countries.[4] In 1986 the combined volume of Chinese exports to and imports from GATT contracting parties was $66.1 billion.

In 1982, China's foreign trade administration was reorganized. The Ministry of Foreign Trade, the Ministry of Economic Relations with Foreign Countries, the State Import and Export Commission, and the Foreign Investment Control Commission were merged into a single ministry, the Ministry of Foreign Economic Relations and Trade (MOFERT). MOFERT assumed responsibility for China's relationships with GATT.

In January, 1984, informal arrangements that had been developed for sharing foreign exchange between the central government and provincial authorities were formalized.[5] Under the regulations, most provincial authorities were allowed to keep 25 percent of their foreign exchange earnings for their own use. Starting in January, 1985, enterprises were given the right to use half of their retained foreign exchange earnings for their own purposes. Provisional regulations for issuing import licenses were also adopted in January, 1984. Imports were classified as restricted or unrestricted, and only those in the restricted category needed MOFERT approval.

In September, 1984, the State Council approved a reform of foreign trade proposed by MOFERT. Under this reform, MOFERT gave up its monopoly of foreign trade. Importers and exporters became free to choose their agents freely among licensed trading agencies other than MOFERT's foreign trade corporations, and certain enterprises were given trading rights. Foreign trade corporations had been established by both provincial authorities and line ministries. The centralized foreign trade corporations had established branches that under the September, 1984, reforms became separate accounting units. Trading corporations became responsible for their own profits and losses and subject to taxes. The foreign trade planning system was shifted toward greater reliance on guidance plans and less on command plans. Through these steps MOFERT reduced its involvement with routine transactions and moved toward concentration on the formulation of overall plans.

Two tariff laws were approved by the State Council in March, 1985, "Regulations for Import and Export Tariffs" and "Import and Customs Tariff."[6] The former established rules and regulations for the formulation of

4. IMF, *Direction of Trade Statistics Yearbook, 1987* (Washington, D.C.: IMF, 1987), 136–37. The portion of China's exports to and imports from GATT contracting parties was: 1980, 84.9 and 90.0 percent; 1981, 86.3 and 92.7 percent; 1982, 84.4 and 90.2 percent; 1983, 83.5 and 91.4 percent; 1984, 85.3 and 91.7 percent; 1985, 85.2 and 92.3 percent; and 1986, 84.7 and 90.8 percent. See also James T. H. Tsao, *China's Development Strategies and Foreign Trade* (Lexington, Mass.: Lexington Books, 1987), 156.

5. See IBRD, *China: External Trade and Capital* (Washington, D.C.: IBRD, 1988), 100–101.

6. See IBRD, *China: External Trade and Capital*, 145–58.

policy and the administration of the system, and the latter established the new schedule of import tariffs and export taxes. The tariff included two schedules, a minimum one for the more than ninety countries with which China has most-favored-nation treatment treaties or agreements and a maximum one for other countries. The tariff rates in the schedules ranged from zero to 180 percent. In addition, commodities falling in some tariff codes were subject to import surcharges that resulted in combined duties of 200 percent. Manufactured items in general were subject to higher duties than agricultural products. Consumer essentials were subject to the lowest rates, while luxury items were subject to the highest rates.

Even though the new trading regime was radically more decentralized than its predecessor, China's foreign trade in the mid-1980s nevertheless remained subject to multiple layers of control. These included: the overall plan and the foreign trade plan, which according to the World Bank covered from 70 to 80 percent of all exports, while about 40 percent of imports were included in a command plan and a relatively large share of the remainder were included in a priority system;[7] the still substantial role of foreign trade corporations, even though their number had expanded from 12 in 1978 to more than 1,000 in the mid-1980s; import licensing, which covered more than forty goods involving approximately 30 percent of imports;[8] tariffs and surcharges; and an administered exchange rate and regulations governing the use of foreign exchange. This is why the World Bank characterized China's revised trade regime as still basically "inward-looking," involving a modified import-substitution trade policy.[9]

Through careful use of international assignments China had developed a number of individuals who were intimately familiar with GATT and its procedures. By this time, Liu Xianming, the first official from the People's Republic to participate in GATT's commercial policy course, had become counselor in the Chinese mission in Geneva and had been given responsibility for China's relationship with GATT. Wu Jiahuang, who had observed GATT during the 1970s, first from a position in the Chinese mission in Geneva and then as a member of UNCTAD's secretariat, had been appointed chief of the division dealing with GATT in MOFERT's Department of International Relations.

Linden and Dunkel Visits, 1984, 1985, and 1986

In 1984, China invited Ake Linden, then the legal adviser to the director-general of GATT, to visit China and to conduct a seminar on the purposes,

---

7. IBRD, *China: External Trade and Capital*, 104–5, and 110–13.
8. IBRD, *China: External Trade and Capital*, 135.
9. See IBRD, *China: External Trade and Capital*, 1–9.

structure, and functioning of GATT. By this time, it was clear that GATT would sooner or later launch another round of multilateral trade negotiations. The United States particularly wanted another round, and a consensus was gradually developing, first among the industrialized contracting parties of GATT and then extending to all contracting parties, that another round should occur. If the Tokyo Round were a precedent, this eighth round of multilateral trade negotiations would probably last at least five years. It would influence the legal framework for international trade into the twenty-first century.[10] The imminence of a new round of negotiations forced the pace of decision in China. In December, 1984, China requested and received permanent observer status with respect to GATT's council and its subordinate bodies. In its request, China indicated that having this status would facilitate a decision on membership in GATT.

Throughout 1985, negotiations were conducted within GATT concerning the launching of a new round of multilateral trade negotiations. These negotiations culminated in a positive decision in December; the new round would start with a ministerial meeting in September, 1986, in Punta del Este, Uruguay. Because of the location of this meeting, the negotiations became known as the Uruguay Round. In November, 1985, Ake Linden returned to China, this time to explain exactly what would be involved in China's adherence to and full participation in the General Agreement on Tariffs and Trade. His visit was followed up in January, 1986, by a visit of Arthur Dunkel, the director-general of GATT, that had the same purpose.

Meanwhile, Western countries had become increasingly interested in bringing China into full participation in the GATT. As several Western GATT representatives in Geneva said, "It is impossible to envisage the international trade system of the early twenty-first century without China being part of it."

In November, 1985, the Working Party on East-West Trade of the Trade Committee of the Organization for Economic Cooperation and Development requested that the OECD secretariat prepare a study of the issues posed by China's possible application to accede to GATT. OECD's members wanted China in GATT; they wanted it to be part of the system, to share in the benefits and the management of the system. At the same time, because of

---

10. For analyses of issues likely to be covered in the negotiations see: C. Michael Aho and Jonathan David Aronson, *Trade Talks: America Better Listen* (New York: Council on Foreign Relations, 1985); J. Michael Finger and Andrzej Olechowski, eds., *The Uruguay Round: A Handbook on the Multilateral Trade Negotiations* (Washington, D.C.: IBRD, 1987); Gary Clyde Hufbauer and Jeffrey J. Schott, *Trading for Growth: The Next Round of Trade Negotiations* (Washington, D.C.: Institute for International Economics, 1985); and U.S. Congressional Budget Office, *The GATT Negotiations and US Trade Policy* (Washington, D.C.: GPO, 1987).

China's potential economic importance, they felt that the negotiations about China's accession had to be approached on a commercial rather than a political basis. They felt that because political considerations had been dominant in the negotiations in the 1970s about the accession of Eastern European countries, Western commercial interests had been slighted. They thought that the protocols of accession for these countries gave too much and required too little. China was so big that a one-sided protocol could be very costly. While the Western states welcomed China's interest in GATT, they were also determined to protect and promote their own economic interests. The OECD study, which was completed in early 1986, helped to lay the basis for the formulation of Western positions in negotiations with China, particularly for those of OECD's smaller member countries, which lacked the bureaucratic expertise to analyze the issues involved in China's application on their own. Preparation within the United States for dealing with China was extensive and already well advanced when the OECD study was launched, so the United States contributed more to the study than it gained.

When Linden and Dunkel were in China, Chinese officials explained to them that China did not want to apply for admission to GATT as a new member. The People's Republic regarded itself as the successor contracting party of the General Agreement on Tariffs and Trade, and it therefore felt that Taipei's act of withdrawal from GATT had no validity for China. At the same time, it recognized that conditions had changed substantially since 1950 and that the members of GATT had made many reciprocal concessions since then. China would be willing to negotiate the conditions of its full participation in GATT and to sign a protocol of accession. Linden and Dunkel explained the nature of negotiations about accession to GATT and the special issues associated with nonmarket economies that would come up.

GATT's purpose is to reduce obstacles to trade. Its basic thrust has been to reduce tariffs, on the assumption that this would increase trade. This assumption tends to be valid in market economies where individual consumers and entrepreneurs make decisions about what and how much to import: presumably lowering the price of imports by reducing tariffs will increase the demand for foreign goods. However, the effect of reducing tariffs is more problematic when: (1) the level of imports is determined even in part by a state plan; (2) foreign trade corporations are interposed between the foreign seller and the domestic buyer; (3) there are substantial licensing requirements; (4) the exchange rate is set administratively; and (5) access to foreign exchange is regulated. Because of this, when nonmarket economies became full participants in GATT, the contracting parties generally insisted that these countries make other arrangements to ensure that their imports would increase in return for tariff concessions on the part of the contracting parties with market economies.[11] Because of uncertainties about the relationship of prices for exported goods to the value of the factor inputs involved in the production of these goods, they also tended to insist that they should have the right to apply safeguards selectively against the exports of these countries.

Hungary was an exception. Hungarian negotiators convinced the contracting parties that their country had made sufficient progress toward the decentralization of its economy and the introduction of markets that it should be able to accede to GATT on the basis of making tariff reductions. The Hungarian accession created a precedent, but a precedent that received mixed reviews. Many GATT observers felt that it was a precedent that should not be repeated.

The Chinese maintained that because so many steps had been taken to decentralize the Chinese economy, tariff reductions would increase the level of imports, and they wanted to make tariff reductions a central aspect of the obligations that they would undertake. Chinese tariffs were high, averaging 44 percent.[12] The Chinese argued that the scope of mandatory planning both generally and for foreign trade had been sharply reduced.[13] They maintained that the number of products for which import licenses were required had been limited. They also pointed out that in China's case the state plan sets the level of imports not by specifying the commodities to be imported but by allocating foreign currency to importing units. They argued that therefore reducing tariff levels would increase imports. They asserted that a rudimentary foreign exchange market had been created. They also claimed that the Chinese trade regime was transparent. They did not believe that publication of the import plan would be essential to maintaining transparency or appropriate, since doing so might give commercial advantages to foreigners.

Chinese representatives indicated, however, that they would be willing to consider other issues, such as adhering to some of the codes that were adopted during the Tokyo Round. Accepting the subsidy code could be important, because China subsidizes some of its exports directly and energy, food, and housing are heavily subsidized. Competitors in contracting parties could feel that these subsidies would give Chinese exporters unfair competitive advantages. China's adhering to the code—which defines permissible subsidies—would provide a framework for settlement of disagreements about

11. These arrangements are described in Eliza R. Patterson, "Improving GATT Rules for Nonmarket Economies," *Journal of World Trade Law* 20 (March–April, 1986): 185–205.

12. U.S. Office of the Special Trade Representative, *National Trade Estimate: 1986 Report on Foreign Trade Barriers* (Washington, D.C.: GPO, 1987), 63.

13. For an example of the line of Chinese argumentation see Chen Dezhao, "China and the GATT," paper prepared for presentation at the 14th Congress of the International Political Science Association, August 28 to September 1, 1988, Washington, D.C.

TABLE 4.2.   Status of Eastern European Countries and Tokyo Round Codes, June 1, 1988

Country	Codes								
	1	2	3	4	5	6	7	8	9
Contracting Parties									
Czechoslovakia	A					A	A		A
Hungary	A			A	A	A	A		A
Poland				A	A		A		A
Romania	A			A	A	A	A	A	A
Yugoslavia	A		S	A		A	A		A
Other Countries									
Bulgaria				A	A				

Source: GATT, *GATT Activities, 1987* (Geneva: GATT, 1988), 138–39.

Note: Codes: 1. Technical Barriers; 2. Governmental Procurement; 3. Subsidies and Countervailing Duties; 4. Bovine Meat; 5. Dairy; 6. Customs Valuation; 7. Import Licensing; 8. Civil Aircraft; 9. Antidumping. Status: A = accepted; S = signed (acceptance pending)

these issues. For the same reason, China's adhering to the import licensing code could be important. Since China is alleged to have exported some goods at costs that are less than those charged on domestic markets, adhering to the code on dumping and countervailing duties could also have beneficial consequences.

Eastern European countries with communist governments have accepted several of the Tokyo Round codes, as table 4.2 shows. Various of these countries have accepted the technical barriers, customs valuation, import licensing, and antidumping codes, as well as the bovine meat and dairy codes. Yugoslavia alone has signed the subsidies and countervailing duties code, and none has signed the government procurement code. As of mid-1989, China had not indicated which codes it contemplated accepting.

Finally, the Chinese said that they thought that China deserved "developing country" status within GATT. Under Article XVIII and Part IV of the General Agreement developing countries that are contracting parties to GATT may take governmental action to promote economic development that would be prohibited to other contracting parties and may obtain certain trade concessions, such as those gained through the Generalized System of Preferences (GSP) granted by industrialized countries, without the necessity of giving reciprocal concessions. In the 1970s, prompted by UN agencies and especially by UNCTAD, most developed countries adopted GSP programs under which imports from developing countries received preferential tariffs that were lower than those on the imports of the same goods from developed countries.

The important meeting that Dunkel had with Zhao Ziyang during his 1986 visit helped persuade the premier that China should move quickly to participate fully in GATT. For his part, Zhao sought to persuade Dunkel that a planned commodity economy, the intended outcome of China's reforms, could be integrated into the market-oriented principles of GATT. Zhao pledged that China's decision to open its economy to the outside world would not be reversed. Somewhat earlier, China had asked the World Bank to analyze the status of "its foreign trade and capital system and, on the basis of this analysis, to make suggestions for further improvements."[14] The commissioning of the study signaled the Chinese government's aspiration and intention not only to maintain the opening to the outside world, but to expand it. The World Bank mission would do its fieldwork in China in October, 1986.

The Chinese Calculus

On July 14, 1986, China formally notified GATT that it had decided to seek the resumption of its status as a contracting party. The Chinese government envisioned a number of benefits from full participation.

— It would complete its entry into the keystone international economic organizations, and symbolize its full acceptance as part of the international economy. Chinese officials felt that China's status as a growing force in the international economy should be recognized by participation in GATT. Moreover, China's acceptance in GATT would bestow international legitimacy on China's opening to the outside world. It would acknowledge that China's economy could be fitted into an organization designed for and primarily comprised of market economies. This legitimacy could enhance China's attractiveness to foreign investors.

— It would provide China greater defenses against protectionist and discriminatory tendencies in developed countries than if it were forced to rely only on bilateral negotiations. China's experience in the Multifibre Arrangement had heightened Chinese officials' awareness of the utility of multilateral forums for formulating rules and bringing pressure on states to comply with these rules.

— It would reinforce China's right to receive unconditional most-favored-nation treatment because the General Agreement requires that all contracting parties should be accorded such status. Even though China had gained MFN treatment from all of its major trading partners by 1980, because of the Jackson-Vanek amendment to the 1974 U.S. trade act, China's MFN treatment by the United States required annual presidential certification that China was not violating

14. IBRD, *China: External Trade and Capital*, vii.

human rights by placing restrictions on emigration.[15] China found this requirement degrading and disliked the uncertainty that it introduced concerning China's access to the U.S. market.

— It would enable China to receive preferential tariff treatment under the U.S. Generalized System of Preferences. By 1980 China had gained GSP treatment from all developed countries that had such schemes except the United States. U.S. law requires that communist countries adhere to GATT principles and be members of IMF to receive GSP treatment.[16]

— It would give China access to GATT's dispute settlement mechanisms. Chinese officials believed that this would be an important asset in warding off protectionism and in dealing with any discriminatory treatment that China might encounter.

— It would enable China to join the debate and fight in the organization against protectionism. Because of its potential economic importance, China's accession to GATT would strengthen the neoliberal international trade regime and make that regime more comprehensive. In the mid-1980s, China deeply feared that developed countries would increasingly take actions to limit China's growing exports. The Jenkins bill, sharply limiting textile imports to the United States, which was on the U.S. congressional agenda throughout 1985 and was finally blocked in 1986 by a presidential veto, fueled this fear.

— It might marginally strengthen the hands of free traders within the developed countries in their domestic political battles against their protectionist opponents. Perhaps having an exaggerated view of their own influence, at least some Chinese analysts believed that full PRC participation in the GATT system would help the free traders abroad allay the fears of their domestic protectionist opponents concerning the possibly disruptive consequences of a disorderly Chinese entry into the markets of developed countries. These Chinese argued that by pledging to adhere to the principles of a free trade system, China would enable such free trade politicians in developed countries as Ronald Reagan to resist adopting protectionist measures against China. After all, the developed countries could hardly expect China to liberalize its import restrictions if the same countries curtail Chinese exports.

— From the point of view of the reformers within China, it would involve China in a series of international obligations that could be used to reinforce the reforms and to make them irreversible.

---

15. The provision of the act necessitating this certification is: United States of America, Public Law 93-618, sec. 402.

16. USA, Public Law 93-618, sec. 502.

Full participation in GATT could also create some difficulties for China. China would have to submit its trade regime to continuing scrutiny by the contracting parties—and in the process make available even more data that continued to be internal (*nei-bu*)—and it would have to make trade concessions, reducing some of its protectionist practices.

These difficulties, however, could be mitigated were China accorded developing country status. Article XVIII of GATT allows developing countries to: protect "infant" industries; impose import restrictions for balance of payments reasons with little international scrutiny; and provide governmental financial assistance to industries for general developmental purposes. Part IV of GATT establishes the principle that the developed countries should not expect complete reciprocity from developing countries in negotiations to reduce tariffs or other barriers to trade. In 1979 the contracting parties decided that developing countries could be accorded preferential treatment without violating GATT's strictures against discrimination, thus legitimizing the GSP programs and preferential arrangements among developing countries. In sum, by invoking development objectives, developing countries can avoid many GATT obligations. No formal GATT procedure has been developed for bestowing developing country status; it has been a matter of self-attribution.

China also indicated that it wanted to participate fully in the Uruguay Round. The contracting parties decided that countries that had given formal notification "at a regular meeting of the Council of Representatives, of their intention to negotiate the terms of their membership as a contracting party," could participate in the negotiations.[17] This decision was crafted to permit the People's Republic of China to participate, and to provide grounds for denying the participation of the Soviet Union and also Bulgaria. The Soviet request to participate in the new round, submitted in August, 1986, was spurned overtly because the Soviet Union had not committed itself to negotiating accession to GATT, although the real reasons for not pursuing the Soviet interest in being associated with the Uruguay Round were a good deal more complicated. Bulgaria had announced its desire to accede to the General Agreement, but had not submitted a formal request to the Council prior to the opening of the Uruguay Round.

Initial Negotiations

In February, 1987, China submitted a memorandum describing its foreign trade regime. This memorandum was the subject of some contention within the Chinese bureaucracy, and it went through several drafts. It required the Chinese to clarify some of the ambiguities in their system concerning the jurisdictions of specific bureaucracies to release information about their pro-

---

17. GATT, *Newsletter: Focus*, no. 41 (October, 1986): 5.

cedures that previously were veiled from the outside world. At least one draft of the memorandum was shown to U.S. diplomats in Beijing, and the Chinese solicited their comments, thereby cleverly engaging the U.S. in the process. A consultant provided under an Australian technical assistance program assisted the Chinese in the preparation of their memorandum. Members of the GATT secretariat helped the Chinese by clarifying GATT requirements and terminology.

In May, 1987, three months after the Chinese submitted their memorandum, GATT established a working party to: examine the PRC's trade regime; develop a protocol setting forth China's rights and obligations in GATT; provide a forum for negotiating a schedule of concessions by China; and address other issues concerning China and GATT. The delay between China's submission of its memorandum and the establishment of the working party was occasioned by disagreement over the terms of reference. Whether or not China was resuming its membership in GATT—as opposed to acceding as a new contracting party—was a major stumbling block.

For different reasons, the concept of resumption posed particular difficulties for Australia, Japan, and the United States. In each case, the difficulties had to do with matters of domestic law. If China resumed its membership in GATT, the legal status of certain actions taken in the interim in each of these countries would be problematic. In addition, the United States might have difficulty continuing to apply aspects of the 1974 trade act. When a country accedes to GATT, under the terms of Article XXXV of the General Agreement a contracting party may declare that it will not apply all of the provisions of the Agreement to the new member. Article XXXV would not be applicable in the case of resumption. During the course of the discussions, it was made apparent to the Chinese that resumption could cause difficulties for their country as well. Would the PRC be liable for a Chinese contribution to GATT during the years that it was absent? Could the PRC continue to forbid trade with Israel, the Republic of Korea, and South Africa? China might also need to have recourse to Article XXXV. In the end, the matter was left to the actual negotiations. The terms of reference of the working party did not mention either accession or resumption.

With the establishment of the working party, the formal negotiations about China's full participation in GATT began. Ambassador Pierre-Lewis Girard of Switzerland was chosen to chair the working group.[18] Unlike the

---

18. For an excellent broad analysis of various issues raised by China's request, see Robert Herzstein, "China and the GATT: Legal and Policy Issues Raised by China's Participation in the General Agreement on Tariffs and Trade," *Law and Policy in International Business* 18, no. 2 (1986): 371–415. See also Penelope Hartland-Thumberg, "China's Modernization: A Challenge for the GATT," *The Washington Quarterly* 10, no. 2 (Spring 1987): 81–98; and J. E. D. McDonnell, "China's Move to Rejoin the GATT System: An Epic Transition," *World Economy* 10, no. 3 (September, 1987): 331–50.

negotiations involving the IMF and the World Bank, these negotiations would be conducted between China and GATT's contracting parties—the members of the organization—rather than the secretariat. They were, as mentioned above, expected to be difficult and to last for some time.

After the establishment of the working group, the contracting parties submitted written questions based on their examination of China's memorandum describing its trade regime. Then China prepared written answers to these questions. When China's written responses had been circulated to the contracting parties, the working group began holding meetings. Its first session was in February, 1988, and it held three more sessions that year and two in the first half of 1989. Additional questions were raised during the meetings of the working group.

By mid-1988, China had been asked more than 1,200 questions, a record number. These had been answered by mid-1989, and the contracting parties had expressed their views on China's responses. Then the more difficult issue of preparing a protocol began.

The United States, the European Community, and Japan submitted the most written and oral questions. Although the OECD Trade Committee's Working Party on East-West Trade continued to study the ramifications of the PRC's application, and various meetings were held to discuss the issues involved, this did not stimulate the smaller member countries of OECD to become very actively involved in the GATT negotiations. OECD's working party was, however, a useful vehicle for the Western countries to share information and discuss strategies.

The developing countries have been relatively passive in the GATT working group, even though many of China's exports are directly competitive with theirs.[19] Developing country representatives in Geneva have regarded China's full participation in GATT as inevitable, and they have lacked the bureaucratic support to seriously investigate China's trading practices. Then too, they could be free riders, confident that the developed countries would force consideration of all of the issues in depth and detail. Moreover, given the norms of Third World solidarity, they would find it awkward to publicly oppose China's application. Developing country representatives have, however, been concerned to ensure that precedents were not established in the agreement that could affect them. They have been particularly worried that an attempt might be made to establish the concept of "graduation." They have also been keen not to have China's desire to be regarded as a developing country examined, preferring to leave this status to be determined by self-attribution.

---

19. See Alexander J. Yeats, "China's Recent Export Performance: Some Basic Features and Policy Implications," *Development and Change* 15, no. 1 (1984): 1–22.

Developing country representatives have been curious to know what positions China would take on issues that would come before GATT and have sought answers when they have encountered Chinese outside of the formal working party. Chinese negotiators, however, have rebuffed all such questions with the response that as long as China was not a contracting party it would be inappropriate for China to give its views: "The issues are matters for the contracting parties, not outsiders, to decide." In conversations with representatives of developed countries, Chinese have stressed that China is not a formal member of the Group of Seventy-seven, the developing country caucus that is so influential in United Nations agencies and especially in UNCTAD. Chinese representatives have also been relatively open in reporting what they regard as the coolness of some developing country representatives toward China's application.

The process of question and response, whether conducted in writing or orally during the working party sessions, has been cumbersome, both linguistically and bureaucratically. Questions, posed in English, have had to be translated into Chinese. Then answers, prepared in Chinese, have had to be translated into English. Nuances have been lost in the process, and the Chinese have often found it difficult to describe their trade regime in the terminology commonly used in discussions in GATT. Preparing responses required considerable coordination among separate bureaucratic entities. Chinese who were unfamiliar with the GATT have had trouble understanding the seriousness of the exercise. An even greater difficulty has been that the central issues in many of the questions have concerned the progress of the reform of the Chinese economy, the very subject that has frequently caused sharp divisions within China.

Many participants in the working party have described the exercise as an educational process for both the contracting parties and the Chinese. The contracting parties have had to learn about the Chinese economy and its likely future nature, and the Chinese have had to learn about the trade regime that GATT established and serves. Some contracting parties believed that the State Council initially gave China's negotiators an extremely constricted brief, allowing hardly any concessions, a brief that the negotiators had to seek to expand. Whether this is correct or not, GATT's director-general, Arthur Dunkel, was invited to make another visit to China in October, 1987, at the time of the Thirteenth Party Congress. When he was there he talked with Chinese leaders about the advantages and obligations associated with full participation in GATT. The Chinese delegations to the working party sessions have been exceptionally large, with the consequence that numerous Chinese bureaucrats have been exposed to the issues that have been raised by the contracting parties. Before the second session of the working party, the Chinese delegation spent a week closeted together in a Beijing suburb rehearsing the questions that they would be asked and the answers that they would give.

China's overture to GATT has been taken with great care and serious-ness. Its request to participate fully in GATT was accompanied by moves to create a reservoir of experts on GATT and its procedures. Groups comprised of scholars and bureaucrats have been set up in Beijing and Shanghai to study the issues involved in the negotiations. The University of International Busi-ness and Economics in Beijing, which is sponsored by the Ministry of Foreign Economic Relations and Trade, has established a research group on GATT, and a similar group has been established at the Shanghai University of Fi-nance and Economics. By 1988 there was already a reservoir of individuals outside of the bureaucracy who were knowledgeable about GATT and could and did provide useful technical support for China's negotiators.[20] In late 1988, the World Bank study, *China: External Trade and Capital*,[21] started in 1986, was published. It had been cleared by the Chinese government. It provided an excellent description for all who were interested of the Chinese trade regime and an analysis of the policy choices available to China for dealing with foreign trade and capital. It was a primer for China's GATT negotiations, one that forcefully advocated liberalizing the Chinese trading regime.

Although the working party has been the formal focal point of the GATT negotiations, many important issues have been raised, clarified, and negoti-ated in bilateral discussions. China had detailed discussions with the United States, Japan, and the European Community. As table 4.3 shows, these three economies, along with Hong Kong, were China's principal trading partners, and accounted for more than two-thirds of China's trade. Many—probably more than half—of China's exports to Hong Kong were re-exported to other destinations, with probably a third of those that were re-exported destined for the United States and most of the remainder for other Western industrialized countries.[22]

The talks with the United States started even before the working party held its first meeting, and by mid-1987 they had gone so far toward framing negotiating issues that they had to be slowed down to allow the talks with other contracting parties to catch up. Though the United States and China each presented their positions forthrightly, and important differences emerged between the two sides, the talks were characterized by a close working rela-tionship. As noted above, the United States was asked to comment on a working draft of the Chinese memorandum before it was formally submitted

---

20. For a sample of the type of careful and detailed analysis prepared by Chinese scholars, see Chen Dezhao, "China and the GATT."

21. IBRD, *China: External Trade and Capital*.

22. IBRD, *China: External Trade and Capital*, 119–20.

TABLE 4.3.   China's Principal Trading Partners, 1987, by Percentage of Total

	Exports	Imports
European Community	9.9	16.8
Japan	16.2	23.3
United States	7.7	11.2
Subtotal	33.8	51.3
Hong Kong	34.9	19.5
Total	68.7	70.8

Source: IMF, *Direction of Trade Statistics Yearbook, 1988*
(Washington, D.C.: IMF, 1988), 136–37.

to GATT, and as early as October, 1986, the two sides began to define the positions that they would take. U.S. negotiators put forward five points that they argued should be incorporated in the protocol defining the terms of China's full participation in GATT.

The American Position

In the U.S. view, China should commit itself to maintaining a single, consistent, effective, nationally applied trade policy. Current problems generated this concern. Foreign businessmen have been plagued, for example, by the discrepancies in customs administration and application of tariff schedules, which vary considerably from place to place or over time at the same port of entry. China suffered from both domestic regional and ministerial protectionism, and the moves to decentralize the Chinese economy gave further scope to these tendencies.[23] The Chinese government has also had some trouble policing its own export licensing regulations, with the result that the central government cannot always enforce its export restraint agreements.

The United States also maintained that the protocol should commit China to improve the transparency of—or the publicly available information about—its trade regulations and the administration of its trade barriers. If this request for transparency extended to such issues as providing information about the prices of major factor inputs, the profits and losses accruing to foreign trade organizations, the foreign trade plan, and which organizations in China have access to import licenses and necessary foreign exchange, it could be a very far-reaching requirement.

U.S. negotiators told the Chinese that the protocol would also have to

---

23. See Gene Tidrick and Chen Jiyuan, eds., *China's Industrial Reform* (Washington, D.C.: IBRD, 1987), 146.

contain a commitment to eliminate over time all Chinese practices that were inconsistent with GATT, such as border charges and taxes not explicitly incorporated into China's tariff system. They indicated that the United States felt that China's reliance on central control over foreign exchange to regulate and restrict the level of imports should be replaced with other instruments.

Finally, the United States raised two other issues. U.S. negotiators indicated that the United States would like China to commit itself to the implementation of a price system in which commodity prices would reflect supply and demand and relative scarcities. And they indicated that because China's economy was not yet based on market prices, the United States felt that the contracting parties should have access to safeguard mechanisms to guard against market disruptions caused by practices that in a market system would be regarded as unfair. What was at stake here was the fear that China's administered prices would mask subsidies for exports.

The Chinese Position in the Negotiations

The Chinese also raised five issues in the negotiations. It was a sine qua non for China that its accession to GATT be regarded as a resumption of China's membership rather than a new application for membership. Second, the Chinese indicated that reduction in its tariff schedules—tariff concessions— should provide the basis for the negotiations. Third, China should be regarded as a developing country.

In addition, the Chinese negotiators indicated that, as a contracting party of GATT, China should receive unconditional most-favored-nation treatment from the United States. The U.S. negotiators explained that this would require that Congress modify the Jackson-Vanek amendment, which was something that they could not promise would happen. If the protocol contained serious commitments from China, American negotiators have felt, a U.S. administration would be in a strong position to ask Congress to modify the Jackson-Vanek amendment, at least as it applied to China. The events of June, 1989, and their aftermath, of course, made this issue much more problematic. If the Jackson-Vanek amendment was not modified, the U.S. would not be able to accord China full GATT privileges, and China in turn would have the right to deny the United States privileges granted to other GATT contracting parties.

The Chinese also indicated that they felt that the U.S. should accord China GSP treatment. The American Federation of Labor–Congress of Industrial Organizations had already announced its opposition to this, but a president committed to free trade might be willing to disregard likely opposition from Congress and various interest groups in return for concessions by China.

The other bilateral negotiations that China conducted over its GATT participation undoubtedly raised additional thorny issues. The European

Community informed the Chinese that it basically agreed with the five points advanced by the United States, and in addition it intended to retain the framework of its existing import regulations relating to China.[24] These regulations establish precise quantitative limits for all categories of China's exports to the members of the European Community. The progress of reform within China will clearly be an important factor affecting the community's willingness to enlarge and possibly ultimately abandon these quotas.

There was broad agreement in the working party that a mechanism should be established after China began to participate fully in GATT to regularly review the functioning of the protocol that would result from the negotiations. Since the United States appeared to be determined to retain the right to impose selective safeguards against China until further progress had been made toward price reform within China, and the European Community seemed determined to maintain its quota system, this mechanism would provide a vehicle for reviewing change within China and, in light of this, considering the appropriateness of restrictions imposed by the United States, the European Community, and other contracting parties. Chinese negotiators felt that this would be a useful device for bringing pressure on contracting parties to accord China full GATT privileges.

Hong Kong and Taiwan

The looming transfer of Hong Kong from British to PRC authority in 1997 was not a direct issue in the negotiations. Hong Kong became a contracting party of GATT in April, 1986, at which time statements were made in the GATT council promising that the territory could retain its separate status after the PRC acquired sovereignty over it. This separate status in reality would be justified only if China gave meaning to its "one country, two systems" pledge and Hong Kong retained a separate economic system; nonetheless, 1997 could possibly serve as an ultimate though informal deadline for the GATT negotiations. If the PRC were not a full contracting party of GATT by 1997, a part of the PRC would be in GATT, but the senior part would be outside the system. Hong Kong's membership in any case would give Beijing at least one foot in the GATT door after 1997. The significance of this issue is underscored by the fact that Hong Kong's exports have often exceeded those of the PRC, and that Hong Kong's economy is inextricably intertwined with that of

---

24. See European Communities Commission, "Commission Decision of 15 June 1987 Changing the Import Arrangements Established by Council Decision 87/60 /EEC and Applied in the Member States in Respect of Imports of Various Agricultural and Industrial Products from the People's Republic of China (87/392/EEC)," in *Official Journal of the European Communities*, no. L 206/34 (Brussels: EC, 1987).

the PRC. As shown in table 4.3, in 1987, 34.9 percent of China's exports were to Hong Kong and 19.5 percent of its imports came from there.[25]

As the negotiations proceeded, an unexpected development occurred. Taiwan evidenced interest in acceding to GATT. In 1987 a Taiwanese representative made contact with the GATT secretariat and asked about the possibility of Taiwan becoming associated with GATT and also the possibility of receiving technical assistance so that Taiwan's legislation could be brought into harmony with GATT procedures and requirements. The secretariat replied that Taiwan's relationship with GATT was within the province of the contracting parties and that under the circumstances the secretariat could not give Taiwan technical assistance.

Representatives of Taiwan have also been in contact with GATT member states and indirectly with PRC officials. Even though in the 1980s Taiwan had a larger role in international trade than the PRC, and many contracting parties would have liked Taiwan to be subject to GATT regulations, none wanted to jeopardize the negotiations with China. The Chinese felt that their negotiations should have precedence, but they have stated that they would welcome Taiwanese officials in Beijing to discuss the matter.

Full participation of the PRC and Taiwan in GATT could pose fewer difficulties than it has in other international organizations. Article XXXIII of the General Agreement allows territories that have autonomy in customs matters to have separate representation. Clearly, representatives in Geneva have envisaged the possibility of Taiwan's being brought in at some point, not always with relish. Discussing the negotiations with the PRC, one representative of a developing country said, "It's not only China we have to think about, it's China, plus Hong Kong, Macao, and Taiwan, and that's a commercial monster." The combined exports of the four in the late 1980s exceeded those of the United Kingdom.

Prospects for GATT Negotiations

Exactly how and when the negotiations about China's full participation in GATT would end was impossible to foresee, especially in mid-1989. In the aftermath of the suppression of the prodemocracy movement, the working party session scheduled for July, 1989, was postponed until September, 1989. The major Western governments had been proceeding in the negotiations on the assumption that, regardless of how much progress toward the reform of the Chinese economy might have been accomplished by the time a protocol was signed, the Chinese leaders were deeply committed to reform and would

---

25. IMF, *Direction of Trade Statistics Yearbook, 1988* (Washington, D.C.: IMF, 1988), 136.

have the political will and legitimacy to implement reform. The events of the summer of 1989 threw this assumption into question and in so doing may have undermined the basis for the negotiations. Even if this proved not to be the case, that the negotiations would be difficult and important was obvious. The issues that would have to be resolved in crafting a protocol were thorny.

Until the summer of 1989, many participants believed that at some point a decision would be made to sign a protocol even if all of the issues were not completely resolved, and they believed that this would occur before or simultaneously with the conclusion of the Uruguay Round.

The fact that the U.S. legislation giving the president negotiating authority would expire at the end of 1990 established a practical deadline for the Uruguay Round. There was also a widespread belief among participants that the thorny issue of resumption versus accession would be glossed over and the protocol would be given an innocuous title, such as the relationship of the People's Republic of China with the General Agreement on Tariffs and Trade, that would allow all parties to retain their respective interpretations for purposes of their domestic law.

Expectations about the type of protocol likely to emerge varied among our respondents. Of the twelve individuals—all non-Chinese—who responded to the statement, "GATT will have to make special arrangements to facilitate China's entry," three strongly disagreed, one disagreed, two took the intermediate position, four agreed, and two strongly agreed. When the respondents who agreed with the statement explained what they meant, it became clear that they had in mind a variety of things, ranging from the U.S. insistence on retaining the right to impose special safeguards to cynicism that in the end a deal would be struck that would accord China many privileges and impose few obligations. Of the six who agreed or strongly agreed with the statement, none expected China to make significant changes in its economic policies as a consequence of its full participation in GATT. Since all of the individuals were professionally engaged in the negotiations for China's full participation in GATT, more than anything their explanations of their answers reflected their sense of the uniqueness, historic importance, and difficulty of their task.

An Appraisal

This story of Chinese preparation for participation in the keystone international economic organizations is an impressive one. The Chinese approached the issues methodically and carefully. Once they decided to seek membership, they sought to move swiftly, but they remained sensitive to the political nuances. Well prepared, they entered the negotiations knowing their objectives, but they did not make egregious demands and were prepared to work within the existing framework of these organizations. They recognized that their understanding of organizational procedures in the international bodies remained limited, and hence—similar to the story of their entry into other United Nations organizations—their initial posture was cautious but determined.[26] With respect to the IMF and the World Bank, they had a fundamental principle to uphold, the expulsion of Taiwan, and a longer-term objective, the attainment over a period of time of status and influence at least equal to India. As Chinese officials acknowledge, India provided the yardstick against which they established their own demands, and the Chinese succeeded in establishing at entry that over time and in a minimally disruptive fashion their position would approximate that of India. China's objectives with respect to GATT were both similar and broader. They sought to maintain their legal claim of governmental succession by insisting that they were resuming their status as a contracting party. More broadly, they sought full acceptance as a developing country in the international trading system.

The KIEOs also behaved responsibly. In all three cases the executive heads of the organizations were receptive to and even encouraged Chinese overtures. The leaders of the KIEOs placed the engagement of China in an appropriately broad context. They did not, however, get too far ahead of the membership of their organizations, and particularly the most important members, the United States, the EEC countries, and Japan. They realized that if these states firmly opposed Chinese entry, it could not occur. Agility was exhibited in the negotiations over such issues as the China quota, disposition of gold, addition of seats on the boards of executive directors, and the gradual accession by China to IDA funds. Confrontations could easily have arisen on each of these issues, but diplomatic tact reduced complex issues to manageable proportions. None of the organizations has so far compromised its basic principles in negotiating the PRC's admittance. None has made commitments that have jeopardized its core principles or missions. Yet the Fund and Bank also demonstrated flexibility and creativity in defining the conditions that made China's membership possible. In short, both sides helped set the stage well for the next phase of initial participation. In addition, China's entry to the International Monetary Fund and World Bank smoothed the way for Hungary's entry into these two institutions in 1982 and Poland's in 1986, and China's GATT negotiations established standards that the contracting parties sought to apply in those with Bulgaria that were started in 1988.

With respect to China's participation in the International Monetary Fund and the World Bank, the criteria for successful engagement set forth at the outset of chapter 3 were largely met. Since the GATT negotiations have not yet been completed, it is too early to render a judgment.

---

26. See Samuel S. Kim, *China, the United Nations, and World Order* (Princeton: Princeton University Press, 1979).

To prepare for our later examination of the broader issues involved in China's relationship with the KIEOs, it is important to underscore that China's overtures to the KIEOs followed rather than preceded its basic decision to reorient and restructure its economy. The only requirements that the Fund and Bank placed on China, beyond meeting the financial obligations involved in its quota in the Fund and subscription in the Bank, were for the publication of data. China agreed to fulfill these obligations, thus respecting the integrity of the institutions' rules, but fulfilling the obligations did not in principle seriously affect the character of Chinese institutions.

The terms of China's full participation in GATT had not been determined by mid-1989, but the outline that had emerged of the prospective protocol would not force China to adopt market principles to become a contracting party of GATT. However, the extent to which it would fully gain GATT privileges would depend upon the progress of reform within China. More Chinese have been involved in the process of negotiating China's full participation in GATT than were involved in the negotiations concerning the Fund and the Bank, and the obligations of GATT could be more substantial, so this negotiation could ultimately have a greater impact within China than the other two. Depending on the terms of the protocol—for instance, in the event that China were given full GATT privileges without having to fulfill GATT obligations—the negotiations could have a major impact on the GATT-organized international trade regime. The character of a future global economic order is much more clearly at stake in the negotiations about China's participation in GATT than it was in the those involving IMF and the World Bank.

Another point that merits emphasis concerns the role of the United States. Though the issue has never been put to the test, U.S. consent—or at a minimum acquiescence—appears clearly to have been a condition for the PRC's full participation in the KIEOs. The importance of the United States stems from its financial contribution to the organizations, its voting strength, and the size of its market in the world economy. This partially supports the arguments of all those who stress the crucial role of the United States in the neoliberal international economic order including hegemonic stability, world systems, and dependency theorists. But while U.S. consent was essential, the KIEOs did not always follow U.S. bidding and occasionally ignored U.S. wishes, as when the IMF delegation ignored Secretary of the Treasury Miller's request to delay the negotiations. Robert Keohane's position that although the U.S. has substantial influence, the institutions have taken on a life of their own provides the more accurate description of the interaction between the United States and the KIEOs during the process of engagement. Moreover, as will be seen, the U.S. role during the process of engagement was greater than during subsequent processes.

CHAPTER 5

The Process of Initial Participation in the KIEOs

Integrating a State into the KIEOs: The Four Stages

Incorporating a member state into an international organization is protracted, involves several processes, and passes through different stages. Though these phases overlap, and may even occur simultaneously, for clarity it is useful to distinguish among them.

First comes *engagement*. Contact is made and both sides prepare for and negotiate over the terms of participation. We have described this stage in the preceding chapters. The next step is *initial participation*, the topic of this chapter. Projects and other activities are started. Data are gathered according to the international institutions' specifications and put in the public domain. Efforts are launched to bring national policies and practices into conformity with the norms set by the organization. The new entrant begins to participate in the policy-making processes of the organization and may begin to have an influence on the outcome.

A process of *mutual adjustment* occurs next. By this time the interaction between the state and the institution is well established. Projects and activities are underway, an ample supply of internationally comparable data is available, and national policies and practices are regularly scrutinized to ascertain the extent to which they comply with international norms. The member is a regular participant in the international organization's policy-making. At this stage the compatibility between the state and the international organization is tested. Can the two join together in a harmonious and mutually beneficial relationship? This is not a question of one side merely adapting itself to the other, but rather of mutual adjustment, so long as this adjustment does not seriously deflect the organization from its purposes or destroy its capability to fulfill these purposes.

A *mature partnership* emerges if the process of mutual adjustments is successful. At this stage the country and the international organization have become partners in accomplishing the organization's assigned mission. The challenge is for the two sides to nurture this relationship, use it constructively for common purposes, and adapt it to changing circumstances. To remain relevant, political institutions need to adjust their policies and procedures to changes in their environments. Policies that were effective in achieving goals in one period may not be in the next. Even some goals may need to change. As urgent problems are solved, attention can be devoted to those that previously seemed less urgent. The objective is to attain an "evolutionary equilibrium." This implies constancy in pursuit of basic goals and adaptation to changing circumstances.

As these stages unfold, dangers arise that could threaten or ultimately destroy the relationship between the state and the international organization. In the initial phases, one major danger is that the member state may prepare for and encourage a pattern of dependency on the international organization. While a dependency relationship may be attractive at the outset for the benefits it bestows, a member state probably would subsequently resent and reject it. Some developing countries appear to have slipped into this type of relationship with the International Monetary Fund. Another danger is that the member state may pledge to adhere to the norms of the organization without the intent or capacity to do so. Many contracting parties feel that this is the case with respect to Poland's, Romania's, and Hungary's accession to GATT. The challenge for the international organization in the early stages is to avoid the extremes of indulgence, on the one hand bending at the whim of the member or, on the other hand extreme arrogance, dogmatically enforcing its doctrines whatever their applicability to local circumstances. The former posture erodes the principles of the organization, and hence would make successful inclusion of the new state a Pyrrhic victory, while the latter may preclude the process from going forward.

This abstract portrayal of the process of incorporating a new member into an international organization places the Chinese case in perspective. At the IMF and World Bank by the late 1980s, the stage of initial participation of the People's Republic was drawing to a close, and the third stage of mutual adjustment was well under way. As the previous two chapters and this one detail, the processes of engagement and initial participation were marked by appropriate caution and vision on both sides, and care was taken to pilot around the shoals. As for GATT, the Chinese involvement was still at the first stage, and the early signs did not permit a forecast as to how smooth the processes of engagement and initial participation would be. Until June, 1989, the early indicators also augured well for the successful creation of a mature partnership, but the use of military force and the resulting deaths in Beijing in June, 1989, also revealed that many Chinese leaders either were not yet understanding of or chose to ignore their international environment. These Beijing events underscored that a mature partnership between the leaders of China and the international economic community had not yet been reached.

The *initial participation, mutual adjustment,* and *mature partnership* stages of incorporating a member state into an international organization tend to involve the political systems of the member state and those of the international institutions more deeply than the stage of *engagement*. The consequences of the interaction for the various systems are potentially much more serious. This chapter describes the interaction, the next probes the consequences. The account and analysis focuses primarily on the interaction between China and the KIEOs as it has applied to China rather than to the broad issues before the KIEOs. Although Chinese representatives have been fully engaged in the policy-making processes within these institutions, as of mid-1989 they had not proposed major initiatives or sought a central role.

The World Bank

Initial Participation

In the World Bank, the first Chinese step after securing its seat was to send a small mission to Washington, led by Pu Shan. Pu had received advanced degrees in economics at the University of Michigan and at Harvard University and had returned to China upon the founding of the People's Republic. His subsequent career had been in the Ministry of Foreign Affairs, and, at the time he led the mission, he was deputy head of the Institute of International Relations, a research agency under the ministry. In recalling the history of China's entry, World Bank officials attach great significance to this mission for its effective exploration of the full range of services the Bank offered. The genesis of many programs, such as the major effort of the Economic Development Institute (EDI) to train Chinese in the techniques of project appraisal and evaluation, can be traced to the Pu Shan mission.

The early Ministry of Foreign Affairs involvement, which continued with the appointment of veteran Foreign Ministry official Chen Hui as the first Chinese deputy executive director, reveals the priority that was attached in the first year to ensuring that diplomatic and protocol issues, such as the way maps referred to the People's Republic and the island of Taiwan, were handled successfully. For several years, the Bank (and IMF also) ceased publishing any statistics about Taiwan. It was only in the late 1980s that the Bank (and the Fund) resumed publishing such statistics, then usually under the rubric "Taiwan, Province of China."[1]

Soon after the mission led by Pu Shan came the July, 1980, Bank mission to China led by Shahid Husain, vice president for East Asia and the Pacific region. The chief and senior economist of the China Division, Edwin

---

1. See IBRD, *World Tables, 1987* (Washington, D.C.: IBRD, 1987), 98–99; IMF, *Annual Report, 1988* (Washington, D.C.: IMF, 1988), 12; and IBRD and IMF, *Finance and Development* 25, no. 3 (September, 1988): 47; and 26, no. 1 (March, 1989): 20.

Lim, as well as several functional division chiefs, spent two weeks in Beijing in extensive briefings. Knowing that McNamara was deeply committed to launching a China program before his impending 1981 departure from the Bank, the two sides agreed the first project should go to the Bank executive directors in less than a year. The delegation journeyed to Sichuan and met the leader of the province, Zhao Ziyang. Zhao already knew he was ticketed for promotion to the premiership, and he demonstrated a keen interest in the Bank's activities in a fruitful discussion with Husain. While in Beijing, the delegation established contact with the Chinese Academy of Social Sciences, especially the leading reform-minded economists Liu Guoguang and Dong Furen.

Prior to its departure from Beijing, the delegation reached agreement with its Chinese hosts over the activities that the Bank would undertake. These included five development projects: a $200 million education loan to improve facilities in universities; a loan to enhance the capacity to handle containerized freight in the harbors of Shanghai, Tianjin, and Guangzhou; an agricultural loan to enable drainage of saline soil in North China; a project to develop agricultural education and research; and a project to enhance the capacity of the China Investment Bank to loan foreign exchange to enterprises for small and medium projects and to provide assistance in ensuring the efficient use of foreign technology.

During the same month that the Husain mission was in China, Margaret and Barend de Vries, staff members of the Fund and Bank respectively, visited China and informally briefed officials on how to deal with Fund and Bank missions. During the course of their conversations they discussed the last project involving the China Investment Bank. They pointed out how the Bank could lend to industry indirectly through a domestic development bank. This idea was later successfully implemented through World Bank loans for industrial development to the China Investment Bank.

The Husain mission also advanced the idea of a major, comprehensive study of the Chinese economy, an idea that elicited the interest and support of Zhao Ziyang soon after he became the premier. A series of Bank missions went to China in late 1980 to examine various sectors of the economy and, in rapid fashion, a draft report was prepared and shared with the Chinese in the spring of 1981. It sought to trace the major features of development since the founding of the People's Republic. Its broad theme was a portrayal of thirty years of socialist economic development.

The report noted the steady and relatively rapid growth of the Chinese economy in the years since 1949 and the relatively equal distribution of income. It stressed China's success in providing health care and education throughout the country. The report analyzed problems that China would face in the pursuit of its objectives in the future and offered alternative projections based on differing assumptions. It stressed that:

> Future growth will inevitably depend mainly on improving the efficiency of resource use, rather than on (as in the past) massive mobilization of resources and fundamental institutional change. The benefits of technological innovation as a stimulus to improvisation have been overtaken by its costs in terms of backwardness and bottlenecks. And the remarkable progress made in industrialization and in meeting basic needs has not been matched by—and has created a demand for—a commensurately rapid rise in general living standards.[2]

It warned that China's ability to depend on oil exports as a source of foreign exchange could be limited by the PRC's own growing energy requirements and suggested that Beijing might have to rely on agriculture to generate foreign exchange or to produce foreign exchange savings.

Initially the Chinese did not wish to publish the report openly, but eventually they changed their minds, and in 1983 the Bank published the report, which was entitled *China: Socialist Economic Development*.[3] It soon became highly sought after, both within and outside of China. World Bank projects primarily involve work at the sector and microlevel of the economy, but preparing this report enabled the Bank to work at the macrolevel and to have access to the strategic planners of the economy.

In June, 1981, the first project, on higher education, went to the board of executive directors for approval. The loan of $200 million was financed through a blend of 50 percent IDA and 50 percent IBRD financing. The funds were to be used by the Ministry of Education (MOE) (reorganized into the State Education Commission in 1986) to assist 150 chemistry, physics, biology, computer science, and engineering departments in twenty-six (later increased to twenty-eight) higher institutions. Specifically, the purpose was to upgrade the quality of graduate training, increase the number of graduate students, and improve management at the university and ministry level. The bulk of the loan was spent on books and equipment to strengthen educational laboratories, to upgrade analytical testing centers, and to equip computer centers.

Some of the most senior and experienced Bank officials in the education area were assigned to work on this first Bank project in China. Whereas one to

---

2. IBRD, *China: Socialist Economic Development* (Washington, D.C.: IBRD, 1983), 1: 13–14.

3. IBRD, *China: Socialist Economic Development*.

two years is a typical period of gestation for a Bank project, only half that time elapsed from the initial broaching of this project by the Chinese to its submission to the board. The Bank relaxed some of its usual procedures, such as monitoring of the architectural designs for the new buildings that would house the new equipment. But it successfully insisted that 20 percent of the loans be devoted to manpower training; the Ministry of Education wanted to spend the entire $200 million on equipment. The ministry accepted other Bank suggestions as well: to include biology as one of the sciences to be upgraded; in an unprecedented action, to form an International Advisory Panel and a Chinese Review Commission to assist and advise the MOE in the implementation of the project; and to include upgrading of university management in the scope of the program. The ministry rejected other Bank suggestions, such as allowing each university to purchase a computer system designed for its particular needs or spending funds to enhance management within the ministry. The ministry allocated the funds among the twenty-eight universities, giving the largest sum to Qinghua University, with which the leaders of MOE have particularly close personal connections. This detail hints at a tough negotiating process; the project was launched because of the flexibility that both sides demonstrated.

With the comprehensive economic study and the education project setting the pace, by the end of the first year of membership, the two sides felt a great deal had been accomplished. To be sure, there were difficulties and problems as well. Honest differences cropped up over some aspects of the report; the top PRC leaders, for example, thought the World Bank's projections of petroleum production were too pessimistic and underestimated the potential of peripheral fields. The Chinese also felt vigilance was required to ensure that World Bank references to Taiwan clearly sustained a "one China" policy. Moreover, while the Bank had begun to establish good relations at the leadership level, had begun to establish links with a few ministries at the working level in project planning, and had reached to the Chinese Academy of Social Sciences and the universities, it had not been as successful in contacting the intermediate levels of line ministries (a ministry with functional responsibilities in a narrow sector such as railroads, metallurgy, or coal), especially their research bureaus, nor had the Bank established firm relations with the pivotal State Planning Commission (SPC). Finally, Bank officials sensed that the release of previously secret data was a painful process for the Chinese and came over the opposition of some leaders and agencies.

The most serious early impediment to rapid expansion of World Bank operations in China, however, was the economic retrenchment ordered in late 1980. The top leaders sought to cool off their overheated economy, marked by inflation, government deficits, trade imbalances resulting in deficits of about $2 billion in both 1979 and 1980,[4] and looming purchases of foreign equipment. They slashed foreign imports and reduced capital investment projects.[5] When the Chinese soon afterward informed the Bank that only the education project would go forward in 1981 and that planning was to be halted for all Bank missions, it sounded to some Bank officials as if the relationship would prove stillborn. The early days of 1981 were anxious ones for the new China Division, which received no message from Beijing for two months. Finally, with the resumption of discussions about the Bank report on the Chinese economy in March, 1981, the Bank realized that it had not been singled out for cutbacks but rather that the Chinese had embarked on a stringent retrenchment on all investments, a program in which the IMF was involved, as will be described in the following section.

During the 1981–82 retrenchment, World Bank lending to China remained at an ebb. Only one project, a $60 million agricultural loan, went forward. In retrospect, this low level of project loans may have been fortuitous, for the time was well spent by both sides in training Chinese personnel to work with the Bank and in acquainting Bank officials with China. Invariably, a trip to China proved helpful in providing a more empathetic view of the Bank's mission in China. Such trips as those by Senior Vice-President Ernest Stern in March, 1982, and President A. W. Clausen in May, 1983, helped to cultivate broad support in the Bank for extending its China operations. Indeed, a parallel exists with the role that Beijing sojourns by high officials play in the Sino-American relationship, a phenomenon which has been described as an exercise in "trip driven diplomacy."[6] Some Chinese officials have complained about the burden these Bank missions have placed upon them in terms of required preparation, the demands for information they engender, and the complex logistical arrangements that have to be made to ensure a smooth visit in a country where making even the simplest travel arrangements requires considerable effort. However, interviews with World Bank and IMF officials suggest the heightened understanding has amply compensated for the effort involved.

The Stern and Clausen visits restored momentum to Bank activities in China. Perhaps more important, Beijing eased its retrenchment policies as

---

4. IBRD, *China: External Trade and Capital* (Washington, D.C.: IBRD, 1988), 116.

5. For details on the 1980 retrenchment, see Bruce L. Reynolds, "Reform in Chinese Industrial Management: An Empirical Report," in *China under the Four Modernizations*, pt. 1, U.S. Congress, Joint Economic Committee (Washington, D.C.: GPO, 1982), 119–37.

6. For a description of the role that missions to Beijing play in U.S. foreign policy see Robert G. Sutter, *The China Quandary: Domestic Determinants of U.S.-China Policy, 1972–1982* (Boulder, Colo.: Westview Press, 1983).

problems of inflation, government deficits, and trade imbalances were brought under control (in 1982 and 1983 China had trade surpluses), while the Reagan administration, having completed its review of the multilateral development banks, softened its own restrictive views toward the Bank and appropriations for the Seventh IDA Replenishment. By mid-1983 the stage was set for an expansion of loans to China.

The Clausen visit also led to the World Bank's second major study of the Chinese economy. Through discussions that Clausen had with Deng Xiaoping and Zhao Ziyang about China's aim to raise its per capita GNP to $800 by the year 2000, agreement was reached that the World Bank should undertake a study of some of the key development issues that China would face and analyze opportunities for dealing with these issues in the light of international experience. This second report, titled *China: Long Term Development Issues and Options* was published in 1985.[7] Edwin Lim, who was then the China Division's chief economist and who subsequently became the Bank's first representative in China, was chief of mission for the report.

The Development of A Policy Dialogue

The second report contained much more data about other countries than the first and put China's development and the choices it faced in comparative perspective. It was more future oriented. It stressed the need to depart from the past emphasis in China's economic development on local self-sufficiency, to abandon local protectionism, and to move toward a broader orientation that would allow greater specialization within the country. It urged that greater reliance should be placed on market mechanisms. This would involve, above all, price reform. The report examined how the role of the state in the management of the economy would change if China pursued the recommended course, showing particularly how the emphasis in planning would shift from the short to the medium and long term. It analyzed the issues that would be involved in increasing the amount of animal protein in the Chinese diet. The report emphasized the need within higher education to recover from the effects of the Cultural Revolution and the need to make efficient use of energy. It laid out the case for greater emphasis on the development of the service sector. The report directly addressed the question of whether or not the benefits gained through the development of China's socialist system—particularly the reduction of poverty and the relatively egalitarian distribution of income—could be preserved if the suggested changes were implemented and argued that they could. The report contained several different projections,

---

7. IBRD, *China: Long-Term Development Issues and Options* (Washington, D.C.: IBRD, 1985).

illustrating the consequences for China's development of different strategic choices.

After completing the second country economic report, the Bank launched a series of sectoral studies, and growing emphasis came to be placed on these studies. Within China, the 1984 decisions to extend processes of restructuring and reform to the urban sector stimulated interest in receiving detailed advice on adjustment within sectors. The 1987 decisions of the Thirteenth National Congress of the Chinese Communist party to continue and intensify the reforms increased this interest. Within the Bank, the members of the China Country Department held a retreat shortly after the department was established. One conclusion of the retreat was that, because of the work that had been done and the data that were available, the Bank had a comparative advantage to offer useful macroeconomic advice on a sectoral level.

In a sense, the emphasis on sectoral studies symbolized achievement of agreement between Chinese and Bank officials on principles according to which China's economy should be organized, such as the principles that prices should be determined by markets and that enterprises should be responsible for their profits and losses. The sectoral studies took these principles as given and concentrated on transitional questions, i.e., how over time to move in the direction of fuller implementation of the principles. The studies were more policy oriented than those sectoral analyses that had provided background for the country economic reports, and they focused on crucial topics in the reform and restructuring process.

The Bank's report on China's external trade and finances has already been mentioned.[8] In addition, by mid-1989 studies of the following had been published: the management and finance of higher education;[9] the livestock sector;[10] finance and investment;[11] and Gansu province, which had the lowest average rural per capita income in China and a rate of poverty far above the national average.[12] Studies of the tax system and social security were under way, and studies of other sectors such as the housing market, agricultural marketing and pricing, the grain situation, transport, and energy pricing were envisaged.

Preparing these reports enabled the Bank to engage in extensive dialogues with knowledgeable Chinese officials and researchers about policy

---

8. IBRD, *China: External Trade and Capital*.

9. IBRD, *China: Management and Finance of Higher Education*. A World Bank Country Study. (Washington, D.C.: IBRD, 1986).

10. IBRD, *China. the Livestock Sector*. A World Bank Country Study. (Washington, D.C.: IBRD, 1987).

11. IBRD, *China: Finance and Investment* (Washington, D.C.: IBRD, 1988).

12. IBRD, *China: Growth and Development in Gansu Province* (Washington, D.C.: IBRD, 1988).

choices concerning crucial sectoral issues. Each study involved extensive fieldwork by Bank staff. Following standard Bank procedure, draft versions of the reports, after being discussed within the Bank, were discussed with various Chinese officials and analysts, and then modified to take account of their views. Eventually, the reports were published and distributed within and outside China. Each report contained detailed analyses of policy choices available to China and of the prospective consequences of these choices. All were timely. The livestock report was published in 1987, amid recurring shortages of pork in China. The report on Gansu province was published in 1988, when there was deep concern about growing regional disparities in the distribution of income. The report on external trade and finance was published in 1988, just as the GATT working party was about to begin preparing the protocol that would define the terms of China's full participation in GATT. All could not help but become factors in the debate about the policies that China should pursue.

The sectoral reports and the discussions about them dramatically under-scored the interrelationships among the various elements of restructuring and reform of the Chinese economic system. This is especially evident in the report on finance and investment.[13] This report stressed that markets could not produce their projected effects of increasing efficiency unless enterprises were responsible for their profits and losses. Enterprises could not become respon-sible for their profits and losses until they were in some way disconnected from the state so that the state would not automatically cover their losses and reap their profits. Making enterprises responsible for their profits and losses could also mean, among other things, that the social security functions for which enterprises were responsible, such as providing education, health care, housing, and a guaranteed income for their employees, would have to be taken care of in some other way. The government could not develop a social security system without developing a taxation system to provide funds to cover the costs of whatever social security functions it might assume. A taxation system would in any case be required to replace the governmental revenues that would be lost by shifting control over the uses of the profits of enterprises from government to the enterprises themselves.

Interlocked with all of these issues were broad questions of how much and what pace of change could be tolerated politically. And as China moved to allow market rather than governmental regulations to determine prices, the politically sensitive issue of how much inflation would be tolerable came constantly to the fore. Each step toward reducing the air lock that insulated the Chinese economy from the international economy ran smack into several of

---

13. IBRD, *China: Finance and Investment.*

these points. Chinese prices had been held virtually constant from 1949 through 1979, while world prices had risen substantially during this period. Removing the air lock inevitably involved upward movement in prices. Moreover, if the government moved to assume social security functions previously handled by enterprises without having an adequate system for raising revenue in place and covered the expenditures simply by printing money, it would seriously exacerbate inflationary pressures.

The developing policy dialogue between the Bank and China addressed the most basic issues in China's quest for a planned commodity economy. The progress of this dialogue encouraged the Bank staff to contemplate additional structural adjustment loans for China. In early 1989 some staff members thought that the volume of such loans could easily and quickly rise to the maximum level of 25 percent of total lending.

The Record of Lending through Mid-1989

Simultaneously, the Bank's involvement in China's development at the microlevel increased. Total new loan commitments in 1983 were $600 million, and in 1984 they reached $1 billion. In 1985 and 1986 they were about $1.1 billion each year, with $423.5 million and $423.3 million coming from IDA. The Bank's level of new lending to China reached $1.4 billion in 1987 and was just under $1.7 billion in 1988. By mid-1989, the total value of approved Bank projects was almost $7.4 billion, with $4.5 billion coming from IBRD and $2.9 billion from IDA.

In 1987, IDA lending accounted for 27.1 percent of the net Official Development Assistance (resources transferred by the governments of developed countries to developing countries at concessional rates) received by China and IBRD and IDA loans constituted 13.8 percent of the total net financial flow to China.[14] After Japan, the World Bank was China's most important source of external assistance. In 1987 China accounted for 6.1 percent of IBRD's lending, 16.0 percent of IDA's lending, and 8.1 percent of total World Bank lending.

Starting in 1988, the Bank began a system of three-year rolling planning for lending in China. According to the Bank's plans for 1989, 1990, and 1991, the volume of lending would be over $2 billion in each of the three years. After June, 1989, it was uncertain whether the annual target of $2 billion could or would be achieved. In June, 1989, the World Bank's management concluded that the Board of Executive Directors discussion of $780.4

---

14. OECD, *Geographical Distribution of Financial Assistance to Developing Countries, 1984–1987* (Paris: OECD, 1988).

million in new loans for China should be deferred. Prior to this decision, twelve projects amounting to $1,348.4 million had been approved in 1989. The Bank's action in deferring additional commitments was relatively unusual and was controversial within the Bank. Some officials and observers felt that the Bank was holding China to a higher standard than it had required of other countries. Others felt that before June, 1989, the Chinese government had elicited World Bank cooperation on the basis of its pledges and performance in implementing reforms and the action in June therefore represented a retrogression that demanded a response. Some in the Bank, as elsewhere in the Western world, also felt a sense of betrayal of trust and confidence.

By mid-1989 the Bank had approved sixty-nine projects for China.[15] Appendix 1 provides a list of these projects. Thus, the Bank had gradually extended its activities and established projects throughout China both territorially and bureaucratically. It had established direct contacts at the basic levels as well as at the ministerial levels in Beijing. It had run training programs for middle-level managers throughout the bureaucracy.[16] It had sponsored joint research involving economists from the Bank staff and from the Institute of Economics of the Chinese Academy of Social Sciences.[17] The initial priorities were in the areas of education, energy (especially petroleum and coal), transportation, and agriculture, but more recently activity has extended to include health, hydroelectric projects, urban development, social services, and natural resource development. Bureaucratically, the Bank had launched projects with the State Planning Commission, the State Education Commission, and a long list of ministries: agriculture, livestock, and fisheries; communications; petroleum; coal; railways; water resources and electric power; public health; and machine building. Bank activities had also extended to some of the most impoverished areas of China. No other external agency had established as wide a range of contacts in China.

Table 5.1 shows the distribution by sector of funds approved by IBRD and IDA for China and compares this distribution with that of funds approved for all other countries from 1981 through 1987. The World Bank's program in China included projects in all of the sectors in which it had activities elsewhere except small-scale enterprises, telecommunications, and the nonproject category. China's first SAL, $300 million for the rural sector, was approved in 1988. As table 5.1 makes apparent, in addition to agriculture and rural

---

15. For a description of the Bank's lending activities in China in the context of China's reform program see Shahid Javed Burki, "Reform and Growth in China," *Finance and Development* 25, no. 4 (December, 1988): 46–49.

16. See especially "A Review of China's EDI Program: Looking Back," in *EDI Review*, April, 1986, 1–3.

17. See Gene Tidrick and Chen Jiyuan, eds., *China's Industrial Reform* (Washington, D.C.: IBRD, 1987).

TABLE 5.1. Comparison of Distribution by Sector of IBRD and IDA Funds Approved for China and for Other Countries, 1981–88

	China		All Others		Ratio of China's Distribution to Others
	Millions of U.S. Dollars	Percentage of Total Funds to China	Millions of U.S. Dollars	Percentage of Total Funds to Others	Percentage
Agriculture and rural development	1,655.0	22.78	28,299.7	24.47	93
Development finance corporations	645.6	8.89	9,786.6	8.46	105
Education	744.2	10.24	4,820.0	4.17	246
Energy	1,573.9	21.67	22,338.9	19.32	112
Industry	484.1	6.66	6,714.9	5.81	115
Nonproject	—	0.00	11,139.6	9.63	0
Population, health, and nutrition	165.0	2.27	1,214.4	1.05	216
Small-scale enterprises	—	0.00	3,488.0	3.02	0
Technical assistance	50.7	0.70	789.8	0.68	103
Telecommunications	—	0.00	1,838.8	1.59	0
Transportation	1,720.6	23.69	13,502.2	11.68	203
Urbanization and urban development	145.0	2.00	6,472.8	5.60	36
Water supply and sewerage	80.0	1.10	5,237.8	4.53	24
Total	7,264.1	100.00	115,643.5	100.01[a]	

Source: IBRD, *Annual Reports,* 1981–88 (Washington, D.C.: IBRD, 1981–89).
[a]Totals more than 100 because of rounding.

development, the Bank's China program has given special emphasis in absolute terms to energy and transportation, areas that Bank analyses identified as bottlenecks to China's development. Compared to the Bank's overall lending, its program in China has given relatively more emphasis to population, health, and nutrition; education; transportation; energy; and industry.

Some Constraints

Several impediments kept annual World Bank lending around the $1 billion level from 1984 through 1986. The Chinese were reluctant to depart from a fifty-fifty blend of IDA and IBRD loans and accept a harder blend (i.e., a higher proportion of IBRD funds) in terms of annual borrowing. While some individual loans could dip below that ratio, the Chinese objective for the late 1980s was for 40 percent of the borrowing to be at IDA's attractive concessional interest rates. The Chinese, however, came to accept that there was a ceiling on IDA loans, and that if they aimed for annual borrowing of more than $2 billion per year, they would have to accept a harder blend than an overall ratio of 40 percent IDA and 60 percent IBRD. They also came to appreciate that even if the IBRD interest rate is sometimes higher than those that they could obtain for bilateral noncommercial loans, since IBRD loans are in convertible currency and are not tied to purchases from any particular country, the total cost of goods obtained via Bank loans is often cheaper than that of those obtained via bilateral governmental loans. Although the Chinese acceptance of a harder blend of IDA and IBRD funds has manifestly been merely recognition of inexorable fiscal constraints, this action and comparable actions by other developing countries have implicitly legitimized donor requests for maturation.

Some Chinese officials stated that a second constraint was the need within China to limit domestic capital construction expenditures. The World Bank calculated that for every dollar borrowed from it, the Chinese must raise two dollars in *renminbi* (RMB) for the internally funded aspects of the project, and some officials were apparently reluctant to tie up a significant portion of central government discretionary investment funds in World Bank projects. To some extent, World Bank projects could crowd out other projects. However, other leading Chinese officials did not consider this a problem. Such officials believed projects backed by the Bank were sound and wished to increase the level of Bank loans. These officials asked the SPC and MOF to identify and reduce the constraints upon World Bank lending.

Internal bureaucratic considerations also constrained Chinese borrowing. The State Council had difficulty developing acceptable procedures for allocating responsibility for loan repayments between the State Planning Commission and the line ministry or province receiving the loan. If the central government required loan recipients to be responsible for repayment of hard currency, then they had to earn the foreign currency to repay the loan. Under these circumstances, provinces and ministries that earned foreign currency (such as the Ministry of Petroleum) inevitably enjoyed advantages in the internal competition for Bank loans. But if recipients bore no obligation, then the loans might have been expended in an inefficient manner. The central government tended to require only those recipients that earned foreign exchange to repay the loans in hard currency. Nonforeign revenue earners, such as the ministries of public health or education, had other repayment obligations. The SPC and MOF found it difficult to apportion Bank loans among the various types of recipients.

The Ministry of Finance also had to engage in time-consuming bargaining with provincial officials to arrange for the repayment of loans. In one case, for instance, a province that earned considerable foreign exchange was slated to be a major beneficiary of an energy project. This governmental unit, however, refused to pledge any of its future foreign exchange earnings to help repay the loan until it was guaranteed the lion's share of output from the new installation. Months of negotiations were consumed ironing out the details, and only a Bank-imposed deadline—the end of its fiscal year—forced a solution. As in other aspects of the Chinese political process, separate deals must be struck among ministries in Beijing or between Beijing and the provinces over each development project. The process for building a consensus to undertake the project was protracted and involved disbursing benefits over a wide range of bureaucratic actors whose cooperation was necessary for the project to be implemented.[18]

Another constraint was that both sides perceived the process of generating acceptable project proposals as cumbersome, although the two sides cited different obstacles. The Chinese side focused on the lengthy and complex initial steps in the project cycle (especially with respect to preparation of feasibility studies and the complex procedures of the bidding process), while some Bank officials claimed that the Chinese pipeline for generating quality project proposals was inadequate. Structural adjustment lending, which is policy rather than project based, bypasses this constraint.

Finally, when China negotiated its Structural Adjustment Loan with the World Bank in 1988 it insisted that the loan should not involve the application of conditionality. Normally the Bank disburses such loans in installments, and specified conditions must be met for the subsequent installments to be disbursed. In the case of China's SAL, $200 million was to be disbursed in 1989, the first year of the loan, and $100 million in 1990 without China having to meet any conditions. The rationale for the Bank's not imposing conditionality was that China had already taken sufficient reform measures to assure the success of the adjustment program. China's posture in these negotiations evidenced a deep reluctance to be put in a position of having to take domestic actions in response to an external authority. Clearly, China will seek to limit its borrowing so that it is not put in this position.

The International Monetary Fund

The early years of IMF membership have also demonstrated a methodical, cautious approach to building a relationship. Pursuant to the negotiations recounted in chapter 3, on September 8, 1980, the Fund authorized a special increase in the PRC's quota from SDR 550 million to SDR 1.2 billion, which subsequently was raised to SDR 1.8 billion in November, and then in 1983 to SDR 2.39 billion.

In the spring of 1981, Beijing received a drawing from the Fund in the

---

18. See Kenneth Lieberthal and Michel Oksenberg, *Policy Making in China: Leaders, Structures, and Processes* (Princeton: Princeton University Press, 1988).

first credit tranche of SDR 450 million and a Trust Fund loan of SDR 309 million, bringing the total to SDR 759 million. The standby arrangement in support of China's 1981 economic stabilization program was negotiated with little difficulty, in part because the retrenchment measures taken by China were very severe. Furthermore, the conditions imposed by the Fund for drawings in the first credit tranche are seldom severe. The success of China's policies was demonstrated in May, 1983, when China announced that it would repay the drawing in the first credit tranche swiftly, a commitment that it fulfilled in 1984. China also used most of its allocation of SDRs in late 1980 and drew its reserve tranche in 1981. Both were repaid by the end of 1984.

Beyond these loans, IMF activities with China through 1985 included the annual consultation required under IMF's Articles of Agreement, the initiation of a publication program of IMF materials in Chinese that were then disseminated in China, and considerable technical training with Fund lecturers going to China and a significant number of younger Chinese attending seminars and courses in Washington. For example, the Fund staff generally, and particularly personnel from IMF's Bureau of Statistics, spent much time with People's Bank officials discussing the "balance of payments" concept and assisting the People's Bank to improve its accounting procedures to record China's balance. In 1980, the People's Bank of China sent two people to learn the methodology of compiling balance of payments statistics according to IMF standards. After they returned to China, the Bank of China compiled and published balance of payments statistics on an internal basis in 1982, 1983, and 1984. Finally, in September, 1985, the People's Bank of China published balance of payments statistics for China for the first time. Also, the Fund staff worked closely with the authorities to improve monetary supply data and external debt statistics.

IMF's managing director, Jacques de Larosière, visited China in October, 1981. During his visit he had discussions with Deng Xiaoping; Li Baohua, president of the People's Bank of China; Shang Ming, vice-president of the People's Bank of China, and Wang Weicai, vice-president of the Bank of China. One outcome of this consultation was a decision that in 1982, the People's Bank of China and the International Monetary Fund should jointly sponsor a symposium in Beijing from October 20 through October 28 on the role of China and of the Fund in the international monetary system and on the outlook for the world economy. Papers were prepared by Chinese economists and by members of the IMF staff. Senior government and banking officials, academics, and postgraduate students attended the symposium. The papers and summaries of the discussions were subsequently published.[19]

In many ways the interaction between China and the IMF in these early

---

19. IMF, *The Fund and China in the International Monetary System* (Washington, D.C.: IMF, 1983).

years can best be described as a mutual learning experience. As China came to publish more and more statistics according to IMF standards, Fund officials came to understand China's economy better; the more contact that Chinese officials had with the Fund, the more that they understood the role of the Fund and the services that it could provide.

This is not to say Chinese-Fund relations were entirely smooth. For instance, an incident occurred at an early stage, when in late 1980 the Chinese decided to establish an internal settlement price or rate of exchange. Fund officials learned of this indirectly, prior to the January, 1981, formal announcement of the decision, and a visiting Fund mission gently indicated that under the terms of accession to Fund membership, China was obliged to inform the Fund of proposed steps such as this one. They claimed that the arrangement constituted a dual exchange rate, which required approval under Fund regulations. Chinese officials responded that they considered this an internal matter. The issue subsided in January, 1985, when China discontinued the internal settlement rate, but at the time the affair suggested to Fund officials that China did not fully understand and/or was not willing to adhere to regulations.

By 1985 the relationship between China and the International Monetary Fund had matured. Also, China had taken further steps toward the decentralization of its economy with the consequence that the government had many fewer direct instruments of control and in the future would have to rely more and more on the indirect instruments commonly used in market economies, such as control of the money supply, interest rates, and taxation.[20] Much of the responsibility for implementing macroeconomic policy through indirect instruments would fall upon the People's Bank of China, which under reforms put into effect January 1, 1984, had in effect become a central bank.[21] Under these circumstances, the advice that the Fund could render became extremely relevant to China.

In late 1984, the Chinese executive director in IMF began discussions with the Fund staff about the possibility of the Fund's conducting a technical assistance program that would deal with the indirect instruments used in macroeconomic policy. The director of the Central Banking Division of the Fund, Linda Koenig, and a colleague visited China in mid-1985. They gave lectures and engaged in discussions with Chinese governmental and banking officials. This resulted in preliminary agreement on a technical assistance program, an agreement that was formalized when Shang Ming visited Washington in the fall of 1985.

---

20. See Luc de Wulf and David Goldsbrough, "The Evolving Role of Monetary Policy in China," *IMF Staff Papers* 33, no. 2 (June, 1986): 209–42.

21. These reforms are described in Luc de Wolf, "Financial Reform in China," *Finance and Development* 22, no. 4 (December, 1985): 19–22.

The program involved Chinese officials spending time in Washington, D.C., in January, 1986, and Fund officials spending time in China in March, 1986. The purpose of the project was to evaluate the monetary instruments employed by and available to the People's Bank of China in terms of the broad framework of Chinese policy. A report was published in May, 1986. Fund officials sought to give the Chinese an analytical framework for evaluating instruments. The Fund undertook a second mission under the project in April, 1987. A projection system was developed in this phase of the project.

The Fund and the People's Bank of China cosponsored a major colloquium in China from November 11 through 17, 1986, on "Macroeconomic Management, Growth, and the Role of the IMF." The symposium covered a range of diverse topics including the role of monetary policy and instruments, the formulation and monitoring of fiscal policy, adjustment in centrally planned economies, and the development policies pursued by Korea from 1960 through 1985.[22] There was a vast leap in sophistication between the symposium that the Fund cosponsored three years earlier and this colloquium. China was more familiar with the Fund. Also, China's economy had changed and as a consequence its needs were more complicated.

In November, 1986, the Executive Board of the IMF approved a standby arrangement for China, authorizing purchases of up to SDR 597.7 million over twelve months.[23] China's balance of payments position had begun to deteriorate in mid-1984, when the current account moved into a deficit position, and this situation persisted in 1985, 1986, and 1987. The 1985 deficit on current account was an astonishing and record $15 billion. In 1986 the deficit on current account was over $13 billion.[24] By 1987 it had declined to less than $4 billion.[25] Chinese officials began to discuss negotiating a standby arrangement in early 1986, and the actual terms of the arrangement were worked out during the annual consultation in July, 1986.

It was determined that the standby arrangement would be in China's first credit tranche. China's balance of payments situation was not so severe as to necessitate a drawing in the higher credit tranches. Perhaps more important, China did not want the more severe conditionality requirements associated with drawings in the upper credit tranches. Drawings in the upper credit tranches are disbursed in installments, and performance criteria are estab-

22. A Chinese language version of the papers has also been published.

23. IMF, *IMF Survey,* November 1986, 357.

24. IMF, *Direction of Trade Statistics Yearbook, 1987* (Washington, D.C.: IMF, 1987), 137.

25. IMF, *Direction of Trade Statistics Yearbook, 1988* (Washington, D.C.: IMF, 1988), 136.

lished that must be met before second and subsequent installments are paid. China's posture with respect to IMF drawings parallels the stance that it took subsequently in the negotiations about its World Bank Structural Adjustment Loan.

Several issues were discussed during the negotiations for the standby arrangement. China refused to allow the arrangement to specify conditions, but was willing to allow the Fund to make recommendations and gave concrete assurances that it would act on these recommendations. One issue involved devaluation of the *renminbi*. The Chinese resisted the Fund's pressure for a substantial devaluation of nearly 30 percent, arguing that the resulting sharp rise in the cost of imported materials and components would have too disruptive an impact on domestic prices. On July 5, 1986, just after the IMF consultation mission departed, however, China devalued the *renminbi* by 15.8 percent against major currencies. Other issues involved increasing internal interest rates and improving China's debt management. China increased its internal interest rates in 1986, though not as much as the IMF would have liked. That same year the Fund and China agreed on a technical assistance project concerning the management of China's external debt. Chinese willingness to permit IMF intrusion into this sensitive area had been stimulated by an IMF mission in early 1986, which estimated that China's external debt had reached $20 billion. One Chinese official claimed that this was impossible, citing China's estimate of a debt of $12 billion. The different estimates prompted a desire to ascertain the real situation. Thus, all three issues had been subjects of discussion between China and the Fund for some time, and Chinese officials had in any case long been considering taking action with respect to them.

As is evident from this account, starting in the mid-1980s, the interaction between the Fund and China increased. As this occurred, the Fund upgraded its capacity to deal with China, increasing the number of staff assigned to this work. Those assigned to China included some of the Fund's most promising younger officials. The interaction between the Fund and China stepped up further in 1988–89 as the rate of inflation within China increased. According to official Chinese statistics, the inflation rate for the first ten months of 1988 was 17 percent.[26] Unofficial estimates of the rate of inflation were even higher. Some Western sources estimated the rate of inflation in mid-1989 to be as high as 30 to 40 percent.[27] IMF's managing director, Michel Camdessus, visited China in April, 1989. Before his visit he stated that the Fund was intensifying its dialogue with Chinese authorities to assist them in their

26. *New York Times*, January 3, 1989.
27. *Wall Street Journal*, June 16, 1989.

efforts to bring inflation under control. He warned that the inflation could derail the entire reform process. He said that China's problem:

> . . . is how to move to an open price system without the checks and balances of a market economy, which are ultimately company profit and loss accounts, and how the central bank can tackle the over-liquidity of the economy in the transitional period.[28]

According to Camdessus all countries moving from central planning toward markets faced problems similar to those that confronted China. He insisted that it was crucial that China should succeed so that other countries could profit from China's experience. The Fund was to sponsor a seminar in China in the summer of 1989 on monetary policy in which such public figures as Paul Volker, the former chairman of the U.S. Federal Reserve Board, and others would share their experience with the Chinese and give their advice, but this seminar was postponed.

GATT

Since China has participated fully only in GATT's Multifibre Arrangement, the record of interaction between GATT and China is much less substantial than that between China and the Bank and the Fund. China has played a relatively modest role in the MFA. Within the framework of the MFA, Chinese representatives have been relatively passive in multilateral discussions, but firm and forceful in bilateral negotiations.

China has brought two complaints before the Textile Surveillance Body. In late 1984, China joined with other developing countries in a complaint against U.S. efforts to restrict quotas on textile imports. The following year, China complained to the board about a U.S. decision to classify luggage made of fabrics as a textile product and therefore subject to an import ceiling. In the first case, the United States was forced to rescind some but not all of its restrictions. In the second, bilateral negotiations occurred that resulted in a compromise. From China's point of view, the outcome of these two complaints was mixed. Because the TSB is composed of an equal number of exporting and importing countries, its decisions tend to be compromises, and China did not receive complete satisfaction in either case.

Because China is such a large country, and politically so important, it is not obvious that when it has disputes with importing countries its short-term interests are better served by bringing the dispute to the TSB rather than by engaging in bilateral negotiations. In January, 1983, when the United States

28. *International Herald Tribune*, April 10, 1989.

imposed restrictions on textiles exported from China, Beijing responded by imposing a ban on imports of cotton, synthetic fibers, and soybeans from the United States, a ban that was not lifted until the PRC received satisfaction from the United States in September, 1983. Despite, or perhaps because of, this experience, the Chinese chose to join the MFA and to participate in its dispute settlement procedure. The Chinese have generally taken the position that they prefer the relative predictability of multilateral procedures to the somewhat greater uncertainty of bilateral procedures.

In keeping with this position, China participated in 1986 in the negotiations for the extension of the Multifibre Arrangement for the period from August 1, 1986, until July 31, 1991. Even though China shared the disappointment of many developing countries that MFA IV could be read as further restricting rather than liberalizing trade in textiles, and was particularly disappointed that ramie fabric—a product made from the fiber of an Asian shrub that is an important export of China—was included in the arrangement for the first time, it ultimately ratified the extension, though only after it had concluded a new bilateral trade agreement with the United States, which allowed an expansion of China's exports of textiles to the United States.

China also let it be known that it would be pleased to have a seat on the Textile Surveillance Body. To fulfill this ambition, however, would require skillful maneuvering through sensitive issues. Four members of the TSB have been chosen from the importing countries that have signed the MFA and four from the exporting countries. China's ambition posed the issues of whether existing patterns of representation should be changed among the exporting countries, or if they should be maintained, whether or not the TSB should be enlarged and the principle of parity between importers and exporters maintained. These were issues upon which agreement would be difficult to achieve.

An Appraisal

The record at the World Bank and the IMF and the brief record in GATT's MFA reveals an orderly process of initial participation by China. The dire predictions from some quarters that Chinese membership would be disruptive have not proven to be correct. Chapter 1 posited four possibilities: (1) that China would be a voice for major change on behalf of developing countries; (2) that it would press for incremental changes so that Chinese traditions and practices would be applied more generally; (3) that China would seek to receive special treatment; or (4) that China would basically accept the existing framework. By and large the fourth outcome is largely what has occurred.

Chinese representatives have certainly not led or even been part of an effort within the KIEOs to transform them to fit the prescription for a New

International Economic Order. Nor have they sought to have China become the model for developing countries. China's voting strength in the Fund and Bank, though greater than it was at the end of Taiwan's presence in the two institutions, was less than had been allocated to it at Bretton Woods. China has not received a disproportionate share of the financial and staff resources of the International Monetary Fund and the World Bank, and the rules of the two institutions have not been bent for China any more than they normally are for large new entrants. Indonesia was such a case earlier. To be sure, special considerations were made to facilitate its initial participation in the Fund and Bank, such as the swiftly processed education loan or the recruitment of talented officers to launch the China programs.

But an orderly entry does not mean that China's membership has been without consequence or challenges for the parties involved. We turn to this topic in the next chapter.

CHAPTER 6

The Process of Mutual Adjustment

Many institutional changes and policy modifications have occurred both within China and within the IMF and the World Bank that have facilitated cooperation between Beijing and the KIEOs. This has entailed a process of mutual adjustment. Its essence involves each actor allowing itself to be influenced by the other.

At the outset we must acknowledge that it is extremely difficult to measure influence, discern motives, and sort out cause and effect. China and the KIEOs undertook some changes purposefully and voluntarily to ease China-KIEO relations. Each undertook a few other measures under pressure to meet conditions imposed by the other side. Finally, each initiated steps without the China-KIEO relationship as the primary or even secondary consideration, but the changes had unintended salutary effects. In particular, many of the reforms undertaken in China began to be implemented before Chinese membership in the Fund and Bank, and they probably would have continued without its involvement in the KIEOs. Similarly, some changes in the IMF's and the World Bank's policies were based on broader considerations than China, yet they eased cooperation with the PRC.

Further complicating the analysis is the perception, held by each of the actors we are studying, that it is of global consequence. None is eager to admit to being affected by the others; each jealously seeks to project an image of its independence. Each quietly and privately harbors a somewhat exaggerated notion of its influence on the others that outside observers can easily detect. Yet particularly in the case of the IMF and the World Bank, there is a strong desire to avoid the publicity of influence out of concern that this would adversely affect the ability to work in China, while many Chinese are eager to underscore their contribution to these organizations in order to demonstrate that the relationship is genuinely equitable. As a result, a good deal of the issuance of demands, the hard bargaining, and the resulting accommodation has gone on quietly behind the scenes and has not been openly acknowledged.

Another major difficulty in assessing the adjustments China has made to facilitate cooperation with the KIEOs is that many other foreign organizations have been involved in collaborative activities with Chinese agencies at all levels of the hierarchy. To be sure, the KIEOs were particularly prominent, enjoyed special access to the top leaders, and earned special trust because many Chinese perceived that the KIEOs do not advance the interests of and are not dominated by any specific country. Yet, many of the other foreign organizations that have been active in China have offered advice that has paralleled or reinforced the views of the KIEOs. These agencies range from international governmental organizations such as the United Nations Development Program and the United Nations Children's Fund, to the ministries and science councils of foreign governments, private foundations (the Ford Foundation is among the most active), universities, corporations, and individual philanthropists. With the welter of foreigners that have sponsored projects in China and showered the Chinese with advice, it is difficult to pinpoint the influence of a single external agent.

An additional consideration burdens the tracing of mutual adjustment. The KIEOs have not formed a cohesive, united front in the advice they have given to the Chinese. Sometimes their recommendations have even appeared to be contradictory. For example, in 1987 the IMF was encouraging measures to recentralize control over foreign currency expenditures in order to bring the current account deficit under control, while the GATT discussions propelled China toward a more decentralized trade regime in order to ease import restrictions. To cite another instance, some Chinese officials believed the World Bank was inclined to use persuasion and reason as the techniques for getting the Chinese to adopt new policies. They perceived the IMF in contrast as inclined to impose conditions. And they believed accession to GATT would necessitate the greatest adjustment. Whatever the merit of these views, it suggests the Chinese distinguished among the KIEOs in the leverage each sought to exercise.

In spite of these analytical difficulties, the evidence does suggest that a process of mutual adjustment occurred, and it is possible to identify ways in which China affected the KIEOs and to list changes the KIEOs helped to produce in China. We must stress, however, that the changes that we see are at the margins. In 1980, when their intersection began, the political systems of the KIEOs and China had substantial momentum, the course of which has been nudged but not deflected by the subsequent interaction. Our respondents reinforced this view. None felt that the KIEOs had changed or would change significantly as a consequence of China's participation, and only a tiny minority felt that participation had caused or would cause China to significantly change the way it managed its economy.

Even minor shifts in course, however, are important, especially in the long term. We now turn to our analysis of the mutual adjustment.

Adjustment in the KIEOs

The general consensus among the executive directors, officers, and staff of the World Bank and International Monetary Fund is that Chinese membership affected the organizations in several ways. First, it legitimized their claim to be genuinely global organizations. By participating actively in the KIEOs, China blunted the charge that they were instruments of Western imperialism and exploitation and helped to squelch the notion central to the demand for the creation of a New International Economic Order that they should be shunted aside or abandoned. China's request for full participation in GATT had a similar effect. It stimulated interest in membership in GATT among other developing countries as well as pushed the Soviet Union toward membership. In doing this, it weakened UNCTAD's case as an alternative forum to GATT for negotiations about international trade issues.

China's move toward the KIEOs brought them closer to being genuinely global international economic institutions. The organizational ethos of the KIEOs, with their acceptance of such concepts as interdependence and comparative advantage, impels their proponents to forge institutions appropriate to interdependency. Those at the KIEOs who worked on the initial stages of Chinese involvement clearly derived enormous intellectual and emotional satisfaction from the contributions they made to what they considered a very worthy, indeed historically significant undertaking.

Second, the timing of the entry in the early 1980s was fortuitous at least in one respect. According to one official, "The World Bank was in a lull in the early 1980s." At a time when morale was suffering and doubts were spreading as to whether the Bank had the wherewithal to contribute to the development process in many debt-ridden, bureaucratically slothful Third World countries, Chinese membership provided a renewed sense of relevance. It helped to restore confidence in the Bank that development assistance can be effective. In addition, because of U.S. strategic interests, China's membership in the Bank may have inclined the United States toward a more favorable view of the Bank than it would otherwise have had. The Reagan administration's review of multilateral development banks specifically mentioned the advantage for the United States of being able to provide funds through them for countries for which bilateral programs would be problematic.

China has been active within the Bank and Fund. Its executive directors and their deputies have received wide praise for their competence from fellow directors as well as from the top officers and staff in the two agencies. They have attempted to articulate the Chinese position, and at the same time, as members of the executive boards, they have sought to maintain the effectiveness of the organizations. Other executive directors state that they have not been ideological and have not introduced extraneous political considerations into debates. For the most part, they have operated under only loose guidance or instruction from Beijing, but under tight control on matters of importance, such as the few issues that come to a vote. And at the annual meetings, the Chinese minister of finance and the head of the People's Bank lead delegations and deliver speeches in their capacity as governors of the Bank and

Fund. The Chinese claim to value the meetings as occasions to broaden their contacts in the international financial community and to acquire additional information on trends in global economic and monetary affairs. Through their playing by the existing rules of the game, China's representatives have blunted pressures for radical revisions of these rules.

Perhaps most significantly—at least prior to June, 1989—China emerged as a responsible spokesman for developing countries. Before he returned to China, World Bank Executive Director Xu Naizhong had become dean of the directors representing developing countries, and he chaired the so-called Group of Ten, the developing countries caucus for the board. While deliberately eschewing the role of middleman or mediator between developed and developing countries, its presence in fact has served to ameliorate North-South tensions. As one executive director of the World Bank put it, "The fact is that China supports the raison d'être of the Bank. Its presence undercuts the rhetoric of other socialist-leaning countries. The Bank can now say with greater credibility that we are willing to do business with countries regardless of their politics. We are just concerned with efficiency." This director noted that the UNCTAD "rubbish" and the debate of the 1970s over a New International Economic Order have now faded. He continued, "The realities of economic difficulties have pushed this stuff into the background. China's coming into the Bank has helped other developing countries look more realistically at development. The United Nations and UNCTAD are now more peripheral, and the rise of China is one development that has brought this about." Because its own development rhetoric still praises self-reliance and prudence and because it is a significant shareholder in the Fund and the Bank, China's has been a voice for moderation and pragmatism.

Some Chinese officials understand this as well. As one put it: "Many in the World Bank are interested in our economic reforms and have sympathetic concern for their future development. But some people from Third World countries do not welcome the introduction of our experience in open forums, because China says nations should be self-reliant and develop a strategy suited to their conditions. The Bank uses China as testimony: If a developing country does what China has done, it can have a better economic situation. So the outcome of the reforms are more commended by developed than by Third World countries."

The pace of China's economic progress through the late 1980s commended China's course, its reforms, and its receptivity to the KIEOs. Table 6.1 compares the average annual rate of growth in China's gross domestic product with that of neighboring countries. In contrast to the period 1965–80, when China's growth rate lagged behind that of many neighboring countries, during the period 1980–86, China led the group. Its economy was one of the fastest growing in the world.

TABLE 6.1. Average Annual Percentage Growth in Gross Domestic Product in China and Other Developing Countries, 1980–86

Country	Growth Rate
China	10.5
All developing countries	3.8
Low income developing countries other than China and India	2.9
Hong Kong	6.0
India	4.9
Indonesia	3.4
Korea	8.2
Malaysia	4.8
Singapore	5.3
Taiwan	6.8

Source: IBRD, *World Development Report 1988* (Washington, D.C.: IBRD, 1988), 224–25. *Source for Taiwan:* Official Statistics of Taiwan.

Yet, the Chinese have also behaved in ways calculated to minimize their potential tensions with developing countries. Thus, at the Bank and Fund, the Chinese executive director has been under instruction never to raise demands that might come at the discernible cost of another developing country or that entail special treatment for China. As one knowledgeable Chinese official put it, "China understands that if it asserts claims, it will bring trouble." For that reason, China is more reluctant to make requests within the KIEO framework than in its bilateral relations. As the same official observed, "In bilateral relations, China is not shy to ask for special treatment, for example in requesting concessional interest loans from developed countries on a bilateral basis. China behaves with greater restraint in structured rather than unstructured situations."

At least partly because China—as many other countries that previously emphasized planning—has placed greater emphasis in recent years on market forces in the management of its economy, the participation of China in the IMF and the World Bank has had relatively little impact on the ideology and doctrines of these two institutions. The Chinese have not brought radically different ideas into these institutions.

As of the mid-1980s, there was a broad similarity of views between those Chinese who were professionally engaged in working with the KIEOs and their counterparts from other countries. Our Chinese and non-Chinese respondents tended to choose similar adjectives to characterize the contemporary international political-economic environment and generally agreed on tactical and strategic maxims for dealing with international political-economic issues.

Reflecting and perhaps explaining this, a majority of our Chinese respondents ($n = 8$) and almost two-thirds of our non-Chinese respondents ($n = 11$) agreed or strongly agreed with the assertion that "ideology is a declining factor in international relations."

There were, however, some differences between our Chinese and non-Chinese respondents. Among the latter, 76.5 percent ($n = 17$) felt that the international economy had a bright future, but only 37.5 percent of our Chinese respondents ($n = 8$) shared this view. While 58.3 percent of the non-Chinese ($n = 12$) agreed with the statement, "We should opt for a faster economic growth rather than for a redistribution of wealth and income to solve the poverty problem," only 25.0 percent of the Chinese ($n = 8$) strongly agreed with this statement and 50 percent of them disagreed with it. The divisions among the Chinese on this and possibly on other questions probably reflected the divisions that exist within China about the exact direction and pace of economic reforms. The Chinese responses also evidenced an enduring commitment among many of them to socialist goals, particularly the commitment to equity, notwithstanding a more recent commitment to increase efficiency in the Chinese economy. Uncertainty about how to step up the efficiency of the Chinese economy without undermining its egalitarian features could explain doubts about the future, doubts that the popular discontents manifested in the events of June, 1989, underscored.

When he was an executive director of the IMF, Zhang Zicun sought to have the Fund staff study differences between market and planned economies and the consequences of these differences for Fund relationships with member countries that had different systems.[1] In his farewell address before the board, however, he concluded that while the staff had changed its views somewhat it still tended to treat market economies as the norm and its policy recommendations followed uniform prescriptions. In its first report on China, the World Bank exhibited a curiosity about how socialist development would occur, but this curiosity was never developed into a strong interest, and the theme has largely disappeared from Bank publications.

As the 1980s drew to a close, staff members of both the Bank and the Fund increasingly came to see China as a laboratory for exploring how countries that had practiced central planning could be transformed in the direction of greater reliance on market forces. Michel Camdessus's public comments prior to his 1989 trip to China (cited earlier) reflected this attitude. The staff members thought that China's experience would be relevant for Eastern Euro-

---

1. For an example of the consequences of his efforts, see Thomas A. Wolf, "Economic Stabilization in Planned Economies: Toward an Analytical Framework," *IMF Staff Papers* 32, no. 1 (March, 1985): 78–131.

pean countries, developing countries such as Vietnam and Tanzania, and ultimately possibly even for the Soviet Union.

China has been a factor in changing IMF and World Bank strategies for dealing with issues. For instance, China's stress on the importance of including policies to promote economic growth in adjustment programs contributed to the Fund's adoption of this strategy in 1985. And China played a role in 1988 in the executive board's decisions to ease the repayment terms for IBRD loans and to reduce IDA's credit charges.

While identifying itself with the position of the Group of Twenty-four— more formally the Inter-governmental Group of Twenty-four on Monetary Affairs, the grouping formed in 1971 of finance ministers from developing country members of the IMF—several examples exist of China using its special status to reduce North-South tensions. China is not a formal member of the Group of Twenty-four or the Group of Seventy-seven, the developing country caucus in the UN. Premier Zhao Ziyang, for example, quietly worked behind the scenes to secure a supplement to the Seventh IDA Replenishment from the developed countries. Zhao contacted such leaders as Prime Minister Yasuhiro Nakasone and President Ronald Reagan. Forgoing a claim on the supplement, the Chinese in this instance spoke on behalf of African and other nations facing a development crisis. But when several Latin American countries began to advocate a moratorium on debt repayment, the Chinese spoke strongly against the proposal and lobbied behind the scenes to dissuade developing countries from this course. For example, both Li Xiannian and Zhao Ziyang included this point in their discussion with the Argentineans. And at least on one occasion, China has played an important role in resolving a North-South confrontation. In 1984, the IMF had reached an impasse over whether to reduce supplemental fund withdrawal rights. A meeting on the subject became deadlocked and threatened to last interminably, when British Chairman Geoffrey Howe turned to the Chinese representative Shang Ming, saying "Let the Wise Man of the East make some remarks." Shang indeed offered the basis for a compromise, a position between those advocated by the developed and developing countries.

While China has its share of nativists who have little inclination to join the international community, the Chinese role reflects the desire of its cosmopolitans to become a constructive part of the world and contribute to it. Here is how one influential Chinese economist sees it:

Without Chinese membership, these economic organizations will not be truly international. Chinese membership strengthens them. Moreover, there are now two economic systems in the world—socialist and capitalist. This is what Stalin said. But it is not easy to set up a socialist international market. I believe there will be one international market, and capitalist countries cannot exclude socialist countries from it.

In sum, the Chinese posture has been to facilitate the work of the World Bank and International Monetary Fund by espousing and adhering to their norms.

This has been the concrete manifestation of the gradual and widening acceptance of the concept of interdependence in China, although a great deal of confusion has continued to exist in China over the precise meaning of the term. Illustrating this, 50 percent of our Chinese respondents ($n = 8$) agreed and 37.5 percent strongly agreed with the statement, "Economies of individual countries throughout the world are becoming more interdependent." All of the non-Chinese respondents ($n = 12$) strongly agreed with the statement.

Even with these considerations, the Chinese entry has had its dislocative effect, and India in particular has paid the price. As one World Bank executive director who is particularly sensitive to this issue put it: "India has borne

TABLE 6.2.   IBRD and IDA Lending to India and China

| | Amount in Millions of U.S. Dollars | | | |
| | IBRD | | IDA | |
Year	India	China	India	China
Cumulative				
through 1980	2,770.6	0.0	8,285.2	0.0
1981	430.0	100.0	1,281.0	100.0
1982	1,264.8	0.0	900.0	60.0
1983	1,087.9	463.1	1,063.0	150.4
1984	1,721.4	616.0	1,001.0	423.3
1985	1,674.0	659.6	672.9	442.3
1986	1,743.2	687.0	625.1	450.0
1987	2,128.0	867.4	677.6	556.2
1988	2,255.0	1,053.7	717.2	639.9
	Percentage Share of Total IBRD and IDA Lending			
Cumulative				
through 1980	4.67	0.00	40.28	0.00
1981	4.88	1.14	36.79	2.87
1982	12.24	0.00	33.50	2.23
1983	9.77	4.16	31.82	4.50
1984	14.41	5.16	28.00	11.85
1985	14.74	5.81	22.22	14.61
1986	13.23	5.21	19.91	14.33
1987	15.00	6.11	19.44	15.96
1988	15.28	7.14	16.09	14.35

Source: IBRD, Annual Reports, 1980–88 (Washington, D.C.: IBRD, 1980–88).

the burdens almost exclusively for Chinese membership." Whereas India previously obtained nearly 40 percent of IDA loans, in the Eighth Replenishment India and China were to share equally a total of 35 percent of IDA loans. From the outset, India has been concerned that Chinese claims would restrict Indian access to Bank and Fund resources. For example, prior to China's first IMF loan, India hastened to make a very large draw. It apparently feared that after China applied, its own borrowing ability would be reduced.

Table 6.2 shows the amount of IBRD and IDA lending to India and China both in dollars and as a proportion of the institutions' total lending. Since the amounts are given in current U.S. dollars, the effect of the decline in IDA funds going to India has actually been greater than the numbers would indicate. Despite this, the Indian government has consistently supported China's participation in the KIEOs. The Indian government has not begrudged China's receiving IDA funds; indeed, it has expressed disappointment that the replenishments of IDA have not been increased to take account of China's needs. Table 6.2 also shows that the total volume of Bank lending to India in current dollars has actually increased in the 1980s, but this increase has been achieved by increasing the level of IBRD lending, hardening the blend, in effect promoting maturation.

India also has exhibited some nervousness about China's prospective full participation in GATT, clearly fearing competition for export markets. This nervousness is shared by some other developing countries. China's exports will undoubtedly compete with those of other developing countries, especially the newly industrialized countries.[2] Sino-Indian tensions have, however, been muted, as both have sought larger IDA funding and both have been willing to yield to the more pressing needs of African countries. The competition has been waged over the pace at which China achieves equity with India, but this battle over the allocation of IDA funds has been fought behind the scenes. In this regard, Britain appears to have been India's chief ally, while Japan appears to have been more favorably inclined toward China. Reflecting their sensitivity to the divisions among developing countries, as well as North-South divisions, 87.5 percent of our Chinese respondents ($n = 8$) strongly disagreed or disagreed with the statement, "There is a growing consensus among nations about global problems and how to cope with them." In contrast, only 25 percent of the non-Chinese ($n = 12$) responded this way.

Several favorable factors smoothed China's engagement and initial par-

---

2. For an analysis of China's present and potential exports see Nicholas R. Lardy, *China's Entry into the World Economy: Implications for Northeast Asia and the United States* (New York: University Press of America, 1987), and Alexander J. Yeats, "China's Recent Export Performance: Some Basic Features and Policy Implications," *Development and Change* 15, no. 1 (1984): 1–22.

ticipation. McNamara and, after a hiatus, Clausen both brought a broad vision to China policy. An excellent staff was assembled under Caio Koch-Weser's and Edwin Lim's capable direction. The entire Bank and Fund were willing and able to make necessary adjustments to accommodate Chinese needs and sensitivities. The adding of a seat for China on each institution's board of executive directors, the awarding of voting rights that were slightly greater than those of India, the rapid launching of the first higher education project by hastening or avoiding some of the usual steps in a project proposal, and the swift extension of IDA and IMF loans helped set the stage for eliciting Chinese cooperation.

By and large, however, the Bank and IMF have not treated China as an "exceptional case." They have treated China sympathetically, but they have not pandered to China. Even though the terms of the PRC's entry into the two institutions increased China's quota and subscription and thus voting power over that ultimately held by Taiwan, they were still less than they had been when the institutions were created.

Our informants implied that behind the scenes, the bargaining has often been tough and some brutally frank judgments have been given. But some instances of special treatment do exist. For example, the International Finance Corporation, an institution within the World Bank group, has launched activities in China even though it was not totally clear that China intended to allow private enterprise to flourish. And some foreign enterprises believe that the Chinese have not had to adhere to Bank standards in the international competitive bidding process. Yet, these and other instances of possible concessions are at the margins. Many of the allowances made for China were similar to those implemented for other large developing country members such as Indonesia and Egypt.

In the years ahead, Chinese influence in the Fund and the Bank could grow. Thus far, due to the pressing need for adequately trained personnel in China, Chinese agencies have been reluctant to allow their officials to resign and become permanent Fund and Bank staff. But gradually, a PRC presence could make itself felt as PRC citizens are hired on the permanent staff. In addition, Chinese have demonstrated an eagerness to join the study missions that are sent to other countries; this was starting to occur in such areas as agriculture and fisheries in the late 1980s. Having already won World Bank contracts for projects in their own country by competing in the international competitive bidding process, Chinese enterprises could compete for contracts for Bank projects in other countries. Further down the road, it would not be surprising were China to assume a more vigorous role. One leading Chinese official who had been centrally involved in the process described in the preceding chapters anticipated the following course of events: "In the near future, China will not seek to become the champion of developing countries.

The focal point of its energies is upon improving its domestic performance, and through this, to acquire greater credibility among developing countries. But after China achieves success, it will seek a greater voice and more power." If this were to happen, prior to mid-1989 it appeared that China would be able to draw on a reservoir of goodwill and respect built up through its unpretentious and professional participation.

This view recalls a poignant exchange the aging Zhou Enlai had in mid-1973 with a visiting American delegation. The premier asked for the youngest member of the delegation and then directed a question at her: "Do you think China will ever become an aggressive or expansionist power?" Full of goodwill and optimism, the young American responded, "No." The premier shot back: "Don't count on it. It is possible, but if China were to embark on such a path, you must oppose China. And you must tell those Chinese that Zhou Enlai told you to do so."

Thus, the early years of China's participation have been beneficial and constructive for the KIEOs, but cosmopolitan Chinese give muted voice to an apprehension that a more assertive China could begin to express itself in the years ahead.

Adjustment in China

The most direct consequence for China of its involvement in the keystone international economic organizations has been connected with the actual activities that the World Bank and the International Monetary Fund have undertaken with China. Substantively, these include development projects, training programs, studies and reports, and consultations and visits concerning economic development issues. These programs were described in chapter 5.

Here we probe their impact. What have been the consequences for China? What have the difficulties been? What adjustments have been made? And to the extent the early years have been successful, what explains the success? We now turn to these questions.

The consequences fall into three categories: effect on policy, effect on the policy process, and effect on institutions.

Effect on Policy

Both the Bank and the IMF have recommended and endorsed the economic reform policies of the Chinese leadership. Expansion of the role of the market, curtailment of the number of centrally planned and allocated commodities, price reform, increase in foreign trade, and prudent foreign borrowing are among the many views advanced by Bank and IMF officials—as well as by many economic theorists in China, the West, and Eastern Europe.

Officials from the two agencies have also cautioned Chinese about problems in their exchange rates, management of foreign currency holdings, foreign borrowing and conduct of trade, and inflation.

The two comprehensive World Bank reports on the economy, especially the second, presented an extensive inventory of the impediments to economic growth, with the clear statement that systematic removal of these barriers would enable China to sustain impressive growth rates for a protracted period. The second report, which was forward looking and prescriptive, gave three alternative projections of economic performance and indicated that without major structural adjustments, growth rates would be considerably less than they could be with appropriate policies.[3] The second report became available while Chinese officials were drafting the Seventh Five-Year Plan (1986–90). Both reports received high praise from the premier and were widely circulated within the leadership. There could be no doubt that the opinions expressed in the second report and the reforms and Seventh Five-Year Plan converged. There has also been a coincidence between the recommendations advanced in the Bank's sectoral studies and Chinese policy.

The question is: What is cause and what is effect? Have World Bank officials actually affected the direction, pace, and details of Chinese development strategy? These are clearly politically sensitive questions, and neither World Bank and IMF officials nor their Chinese partners from the premier down wished to project an image of extensive influence of foreigners over domestic policies. World Bank officials recognized the inherent dangers should their organization become identified as the source of policy initiatives. They would bear the brunt should the policies encounter difficulties.

Our extensive interviews suggest that the World Bank and IMF, while influential, have *not* been the source of the reform program which, after all, began before China's participation in the KIEOs. Rather, there has been a convergence of views. Had the World Bank and IMF not happened upon the scene, Deng and company probably would have launched many of the changes in any case. After all, the two Bank reports were written in close consultation with the Chinese, and several of their recommendations emanated from such economists as Dong Furen, Liu Guoguang, and Ma Hong. In 1988, Dong Furen was director of the influential Institute of Economics in the Chinese Academy of Social Sciences. Liu Guoguang, a former director of this institute, was Vice President of the Chinese Academy of Social Sciences with supervisory responsibility for all its six economic research institutes. Ma Hong, former President of CASS, was director of the Center for Economic, Technological, and Social Development, a major think tank under the State

---

3. IBRD, *China: Long-Term Development Issues and Options* (Washington, D.C.: IBRD, 1985).

Council. All three were longtime, leading economists who were proficient in Marxist economic theory and more recently had trained themselves in Western economic thought. The ideas contained in the Chinese "Year 2000" study filtered into the second Bank report. Zhao Ziyang and his advisers in effect elicited external views that were compatible with their thinking. The external advice has drawn upon and reinforced the predilections of the reformers and provided them with additional valuable evidence and argumentation to rebut their internal critics. In that sense, the visits by McNamara, Clausen, de Larosière, and Dunkel; the reports; and the annual meetings and consultations have increased the self-confidence of the reformers to persist in their course and to battle their bureaucratic opponents. This, at least, was the interpretation of both the Chinese and World Bank and IMF respondents.

Chinese officials elaborate on this view by noting that membership in the World Bank and IMF has provided valuable new perspectives on the development process and strategies available to them. During the decade and more of isolation, Chinese economists and planners had little contact with their counterparts in other countries. As one interviewee put it, it came as somewhat of a revelation to learn that China confronted problems faced by many other developing countries, and that a variety of measures were available to manage them. Membership in the World Bank and Fund, and the access to information that came with it, encouraged the Chinese to fashion developmental policies from fresh perspectives.

One can also point to several instances in which the Chinese adopted specific policies on recommendation of the international organizations. For example, elements of the coal price reform of 1983–84 came at the request of the World Bank as part of its willingness to extend loans for coal mine development, though the first step in coal price reform was taken in 1979. The 1986 devaluation of the RMB, increases in internal interest rates, and steps to improve China's data management were measures that the IMF had encouraged. The two World Bank reports contain many quite specific opinions, as do the sectoral studies, and suggestions have been voiced regularly in the dialogue between China and the Bank and during the annual consultations between the Chinese and the International Monetary Fund. According to one Chinese official, "All these suggestions were taken very seriously, and where it was appropriate, the suggestions were adopted." China's revision of its customs regulations and tariffs in 1985 was undertaken in anticipation of its bid for full participation in GATT.

Several Chinese bureaucrats highly praised the technical assistance that they have received from the Bank and Fund. The Chinese have received strong encouragement to use a portion of their loans on manpower training abroad and on inviting technical experts to China. One official, whose primary familiarity was with the IMF, referred to this advice in these terms: "I attach great weight to the technical assistance, and I believe that, to some extent, it is even more important than the financial assistance." Another Chinese official, whose experience was with the Bank, criticized an early draft of this study for not having emphasized the importance of technical assistance, particularly in the realms of project financing, project evaluation, and absorption of foreign technology. The official noted, "With the Bank's assistance, we have come to understand that just importing equipment is not enough. Management is also important. So, the Bank insists that with every project, there must be a training component. This focus on how to manage a project is crucial. Previously, there had been much waste of material in capital construction projects, but foreign management techniques help us to reduce waste. So, competitive bidding, foreign consultants, training of personnel have changed our minds about undertaking projects and taught us how to reduce costs and improve quality. With the World Bank approach, we would have avoided the errors we made at the Baoshan Steel Mill."[4]

Prior to June, 1989, the prospects were for increasing World Bank and IMF influence on policy in the 1990s. First, with Chinese cooperation, the Bank was augmenting its role in the early stages of project planning. The State Planning Commission welcomed its involvement in stimulating project proposals and suggestions of which projects should go forward. Second, the Bank in cooperation with the SPC had conducted and was planning several studies of sectoral development strategies: transportation, natural resource development, finance, and so on. These two developments suggested the Bank had firmed its relationships with bureaucracies where it was initially weak, namely the SPC and planning and policy research bureaus in line ministries. The 1988 Structural Adjustment Loan facilitated the Bank's engaging in broad macrolevel discussions with Chinese officials about the rural sector. As mentioned above, with the decentralization of China's economy, the IMF's experience in giving advice on macroeconomic policies became more relevant to the Chinese situation, and China has increasingly sought advice from the Fund's staff.

Clearly, China's full participation in GATT will have the potential for even greater consequences for Chinese policy. Responding, even partially, to the positions that the United States and other Western countries have advanced in the accession negotiations would culminate in significant modifications in current Chinese policies and practices. China has already taken several steps in anticipation of its request to resume its seat in the organization,

---

4. Baoshan is a major steel mill whose construction began in 1979. It has encountered many difficulties and received much criticism for being poorly planned. It is now beginning to produce steel, however. See Chae-Jin Lee, *China and Japan: New Economic Diplomacy* (Stanford, Calif.: Stanford University Press, 1984), 30–75.

such as revising its export and import regulations and publishing new customs tariffs in January, 1985. The Chinese have announced a willingness to negotiate a reduction of their tariffs and have hinted that they might be willing to contemplate agreements easing nontariff barriers. Exactly what the contracting parties to GATT will ask China to give in return for the privileges that full participation in GATT would provide has not yet been determined. It is possible, however, that their demands could necessitate changes in current and often major protectionist practices in Beijing's trading system.

Many Chinese appeared to be increasingly receptive to such changes. Interestingly, more and more attention has been paid in China to Ricardo's theory of comparative advantage.[5] Classical Marxist ideology and China's historical circumstances both led the PRC in its early years to place little emphasis on foreign trade. Marxism viewed trade between developing and industrialized countries primarily as a form of exploitation. The expansion of China's trade in the nineteenth century was associated with various evils, including the unequal treaties. Ricardo's theory, in contrast, stresses the mutual benefits to be gained from trade. While Marxism leads to trade-aversion policies, Ricardo's theory provides the basis for trade-expansion policies. Ricardo's theory is the underpinning for Western liberal theories about international trade.

The acceptance of Ricardo's theory of comparative advantage by many Chinese economists put in place a common foundation for dialogue between them and Western economists. The key issue in the acceptance of Ricardo's theory was the conclusion by Chinese economists that trade could be conducted on a basis of equality because it was reasonable to assume that world market prices could be an adequate proxy for an "average unit of universal labor," a conclusion that Eastern European economists had reached in the 1950s.[6] The argument, espoused by such writers as Shamir Amin and Arghiri Emmanuel,[7] that trade could not be equal because of the distortions in markets was explicitly rejected. The acceptance of Ricardo's theory meant that Chinese-Western discussions about trade increasingly could be based on commonly held assumptions. Within China, the acceptance of the theory of comparative advantage provided an additional stimulus for price reform because

---

5. See Shu-yun Ma, "Recent Changes in China's Pure Trade Theory," *China Quarterly*, no. 106 (June, 1986): 291–305.

6. For a brief account of the debate among Chinese economists see "The Evolution of Chinese Trade Theory," in IBRD, *China: External Trade and Capital*, 98–99 (Washington, D.C.: IBRD, 1988).

7. See Shamir Amin, *Unequal Development: An Essay on the Social Formations of Peripheral Capitalism* (New York: Monthly Review Press, 1976); and Arghiri Emmanuel, *Unequal Exchange: A Study of the Imperialism of Trade* (New York: Monthly Review Press, 1972).

price reform would be essential for a clearer understanding of China's comparative advantages in world trade.

Policy Process

While the effect on policy has been somewhat amorphous, the effect on the policy process has been more evident. This centers on data: its organization, dissemination, and use. As one official noted, "This is not just a statistical issue, but a theoretical, policy, and economic issue." Previously the State Statistical Bureau, the Ministry of Finance, and other organizations did not always employ internationally recognized categories for compiling their data. Frequently, the Chinese employed Soviet categories, a reflection of the continued Soviet and Marxist influence on the economic system. For example, the Chinese did not measure their gross domestic product; instead, as in the Soviet Union, they measured their net material product (NMP). Or, in measurement of agricultural production, some rural small-scale industries were included in agriculture rather than, as in most other countries, in industry. And as we noted earlier, Chinese methods for calculating their current accounts in international trade did not reflect international practices. These are but three of many examples where the Chinese have been successfully encouraged to absorb international practices.

Since some of these accounting procedures are intimately related to ideological issues—such as how to value labor or how to measure the service sector—the Chinese have not jettisoned the previous system, rooted in Marxist-Leninist categories. Rather, they have continued to gather and classify production statistics as before and they have also begun to generate statistics in ways that facilitate comparison with other countries. And this has affected policy.

Nor was this conceptual change entirely forced on the Chinese. Several economists had previously argued for the advantage of the Western concepts, although many other leading economists and agencies stuck dogmatically to the virtues of the Soviet approach. After the Chinese were required to provide GDP statistics to the IMF and World Bank, more and more Chinese came to understand the advantages of the concept. As one put it, "Using the World Bank and IMF yardsticks enabled China to compare itself to other developing countries. We wanted to know what place we occupied in the world economy." Thus, in one of the most important facets of a country—how it describes itself to the outside world and how it evaluates itself—World Bank and IMF memberships have prompted the Chinese to adopt universal standards of measurement.

The different accounting systems opened new insights for the Chinese into the operation of their economy. For instance, a principal difference between net material product and gross domestic product is that the former does not include many services that are included in the latter.[8] As GDP and GNP data became available, and Chinese data were compared with those from other countries, Chinese officials came to better understand the importance of the service sector of the economy and gave greater attention and emphasis to it, a shift strongly urged in the second World Bank report. Transportation, tourism, repair services, and commerce began to receive greater emphasis in development plans as a result. In particular, because of the shift in their angle of vision resulting from their using GDP and GNP rather than NMP data, Chinese officials have seen the merit of devoting greater priority and resources to transportation and distribution systems in development plans and strategies. Tourism also has received increased attention. Precisely because of the way it affects thinking about development strategy, some Chinese economists had, since the late 1970s, advocated using GDP and GNP statistics.

With the IMF demand for trade, currency, and credit data as a condition of membership, the government released information that previously had been unavailable not only to foreigners but to many Chinese as well. The two World Bank studies also necessitated provision of substantial data that had previously been classified and kept within the bureaucracies concerned. Chinese officials insisted that the trend toward greater openness predated membership in the international financial institutions, and some Chinese respondents asserted that the release of data would have occurred in any case. But the World Bank and the IMF have unmistakably pressed for release of data, often to the consternation of Chinese officials. Several of our interviewees complained about the amount of data that World Bank and IMF delegations seek when evaluating specific projects or when preparing sectoral studies. These Chinese believed the requests frequently went beyond the boundary of legitimate inquiry and intruded into areas of national security concerns.

The effect of this pressure to release data has not just been to make the Chinese system more transparent to external observers. Within China, more people have had access to data, and the principal beneficiaries have been economists in research institutes and universities. Partly as a result, they have become more involved in the policy process, serving as consultants, using the data for independent work, and occasionally volunteering policy advice that has drawn the leaders' praise. Again, the influence of the IMF and World Bank has been to reinforce trends the reforms were generating in any case, but in this instance we have tentatively concluded that the influence has been quite significant in broadening participation in economic policy-making to include

---

8. A good description of the differences between the two concepts is given in IBRD, *China: Socialist Economic Development* (Washington, D.C.: IBRD, 1983), 1:244–54.

researchers outside line ministries and in encouraging a consultative decisional process. As their knowledge has increased, the views of economists in research institutes and universities have become more respected and they have more often been invited to participate.

The World Bank has also greatly encouraged the use of feasibility studies emphasizing cost-benefit techniques of analysis in appraising project proposals. Its insistence that projects vying for Bank loans be accompanied by feasibility studies and its training program for Chinese officials in project evaluation have helped to produce a more rigorous planning process, in which the finances of the project and its costs and benefits receive much greater consideration than in the past. A similar process has occurred with respect to competitive bidding. International competitive bidding is required in World Bank projects. Chinese officials have been so impressed with the beneficial results of international competitive bidding that they have used the technique in other projects requiring foreign exchange and are even applying the concept of competitive bidding to projects that are operated exclusively within China.

But Bank and Fund advice in the use of data has not always or automatically been accepted. A prime example is in the reporting of government deficits. For a long time, Chinese treasury officials and economists have followed the Soviet formula for calculating the government budget. Under this system, when revenue plus government bond sales equal expenditures, the budget is balanced. The IMF missions especially have attempted to convince Chinese officials not to treat bond sales as revenue. Chinese economists in academic institutions have long been aware that the Soviet method of accounting camouflaged the seriousness of fiscal problems, hid subsidies, lodged excessive purchasing power in the populace, and required involuntary savings through mandatory bond purchases. These economists had already made proposals to modify budgetary concepts before China's participation in the IMF and World Bank, but their voice was weak and not taken seriously. As of the late 1980s, the issue was being debated within the bureaucracy, especially at the People's Bank and the Ministry of Finance. The top leaders learned of the issue during their meetings with Fund and Bank officials. Any change would require approval by the State Council, and this had not yet occurred.

Institutional Changes

Finally, China's involvement with the KIEOs has had a discernible impact upon the institutional landscape in China. To start with, the government had to create bureaucratic structures to deal with the World Bank, IMF, and GATT. After some uncertainty, with the State Capital Construction Commission (now abolished) also making an obvious and energetic bid, the Ministry of Finance became the counterpart of the World Bank. Its External Finance Department grew to a fifty-member bureau consisting of four divisions. Division One studied World Bank policies, prepared for the annual meetings in Washington, and made the arrangements for Bank top management and program lending missions to China. Division Two was responsible for social, agricultural, health, and educational projects. Division Three was in charge of industrial infrastructure projects—transportation, energy, and so on. Division Four was concerned with financial matters, especially planning for the repayment of loans. Policy for allocation of IDA and IBRD money among ministries is the responsibility of the entire department. Also at the Ministry of Finance, the Bureau of Education assumed responsibility for managing a major cadre training program sponsored by the World Bank's Economic Development Institute.

The People's Bank of China and MOFERT established departments to manage China's relationships respectively with IMF and GATT. In addition, a State Council interagency working group on GATT was formed in 1985. It was headed by State Councillor Zhang Jingfu, and was in charge of coordinating China's position for the accession negotiations. The interagency group included representatives from MOFERT, which was the lead agency, and the State Planning Commission, the State Economic Commission (SEC), the Ministry of Finance, the People's Bank of China, the State Price Commission, the Foreign Exchange Control Commission, and several line ministries. In 1986 two study groups on GATT were formed, one in Beijing and the other in Shanghai. Both are broadly based, involving governmental officials, senior staff from research institutes, and university faculty members. Their purpose was to prepare studies that will support and advise MOFERT and the interagency working group on GATT. Research institutes on GATT were created in Beijing and Shanghai.

Other ministerial level bodies that have spawned bureaus or offices to deal with IMF, the Bank, and GATT include the SPC and the Ministry of Foreign Affairs. Moreover, as the World Bank established liaison with and extended loans to a particular line ministry, specialists have congregated in a special section or office of that ministry for World Bank activities. Thus, the ministries of agriculture, communications, education, petroleum, and transportation, beneficiaries of several Bank loans, all developed a small core of personnel who were increasingly familiar with Bank practices.

The Fund and Bank also directly engaged in institution building. The landmark creations were the Chinese Investment Bank, which was pioneering a new method of commercial lending directly to enterprises, and the Shanghai Institute of International Economic Management (SIIEM), an institute within the Shanghai University of Finance and Economics. By 1988, it and a sister program in Beijing, the Central Financial Institute, funded by the United

Nations Development Program, had trained over 1,500 people. The SIIEM sponsored five courses a year for middle-level officials: engineers, accountants, economists, and so on. The curriculum aimed at enhancing project management skills, using the World Bank project evaluation techniques. To hasten the dissemination of these skills, the Ministry of Finance's Bureau of Education, which oversees the project, cooperated with EDI and SIIEM to compile textbooks on such topics as transportation economics evaluation and international project management. Another EDI project involved the preparation of case studies using Chinese materials. These texts draw upon the lectures given at the SIIEM. The courses and materials provided a broader impetus toward a more practical and less theoretical educational orientation. The World Bank's appraisal and evaluation techniques were absorbed by the China Investment Bank and the Agricultural Banks, both of which wrote manuals for their loan officers based on SIIEM materials.

To be sure, the training programs had only a short duration, and the project managers returned to the same environment whence they came. How much of the theory that they absorbed could actually be applied in the Chinese context remained unclear. And the SIIEM faced problems in encouraging line ministries to send the right personnel to attend the courses. Nonetheless, both the World Bank and Chinese officials involved in this program were proud of their accomplishment, and it appeared the SIIEM would persist even as EDI funding began to diminish. In 1987, fully 25 percent of the EDI budget was dedicated to training programs for Chinese officials, including expenditures for seminars for high-level cadres run in Washington. Four such seminars had been held by mid-1989: World Bank Project Management (1981), Economic Development Strategy (1985), Education Management (1985), and Comprehensive Transportation Management (1986). China was the only single country to have its own EDI program; all other countries were included in regional groupings.

An additional, significant influence on institutional arrangements came about as part of the negotiations concerning the November, 1986, standby arrangement with the IMF. Both Bank and IMF officials were concerned about what they perceived as inadequacies in Chinese management of foreign loans and borrowing. Knowledgeable officials in the SPC, Ministry of Finance, and State Council shared these concerns, and welcomed and supported IMF recommendations that the State Council establish greater coordination and control over expenditure of foreign reserves and over foreign borrowing. The situation had become somewhat chaotic. The IMF and Bank held a number of seminars on this topic, with more in the offing. They introduced the Chinese to diverse institutional models: French, Swedish, Brazilian, and so on. In 1986, the State Administration of Exchange Control was given responsibility for gathering comprehensive statistics on China's foreign debt and approving all uses of foreign exchange.

Our research enables us to shed some light on important questions about institutional changes in China resulting from cooperation with the Bank and IMF. Namely, has the involvement of the Fund and Bank in some sense altered the relative distribution of influence within China? Have some ministries gained and others lost? If so, which ministries are the winners and losers? Similarly, has the Bank weakened or strengthened the center vis-à-vis the provinces? One might hypothesize that the Ministry of Finance and the People's Bank of China would probably benefit, possibly at the cost of the SPC and SEC, while the channeling of loans through the central government would probably strengthen it vis-à-vis the provinces. Reality appears to be more complicated. Involvement with the Fund and the Bank has been only one, and not necessarily the most important, of the factors affecting institutional relationships within China during the 1980s; the economic reforms and the public reaction to them have been far more significant.

It is difficult to identify clear winners and losers among the economic bureaucracies as a consequence of China's involvement with the KIEOs. Rather, many gradually benefited from and acquired an interest in World Bank and IMF activities. While the reforms in general increased the importance of the instruments of national fiscal and monetary policy and changed the role of the plan in management of the economy, thus inserting the Ministry of Finance into the planning and decision-making process at an earlier stage than before, the IMF and World Bank involvement was not primarily responsible for this development. Indeed, the origins of this change antedated China's joining the IMF and World Bank. Nor did the channeling of loans through MOF necessarily increase its power. The SPC retained control over the foreign currency for repayment of these loans. As to the effect on central-provincial relations, the direct contact that the World Bank had with line ministries to stimulate project proposals might appear to have eroded the center's influence, while the strengthening of the China Investment Bank stimulated local entrepreneurial activity to the detriment of central control. On the other hand, the improvement of project planning enhanced the quality of control by the SPC and the line ministries.

Perhaps in light of these complexities, one Chinese official effectively summarized the institutional consequences of World Bank activities in China. He stressed that the Bank had strengthened coordination between the SPC and the MOF and among these two and the line ministries. In the past, the SPC decided on which projects should be undertaken and arranged the sequence for initiating major capital construction projects, while the MOF decided on how to include the projects in the budget and to provide the funds to sustain the construction. Coordination between these functions came late in the decisional process. Now, when the SPC receives proposals from line ministries, it elicits MOF views on the likely World Bank reaction. The SPC Bureau of Foreign Loans consults with the sectoral bureaus in the SPC, and it then deals with the External Finance Department in the MOF.

World Bank views on individual projects, according to several knowledgeable Chinese officials, also help to ease the inevitable bureaucratic disputes that surround selection of capital construction projects and to facilitate the reaching of agreement. The World Bank's presence, as one Chinese put it, "tends to keep the debate more honest, as it ferrets out hidden weaknesses in project proposals."

The intrabureaucratic consequences of China's full participation in GATT have just begun. The process of formulating China's memorandum describing its trade regime gave some hints concerning their general direction. Some ministries with responsibilities involving the production of commodities such as the ministries of metallurgy or machine building predictably were concerned about their enterprises being subjected to competition from external sources. If as a consequence of pressures exerted in the accession negotiations China moved toward national, uniform tariff and customs treatment, those regions enjoying special status would suffer while national bodies would have their authority augmented. On the other side, ministries and localities that were major exporters perceived themselves as likely winners. MOFERT, as the coordinating agency, sat astride the negotiating process, and the unified position that it must present externally was the result of intense internal discussions among potential winners and losers.

Changes among Economists

Implicit in the above discussion is a significant intellectual development that several of China's highest leaders encouraged the World Bank, the IMF, and such other external organizations as the Ford Foundation and American universities to sponsor. Communities of economists conversant with non-Marxist, Western theory have been developed. These economists became important policy advisers to Zhao Ziyang and other top policymakers. Their institutional affiliations have included Beijing and People's universities; the Institute of Economics and its sister institutes in the Chinese Academy of Social Sciences; various research institutes and policy research offices in the Bank of China, the Ministry of Finance, the People's Bank, and the Ministry of Foreign Economic Relations and Trade; and the pivotal Commission for Restructuring the Economic System (the *tigaiwei*), the Rural Policy Research Office, and the Center for Economic, Technological, and Social Development, all three of which reported directly to the top leaders. The Bank and

Fund have held seminars, workshops, and training courses for the members of these informal communities. The members of these communities have participated in joint research projects with foreign economists and their units have received funds to facilitate travel abroad. By the late 1980s, many from these units were pursuing Ph.D's in economics in Western universities, though not many had returned.

Nina Halpern has demonstrated that these policy communities trace their origins to the precommunist period, took initial shape in the 1950s, had discernible influence on policy in the 1960s, and after a hiatus during the Cultural Revolution began to regroup and take on major responsibilities in the early 1970s.[9] The small group under the aegis of the Bank of China that studied China's entry into the KIEOs from 1972 through 1976 drew upon these communities of economic experts. And, as Halpern notes, many of the early ideas for the reforms can be traced to the work of these experts in the 1960s and mid-1970s.

Thus, China's involvement with the KIEOs did not lead to the creation of these informal communities of economic experts. But, as with the growth of the community of foreign policy experts, the contact with the outside world enhanced their political influence and deepened their expertise. Joining with the other external agents of change, the Bank and Fund affected the internal composition and relative influence of different individuals and groups among the economic experts.

Our research revealed that the communities of economic experts in China were hardly homogeneous. As is true elsewhere in the world, they had diverse educational backgrounds, career paths, personalities, policy preferences, and institutional and patron-client loyalties that prevented these professionals from acting as a cohesive and unified force in Chinese politics. While there is no easy way to characterize the qualities and differences among the communities of economic experts, several of our Chinese colleagues outlined a roughly similar story of this profession's evolution since 1980. At that time, Chinese economists included a minority of older professionals who had been exposed to non-Marxist economics before 1949, either through education abroad or in Western oriented universities in China. Most in this category had explicitly rejected Western economics and embraced Marxist theories. Due to their exposure to non-Marxist ideas, however, many economists in this category had become politically suspect after 1949 and suffered political reversals during the various ideological campaigns of the Maoist era. The majority of economists had entered the profession either during the Yan'an guerrilla days or through their formal education or on-the-job training after 1949. These

---

9. See Nina Halpern, "Economic Specialists and the Making of Chinese Economic Policy, 1955–1983" (Ph.D. diss., University of Michigan, 1985).

economists either had been exposed exclusively to the Marxist analytical categories and framework, or else they had a brief exposure to non-Marxist courses that continued to be offered from 1949 to 1966 in a few universities as a strictly academic exercise. The top leaders tended to trust the economists who had matured entirely within the Marxist tradition or who had clearly rejected the previous, non-Marxist influences upon them.

But in the Deng reform era, China's leaders began to familiarize themselves—at their own initiative—with non-Marxist concepts. They were influenced by translations of both popular writings, such as Alan Toeffler's *Third Wave*, and of classical economic works, such as Paul Samuelson's basic textbook on economics. As the political leaders began to examine their economic assumptions, they naturally sought out from the communities of economic experts those who had some prior exposure to Western or non-Marxist thought. To repeat, these economists were Marxists, but they had the virtue of understanding and being able to explain non-Marxist theories. And it was natural for these economists to serve as the intermediaries between China and the KIEOs. Thus, the involvement with the KIEOs has been one factor in enhancing the relative influence in the policy process of economists with prior exposure to non-Marxist economics. Further, it strengthened the stature of Marxist economists such as Sun Yuefang and his many disciples who had sought to assimilate various Western economic notions within a Marxist framework. Their efforts, which dated back to the 1950s and early 1960s, had come under severe attack during the Cultural Revolution.

The Trouble Spots

Not all of the interaction between China and the KIEOs has been smooth sailing. We do not mean to suggest that, as far as the Chinese are concerned, their entry and early years have been trouble free. Here is a list of the difficulties and challenges that our respondents identified. Different interviewees mentioned different issues.

> — The early stages of the project cycle took too long and were excessively cumbersome. As long as two to three years were required to get a project approved and under way. This delay caused those ministries that anticipated a high rate of return from a project and anticipated its product would earn foreign exchange to press MOF, MOFERT, and the specialized banks to permit financing through foreign commercial lenders rather than through the World Bank. But the MOF and SPC strongly preferred turning to the World Bank, not only because the interest rates were lower but because they appreciated the discipline of Bank procedures. The bureaucratic tensions

were alleviated through a speedier but presumably no less efficacious procedure and through the plan to transfer more funds to China through structural adjustment lending.

— The pressure to supply data continued to be vexing. This applied not to the normal national-level aggregate data, but rather to data about particular localities and sectors; for instance, concerning traffic at ports other than those involved in a particular project. Bank officials maintained that such data were essential to evaluate the relative merits of proposed projects. Though our interviewees did not articulate the thought, there appeared to be some resentment over the commanding or imperious tone of the requests and over the idea that an external agency had a right to this information. The intrusion on national sovereignty, a core concept of the Chinese revolution, was an emotional matter.

— While understanding the reasons, the Chinese were disappointed that their access to IDA funds had reached a plateau and that they would not be able to maintain even a forty-sixty blend of IDA and IBRD loans.

— China's pricing system made investment decisions difficult for the World Bank. With prices that were set administratively, it was hard to calculate real rates of return on projects. The Bank did not want to support projects if their effectiveness could be undermined by inappropriate prices. The Bank preferred a pricing system that more accurately reflected factor costs, and difficult discussions about prices were an aspect of many negotiations about Bank projects.

— In the absence of an internal capital market and of price reform, the Ministry of Finance had difficulty calculating the likely profitability of competing projects and deciding on the interest rate to charge a ministry on a World Bank loan. MOF experimented with three methods of assessing the internal repayment rates, and none proved satisfactory.

— While neither the World Bank nor the IMF imposed stiff conditions or required significant policy changes, some Chinese officials— particularly those dealing with the Fund—expressed apprehension that conditionality might be looming and that the foreign lending agencies might not take adequate account of China's desire to remain a socialist, planned economy with market features.

— Underlying several of these trouble spots were deeper issues about the course of reform in China. How much change will the Chinese populace accept, and how rapidly will they accept it? Can an economy move from reliance on central planning and mandated prices to a mixed-market system without passing through a period of very high inflation? What level of inflation would the Chinese populace endure? Is it possible to set some prices administratively and others through market forces without maintaining serious distortions in incentives and perhaps even creating new ones? Will these distortions invite corruption? Within the Chinese context, is it possible to ensure that decentralization does not simply result in the transfer of authority from the central government to provincial governments, but instead transfers authority to enterprises and individuals? How can China manage the process of making enterprises responsible for their losses and allowing them to determine the uses of their profits rather than having the central, regional, and local governments perform these responsibilities? If governments no longer have access to the profits of enterprises, how will they obtain the revenues they need to conduct their functions? How will the social service functions previously performed by enterprises be carried out if enterprises must shed them to achieve a realistic assessment of the profitability of their commercial activities?

The economic difficulties that China encountered in the late 1980s—growing inflation, sharply distorted prices, increasing corruption, and insufficient governmental revenues—that were factors leading to the events of June, 1989, underscored the complexity and importance of these issues. China's economic difficulties and the events of June, 1989, also underscored an important limitation on the contribution that international institutions can make to their member states. International institutions can provide financial and technical assistance to states. They can strengthen administrative structures. They can provide information and technical advice about the foreseeable consequences of policy choices. Beyond this, however, there is little that they can contribute to making difficult choices, forging agreement about what should be done, and gaining popular support for the policies that are chosen. These are the tasks of indigenous political coalitions and leadership. Put as an aphorism, international institutions can make major contributions to state building, but their contribution to nation building and political development is much more circumscribed.[10] The broader issue that the events of June, 1989, raised was whether it is possible to move toward greater economic decentralization without simultaneously moving toward political pluralism.

---

10. For an analysis that reached the same conclusion in a different context see Harold K. Jacobson, "ONUC's Civilian Operations: State Preserving and State Building," *World Politics* 17, no. 1 (October, 1964): 75–107.

Reasons for Success

Until June, 1989, the vexing problems were overshadowed by the accomplishments. The World Bank had become a major source of foreign borrowing. Its total commitments were $7.4 billion by mid-1989, with over $3.2 billion already dispersed. By that date it had become involved in sixty-nine projects and, as we have already noted, its impact went beyond its project activity. The participants would not have predicted such an outcome. What explained it? Put more generally, judging from this case, what set of factors internal to the country appears to facilitate effective Bank and IMF operations?

Above all, the changes that the World Bank and IMF suggested were compatible with internal trends. There was a convergence between the views of China's leaders and the international organizations concerning the measures necessary to sustain and accelerate growth. Further, the mode of World Bank and IMF operation was to engage in dialogue rather than to impose conditions, to convince rather than to demand. Confrontation did not occur over China's commitment to a socialist economy; rather there was a process of mutual education and mutual recognition that China's membership in the World Bank and Fund entailed a great challenge of incorporating a large, developing, planned commodity economy into these international organizations in ways that would not be disruptive.

A prerequisite for dialogue rather than dependence or confrontation and conflict is self-confidence and mutual respect. Our World Bank and IMF interviews stressed the importance of Chinese self-confidence. Possessing dignity, cultural pride, and a sense of place and having been tempered by the communist revolution, the Chinese officials with whom World Bank and Fund officials dealt were self-critical and willing to hear criticism. Perhaps their absence from office during the Cultural Revolution and its aftermath (1966–76) contributed to this attitude. For the most part, they did not display a vested interest in the details as opposed to the broad goals of the existing system. Whatever its origins, Chinese self-confidence stands in sharp contrast, many Bank and Fund officials note, to the defensiveness and self-doubt of officials from many other developing countries. For instance, the World Bank has never been given permission to publish its country studies of India. China has welcomed critical analyses of its economic policies and far-reaching appraisals of the policy choices it faces and has quickly agreed that these should be made public.

Other qualities of the political elite were germane. They have appeared to be basically honest. To be sure, favoritism was present; children of the powerful enjoyed great career advantage. But there was no massive capital flight from China, and corruption, while growing and vexing, remained relatively modest in comparison to many other developing countries. In many other developing countries, conditions have led World Bank and IMF officials to despair about prospects for effective development assistance. Finally, an institutional infrastructure was put in place to permit policies to be implemented, albeit imperfectly, slowly, and unevenly. No single one of these factors appears to have been more crucial than the others. Rather, the combination appears to have produced a propitious environment for Bank and Fund cooperation with China. Mutual adjustment was occurring.

CHAPTER 7

Implications for the Future

China has been involved with the KIEOs for almost a decade. What conclusions can be drawn from the record of this interaction about the capacity of the neoliberal international economic order to welcome China into its midst and the ability of China to make the inevitable internal adjustments to its changed external role? What can be said about the possible transformation of the current neoliberal international economic order into a global economic order? Can projections be made about likely future developments?

Above all this study has highlighted the significance of purposeful political action in international affairs. There was nothing automatic about the processes described in the preceding chapters. The sequence of events that unfolded between China and the Fund, Bank, and GATT was not fated to happen. Nor is the future for China and the KIEOs predetermined, as the events of June, 1989, dramatically illustrated.

The trends of China's involvement with the KIEOs, however, provide a basis for reasoned speculation about likely future developments. Viewing the record of the past makes it possible to identify factors or considerations that could shape the future path of cooperation between China and the KIEOs. And in this light, it enables some observations about the possible inclusion of the last major economic power—the Soviet Union—that remains outside the international monetary, financial, and trading order which the KIEOs support.

Implications for Perspectives about International Political Economy

Analysis should start at the broadest level. Various perspectives drawn from the theoretical literature on international political economy and on international institutions to which this story is relevant were identified in the introductory chapter. What are the implications of this case study for those perspectives?

We postulated that dependency, neo-Marxist, world systems, classical liberal, and neo-mercantilist theorists would have thought that the effort to wed a socialist China and the neoliberal international order would prove disruptive to one or the other. The task was impossible. The dependency, neo-

157

Marxist, and world system theorists would have suspected that the KIEOs would corrupt China, while those devoted to liberal principles would have feared that the effort to incorporate China into the international economy would further deflect the KIEOs from pursuit of these principles. Neomercantilists would have worried that concessions to China would sap American vitality and divert the United States from pursuit of its enlightened interests. Only the hegemonic stability or the regime self-maintenance theorists would have believed that the incorporation was possible either under the aegis of the United States or in accordance with the terms stipulated by the KIEOs.

Our case suggests that these theories tend to pose the issues at stake too sharply, simplistically, and unrealistically. China's participation in the KIEOs has neither converted China to capitalism nor subverted the international institutions from their basically neoliberal orientation nor led the United States astray.

More than a year before China assumed its seats in the Fund and the Bank, it had taken fundamental decisions to reorient its domestic economy. Joining the Fund and the Bank was part of China's new broad economic strategy. Throughout the interaction, the Fund and the Bank have been careful to respect China's sovereignty and commitment to a socialist economic system. They have praised China's success in reducing poverty and providing widespread access to basic education and health care. They have refrained from commenting on China's system of public ownership of the means of production until asked to study its efficacy through joint research projects with Chinese economists. The Fund and the Bank have, however, reinforced those within China who have supported reform and expanded their vision of what the reforms could entail.

China has clearly increased its involvement in the international economy, but the decisions leading to this began in the early 1970s. Looking ahead, becoming even more involved in the international economy and benefiting fully from GATT requires adapting to GATT norms. The issues at stake in the negotiations center on China's price system and tariff and nontariff barriers. Full GATT participation could exercise a strong pressure on China, as dependency, neo-Marxist, and world system theorists would argue. But the non-Chinese participants in the GATT negotiations see the discussions as an effort to reach a contractual agreement on the balance of privileges and obligations for the parties involved. It will be China's choice as to how many obligations and hence how many privileges it will accept.

Nor have the IMF and the World Bank noticeably changed their orientation as a consequence of China's entry. Both had a prior commitment to the alleviation of poverty and a relatively egalitarian distribution of income within member nations. China's participation has not increased this commitment. Nor have the two organizations altered their views of the merits of markets and guidance planning. But China's membership has modulated the tenor and thereby improved the quality of debate in these organizations and their ability to carry out their mandates.

The impact of China on GATT, however, remains an open question; much depends on the terms of participation. The GATT negotiations, therefore, could serve as a litmus test. Thus far, the China case supports neither the dependency, neo-Marxist, or world system theorists on one side nor the classical liberal theorists on the other. That in itself is an important finding. But the real challenge looms ahead in crafting a protocol that will preserve the basically neoliberal orientation of the international trade regime.

The case underscores that the United States played a leading but not decisive role in the KIEOs. Without the support—or at least acquiescence—of the United States, China's incorporation probably could not have occurred. At the same time, it is evident that the KIEOs have a much broader base than that provided by the United States: they are firmly part of the contemporary international political economy, and China's move toward them has solidified their place. Further, the role of the United States dropped sharply once China was engaged; the United States had little impact on the day-to-day interaction between China and the IMF and the World Bank other than its broad influence in determining the level of funds available to the two institutions. Our case therefore portrays a more complicated reality than that of a single hegemonic power acting alone to determine the international economic order. The United States was quite influential but not all powerful. This case study lends weight to Robert Keohane's version of the relationship between regimes and hegemonic power; namely, that once in place, international institutions can assume a life of their own.

The case also supports a view of international institutions that emphasizes how they result from and contribute to social learning; this view stresses their role as instruments for achieving noncoerced cooperation among sovereign states through the collection and dissemination of information and by providing a forum for reaching consensus.[1] The Fund and Bank have shared their experiences in economic development and management with China, and China's experience is becoming part of the global repertoire. The GATT negotiations are an exercise in sharing information about China's economy and the international trade regime and in crafting norms for mutually beneficial commercial interactions. Institutional adjustments have occurred within China—as the perspective forecast—to facilitate information exchange and social learning. The case highlights the importance of the KIEOs remaining

---

1. See Harold K. Jacobson, *Networks of Interdependence: International Organizations and the Global Political System*, 2d ed. (New York: Alfred A. Knopf, 1984).

vigilant, agile, and bold in defense and pursuit of their mandates and values if they are to remain a vital force. These are precisely the roles that the leaders and staff of the IMF, Bank, and GATT have played in their opening to China.

This exercise of relating our findings to broader theoretical perspectives about international political economy and international institutions pinpoints three pivotal considerations in world affairs that will be crucially important in determining whether the incorporation of China in the KIEOs specifically and the international economy more generally will continue to be a success story in the 1990s: the way the GATT negotiations are handled; the posture of the United States and the other industrialized democracies; and the independent leadership provided by the KIEOs themselves.

A Cautionary Note

Not surprisingly, international political economy perspectives direct us to look at China's world environment. But our case study indicates we also must focus on political and economic developments in China. What land mines on the Chinese side might prevent the promise of the first eight years from being fulfilled? Our study has identified a number of factors that were favorable to a smooth Chinese entry into the KIEOs but that could easily turn sour in the 1990s. What are these considerations?

It is by no means clear that the Chinese domestic scene will continue to be as propitious. Well before the events in Beijing in June, 1989, our research left us with some foreboding that, down deep, many Chinese officials outside the KIEO policy specialists and the current top leaders remained skeptical of notions of interdependence and an evolving international division of labor. The bureaucratic interests in developing a comprehensive national economy are very strong. Thus, much depends on the succession to Deng Xiaoping and the emergence after Deng of strong leadership committed to economic and political reform at home and China's entry into the international economy.

Political developments in China after 1986 have signaled the continuing strength of conservatism. For reasons that are not well understood probably even by the participants themselves, two succession arrangements went awry, and the tumultous protest movements and subsequent leadership reshuffling in 1989 left Deng Xiaoping without a credible and orderly plan for transfer of power upon his death. In 1986, a viable arrangement appeared to be in place. A duumvirate of General Secretary Hu Yaobang and Premier Zhao Ziyang worked in somewhat uneasy tandem to advance a broad agenda of political and economic reform. Egged on by several conservative octogenarian associates, Deng grew increasingly discontented with Hu Yaobang's performance in managing a series of economic, foreign policy, and political issues. Hu also apparently did not enjoy the confidence of senior military officers. In addition, the general secretary became increasingly supportive of and energetic in implementing Deng's own instructions to carry out political reform and permit limited cultural diversity. When these policies encountered problems, Deng sacrificed his agent. Student demonstrations in late 1986 and early 1987 provided the pretext to remove Hu Yaobang as general secretary.

That change proved to be very costly to the reform effort. The new duumvirate—Zhao as general secretary and Li Peng as premier—brought together individuals with quite different orientations to the reform process. Li clearly was the more cautious, skeptical of the rapidity and desirability of many major reforms with which Zhao was identified: price reform, introduction of capital and labor markets, and changes in the government revenue system. The removal of Hu Yaobang also essentially terminated the steps toward political reform. Meanwhile, in 1987–88, the leaders confronted increasingly severe economic problems: lagging agricultural production, some undisciplined foreign borrowing, government deficits, accelerating inflation, and growing social disorder. The populace perceived also that their leaders were increasingly corrupt and engaged in nepotism. And many among the leaders saw the populace as increasingly corrupted by foreign culture and values. The top leaders became deeply divided over how to respond to these mounting problems. Some, such as Zhao, believed only additional reform could remedy the problems, while others, such as Li and increasingly Deng, believed retrenchment on both economic and political fronts was the only answer.

The result by early 1989 was Deng's decision to weaken and probably remove Zhao. The power struggle at the apex coincided with and probably was related to the demonstrations that swept Beijing in April and May, initiated by mourning of the death of Hu Yaobang. When Zhao refused to participate in the crushing of the demonstrations, his fate was sealed. But his departure from his leadership position removed the single leader most identified with China's involvement with the KIEOs. The think tanks that helped the World Bank had close links to Zhao Ziyang and many of their intellectuals were closely identified with him. To be sure, many Chinese economists as well as IBRD and IMF officials saw much merit in Li Peng's conservative and recentralizing proclivities in 1987–88 as the best route to bring inflation, deficits, and foreign borrowing under control. Nonetheless, Zhao's removal was a major blow to the forces of reform in China, and it raised questions about whether the Chinese trajectory will move away from that of the KIEOs in the post-Deng era.

In addition to political considerations, economic factors dictate a sober assessment of China's economic relations with the outside world in the 1990s. For example, China has the capacity rapidly to increase its market share in select commodities—as it had done in the 1980s in textiles. China has huge needs for imports,[2] but precisely because of this, it may be tempted to expand its exports by whatever means are available to earn needed foreign exchange. Thus, China's development strategy—still to a considerable extent an import-substitution strategy—suggests that the 1990s could pose a greater challenge to the international economy than the 1980s, with China possibly exhibiting both protectionist and aggressive marketing behavior.

Thus, for domestic political and economic reasons, the Chinese leaders may not continue to pursue their program with the same vigor or foresight during the twilight years of Deng Xiaoping or under his successors. The Chinese may also confront systemic constraints upon their ability to continue to expand their relations with the International Monetary Fund and the World Bank. The initial encouragement to release data or to engage in feasibility studies posed a relatively low cost to China and therefore elicited a ready response, but the subsequent encouragement to devalue the RMB, raise interest rates, impose coordinated external debt management, and change prices so that they better reflect costs of production posed more difficult problems.

Further, China may be approaching the limits of its organizational capabilities to sustain the expansion in its opening to the outside world. The generational succession now underway has meant that some of the most sophisticated and knowledgeable officials have begun to retire, and the shortage of capable personnel in their forties and fifties and the inadequate implementing capacity of core agencies has become increasingly evident. On the World Bank side, the total funds that will be available for lending remains somewhat unclear: the claims of Africa upon Bank resources have grown, and competition between India and China could conceivably stiffen. All these factors, derived from seasoned observers, suggest even more consummate skill than that manifested in the 1980s would be necessary in the 1990s to keep the process going forward.

A Shared Responsibility

Our study suggests therefore that the leaders and pivotal administrators in the KIEOs, China, and the industrialized democracies share in the responsibility for a continued, successful integration of China into the KIEOs and the international economic system. The process will not go forward automatically. What, then, are the factors that must be present?

Continued perception of the convergence of strategic interests among

---

2. For on-going analyses of the China market, see *China Business Review* and *China Newsletter*. The former is a bimonthly publication of the National Committee on US-China Relations, while the latter is published by the Japan Economic and Trade Research Organization (JETRO).

Washington, Tokyo, Beijing, and the EEC capitals is probably necessary to encourage all the countries involved to make the necessary and difficult compromises looming ahead. The overwhelming conclusion of our study is that the political leaders of the industrialized democracies and of China must remain convinced of the strategic benefits to be derived from China's full participation in the KIEOs. Without that conviction, the pertinent instructions will not go out to their representatives to the KIEOs nor will the political leverage be exercised to overcome recalcitrant forces at home.

The participants will have to be mindful, as were their predecessors in the 1970s and early 1980s, of the historical significance of their activities. The stakes for China's successful incorporation into the KIEOs are high and certainly exceed the magnitude of the funds involved. At stake is the opportunity to forge a global economic order in which all the participants adhere to the same set of norms. The ramifications of such a world—unattainable though it may seem today—are obviously profound and would extend to the internal organization of the countries involved. However, to attain that vision requires the KIEOs to remain true to their purposes. Quick accommodations to incorporate a nation that does not support the purposes of the KIEOs is not the solution.

But the KIEOs cannot acquire an exaggerated sense of their role or leverage in this process. Our case suggests the KIEOs can play their role only if Chinese leaders, out of internal considerations, continue to believe their interests coincide with full membership in the KIEOs and if the international strategic setting remains conducive to inclusion. The KIEOs, in the final analysis, cannot force the pace of integration. They ratify and cement relations rather than create them. But they can play an influential role in easing the process forward and institutionalizing it.

The rewards to China will have to be tangible and commensurate with the costs the leaders perceive they bear in responding to external requests from the KIEOs for change. The domestic costs may not be monetary in form; they may be political, such as in the using up of their political chits on behalf of KIEO involvement to overcome domestic opposition. In the case of the GATT negotiations, it will be hard to convince the Chinese to open their domestic markets and accept the notion of an evolving international division of labor if the developed countries simultaneously succumb to protectionist impulses and deny China increasing access to their markets.

The leaders of China also will bear a complicated burden in continuing to keep their domestic house in order and in being an effective partner of the KIEOs. Behavior ranging from widespread, growing corruption to suppression of dissidents, persecution of intellectuals, forgery of export licenses, inconsistent application of regulations, and violation of contractual obligations all would damage China's reputation and credibility. Not only did the ordering of tanks into the streets of Beijing produce moral outrage among the leaders of developed countries; it caused them to question the judgment and integrity of China's leaders. One immediate result was postponement of initiatives in the KIEOs: new IBRD loans, the IMF seminars and technical assistance projects, GATT negotiations.

Another difficulty arises from the central government's eroding authority over the provinces. Previously, the view that China could use foreign assistance and advice effectively and could absorb foreign technology and equipment efficiently had encouraged the World Bank to launch its programs vigorously. The leaders seemed able to elicit compliance from their provincial officials. But only partly in response to GATT pressures, and more largely due to internal considerations, not only had China's trade become more decentralized but the authority of provincial officials had expanded in other realms as well. As fewer and fewer of China's commercial and monetary exchanges with the outside world fell under the central government's control, the appropriate standards of behavior became more difficult for Beijing to enforce. And this meant the Chinese government would have to become more open and vigorous in its endorsement of the norms of the KIEOs and in its internal injunctions in support of adherence to these norms. Thus, even if the June debacle had not occurred, KIEO confidence in China's capacity to deliver on its commitment would have eroded somewhat.

Finally, assuming China were able to restore confidence in its ability to behave in a responsible fashion, it would be important for the KIEOs to respect China's deep preference for dialogue rather than conditionality, for persuasion rather than imposition of demands. Much more than sensitivity to Chinese pride would be involved. Chinese proponents of reform would quite often remain politically vulnerable, and placing them in a position where they *must* argue on behalf of accepting externally imposed conditions would undercut their legitimacy. At the same time, the effort to persuade would often have to be made vigorously, with the possibility of applying conditions kept prominently in the background. In this way, some of the onus for unpopular changes could be shifted to the external agent; the internal proponents of reform count on the foreigners to help them secure adoption of the new policies.

Implications for Soviet Union Entry into the KIEOs

China initiated its move toward the KIEOs before the advent of Mikhail Gorbachev, *perestroika*, and *glasnost*. At that time, Soviet membership in the KIEOs seemed a remote or impossible development. But the issue was broached in 1986 through Soviet expression of interest in eventually joining the GATT. Soviet participation in the KIEOs become a lively issue in

Moscow in the late 1980s, and the topic frequently arose in conversations between high-level Soviet officials or Gorbachev's leading advisers and Western visitors.

There was no standard Soviet line on the issue. Some asserted that much progress had to be made in *perestroika* before membership in the GATT was worth formal discussion. Others, however, pressed for rapid initiation of negotiations.

Chinese membership in the IMF and World Bank and the negotiations on full participation in the GATT unquestionably were important stimulants in prompting Soviet interest in the KIEOs. In the mid-1980s, the Soviet Union became the laggard, the last major nation outside the KIEO framework. And Western proponents of a forthcoming posture toward the Soviet expressions of interest have cited Chinese membership in the IMF and the Bank as a precedent for receptivity to Soviet overtures.

Care must be taken in lumping the Chinese and Soviet cases together, however. This study highlights some significant differences between China at the time of its entry into the IMF and the Bank in 1980 and the Soviet Union in the late 1980s. While the Chinese case does mean it is not entirely quixotic to think of one day incorporating the Soviet Union into the KIEOs, many, many changes must first take place in Soviet domestic and foreign policies.

Our case study demonstrates that the process of preparation for including a large, new entrant into the KIEOs is a protracted one. In the Soviet case, it must include, first, changes in the strategic relationship between the principal guarantors of the KIEOs—the United States, Japan, and the EEC—and the Soviet Union, and second, both a redirection of trade of the Soviet Union so that it would already be a heavy trader with market economies at the time it sought membership in the KIEOs and a reorientation of the modalities of conducting trade to ensure that economic motives were the dominant forces shaping the direction of its trade. These major changes would be necessary to provide some assurance that the Soviet Union would have acquired some vested interest in promoting freer trade conducted according to economic interests and liberal international monetary and financial relationships. In 1985, almost two-thirds of the Soviet Union's trade was with members of the Council for Mutual Economic Assistance,[3] and a high proportion of Soviet trade was the result of long-term trade agreements, barter, or countertrade. In the same year, less than 8 percent of China's trade was with members of CMEA.[4] Table 7.1 shows the destination and origins of Soviet and Chinese exports and imports. In sum, entry into the KIEOs should come relatively late

3. IMF, *Direction of Trade Statistics Yearbook, 1988* (Washington, D.C.: IMF, 1988), 399–400.

4. IMF, *Direction of Trade Statistics Yearbook, 1988*, 136–37.

TABLE 7.1. Soviet and Chinese Trade with CMEA Members and Affiliates, by Percentages of Yearly Trade

	USSR			China
	1965	1985		1985
		Imports		
From CMEA[a]	69.01	63.90	From CMEA[b]	4.68
From China	2.80	1.20	From USSR	2.57
From Others	28.19	34.90	From Others	92.75
Total	100.00	100.00	Total	100.00
		Exports		
To CMEA[a]	68.17	64.40	To CMEA[b]	3.15
To China	2.30	1.07	To USSR	2.38
To Others	29.53	34.53	To Others	94.47
Total	100.00	100.00	Total	100.00

Source: United Nations, *International Trade Statistics Yearbook 1965*, *International Trade Statistics Yearbook, 1985* (New York: United Nations, 1966, 1986).

[a]CMEA members and affiliates include German Democratic Republic, Czechoslovakia, Bulgaria, Poland, Hungary, Cuba, Yugoslavia, Romania, Mongolia, Vietnam, Finland, Afghanistan, Angola, Ethiopia, Laos, Mozambique, People's Democratic Republic of Yemen, Iraq, and Mexico.

[b]Not including USSR

in the process of entering the international economy, and not as an early step—as the Soviet Union at one point seemed to prefer. In the late 1980s the Soviet Union appeared to be moving toward more diversified involvement in the international economy, although as table 7.1 shows it had a long way to go to reach the extent of the Chinese connection with Western countries. Moreover, Soviet patterns of trade would be difficult to change; they had been relatively constant for more than two decades.

Further, in terms of the sequence of participating in the KIEOs, the Chinese appear to have gone about it in a sensible sequence: the IMF and the Bank, and then GATT. The degree of transparency and extent of internal adjustments necessary for effective membership increase in that order. Commitment to the maintenance of a relatively open market would appear to precede being able to enjoy the benefits of increased and stable access to the markets of developed countries.

Finally, the Soviet Union would have to give sustained signs of accepting the underlying principles of the international economic order the KIEOs seek to maintain. It would have to be willing to accept the conceptual implications of the way these organizations keep their accounts, which entails—as in the Chinese case—a departure from Marxist-inspired methods of measuring economic performance. It would have to agree that the principles on which the KIEOs are based provide legitimate guidelines for the conduct of international monetary, financial, and trading relations. In this regard, of course, as

its record in UNCTAD and in UN debates on the international political economy still demonstrates, the Soviet Union does not fully accept the principles
of the KIEOs. Not only in rhetoric but in deed, the Soviet Union probably
would have to alter the basis of its economic relations with the Eastern
European countries, carrying out this trade more on the basis of market
principles than through state negotiated agreements. And the Soviet Union
would have to undergo the internal transformation that China exhibited after
1971 and especially from 1977 to 1979 before the USSR could credibly
assume a responsible role in the KIEOs.[5] These actions taken together comprise a tall order.

The net effect of these considerations is that China's entry into the
KIEOs makes contemplation of Soviet entry more plausible. But the Chinese
case does not serve as an immediate precedent for Soviet entry, for it occurred
in ways that the Soviet Union, even with Gorbachev's dynamic urgings, may
likely find difficult to emulate for the foreseeable future.

Toward a Global Economic Order

China's successful initial entry into the KIEOs is an encouraging development
for those who seek a global economic order that would incorporate all major
powers. It serves as a useful reminder that enlightened leadership can effect
change in the world. But any optimism must be swiftly dampened in recognition that the process of China's inclusion in the world economy will probably
face more difficult challenges in the 1990s than in the 1980s. And the Chinese
case offers little hope that inclusion of the Soviet Union could be anything
other than a protracted and difficult matter under the best of circumstances.

The key immediate test will be the negotiations concerning the protocol
setting the terms for China's full participation in the General Agreement on
Tariffs and Trade. Should China's quest to expand its role in the international
economy be thwarted by an inability to gain greater market access, the whole
effort to forge a global economic system could be aborted. Even though
China's relationship with the KIEOs is only one factor shaping the evolution
of the international economic order, because of the size and potential of
China's economy, the terms of the GATT protocol could fundamentally affect
whether or not the term neoliberal would continue to be an apt description of
the character of this order. Increasing governmental intervention in international trade has already led to deep concern about the erosion of liberal

---

5. For a discussion of the progress of economic reform in the Soviet Union see Timothy J.
Colton, *The Dilemma of Reform in the Soviet Union*, rev. ed. (New York: Council on Foreign
Relations, 1986); and Ed A. Hewett, *Reforming the Soviet Economy: Equality versus Efficiency*
(Washington, D.C.: Brookings Institution, 1988).

principles; there are ample forces within the Western industrial states pushing in the direction of a neomercantilist rather than a neoliberal system. A protocol that meant that trade with China, though allowed to expand, would be within frameworks established by governmental agreements or one that caused Western entrepreneurs to feel that China had unfair advantages that had to be countered by protective actions could be the final weight tilting the scale in the neomercantilist direction. On the other hand, a protocol that brought China into the GATT trading regime and preserved GATT principles would be a major step toward the creation of a global neoliberal economic order.

The limited influence of the KIEOs to bring about a global economic order must also be kept in mind, however. Occasionally, analysts ascribe excessive influence to the KIEOs. For example, in the wake of China's domestic crisis of 1989, it is predictable that some analysts will either attribute the onset of the crisis to the KIEOs or demand KIEO actions that, they will claim, would return China to the path of reform. Both analyses will be wrong. The deep cleavages that became manifest in the streets of Beijing in the spring of 1989—between leaders and led, between elder revolutionaries and the youth of China, between urban and rural societies, and between modernizers and conservatives among the leaders—existed before China's opening to the outside world, and in fact were at play during the Cultural Revolution as well. The opening to the outside world and the economic reforms undoubtedly exacerbated some of these cleavages and introduced new problems to China. But it must be remembered that these policies were chosen by the leaders of China and were not forced upon them by the KIEOs. Moreover, rapid economic growth produces dislocations and social unrest under *any* circumstances. The populace attributes its grievances to inadequate political leadership and seeks solutions from the government, but in reality the sources and solutions to the problems must be found elsewhere. Further, to the extent that one can distinguish among the influences of the KIEOs, American organizations such as the Ford Foundation, Overseas Chinese, individual governments, and others, the KIEOs were at the forefront in cautioning China about the difficulties in managing the modernization process well. The IMF, for instance, vigorously pointed to the dangers of inflation and undisciplined foreign borrowing from an early date, and GATT negotiators pointed to the dangers of permitting internal, nontariff trade barriers to grow. Nor can the KIEOs keep China on the path of economic reform. That resolve must come from within, though the KIEOs can facilitate the maintenance of that resolve.

The underlying issues that the Soviet and Chinese leaders must decide— and it is a difficult strategic question that only they can resolve—is the appropriate sequence of their respective reform strategies. Put oversimply, how do the leaders in Moscow and Beijing wish to interrelate political and economic reform. Deng Xiaoping placed economic reforms ahead of political reforms. This yielded him a high growth rate. And as our case study demonstrated, it facilitated China's rapid entry into the international economic system and participation in the KIEOs. The price for this strategy became visible in May and June, 1989.

Gorbachev placed political reforms ahead of economic reforms. This yielded him low growth rates, slow entry into the international economic system, and no membership in the KIEOs. But it also enabled him to address the issue of political participation and bring dissidents into the system—as well as increase pressures from national minorities acting upon their new political freedoms and intensify opposition to him among the entrenched Party bureaucrats.

Our study, undertaken in the midst of enormous transformations within both China and the Soviet Union, must therefore end on an inconclusive note. Will China's leaders decide to add political reform to their agenda and draw upon the support the KIEOs and many other institutions offer to continue the process of economic reform? Will the Soviet leaders be able to implement economic reform and thereby create the conditions for the process of engagement, participation, and mutual adjustment with the KIEOs to begin? On the answers to these questions hinge the prospects for creating a global neoliberal economic order. Our study suggests the goal is realistic and worthwhile, but the path will be arduous and full of unanticipated twists and turns.

Appendixes

APPENDIX 1
World Bank China Approved Projects

FY	Date of Signing	Project	US$ Millions		Subtotal by FY		
			Bank	IDA	Bank	IDA	Total
1.							
	81	11/04/81	University Development	100.0	100.0	100.0	100.0	200.0
2.	82	06/23/82	North China Plain Agriculture	—	60.0	0.0	60.0	60.0
3.	83	11/16/82	Three Ports	68.0	—			
4.	83	11/16/82	Agri. Education and Research	—	75.4			
5.	83	12/28/82	Industrial Credit I (CIB I)	40.6	30.0			
6.	83	03/08/83	Petroleum I (Daqing)	162.4	—			
7.	83	04/15/83	Petroleum II (Zhongyuan-Wenliu)	100.8	—	397.1	150.4	547.5
8.	83	05/20/83	State Farms I (Heilongjiang)	25.3	45.0			
9.	84	10/17/83	Polytechnic/TV University	—	85.0			
10.	84	10/17/83	Technical Cooperation	—	10.0			
11.	84	01/05/84	Rubber Development	—	100.0			
12.	84	03/12/84	Lubuge Hydroelectric	145.4	—			
13.	84	04/13/84	Railway I	220.0	—			
14.	84	06/01/84	Rural Credit I	—	50.0			
15.	84	06/01/84	Rural Health/Medical Educ.	—	85.0			
16.	84	06/25/84	Petroleum III (Karamay)	99.5	—			
17.	84	06/25/84	Industrial Credit II (CIB II)	105.0	70.0	615.2	423.5	1,038.7
18.	84	07/09/84	Agri. Education II	45.3	23.5			
19.	85	12/03/84	Agri. Research II	—	25.0			
20.	85	03/15/85	Power II	117.0	—			
21.	85	03/15/85	University Development II	—	145.0			
22.	85	05/20/85	Changcun (Luan) Coal Mining	120.5	—			
23.	85	05/09/85	Seeds	—	40.0			
24.	85	05/09/85	Rural Water Supply	—	80.0			
25.	85	09/05/85	Highway I	42.6	30.0			

(continued)

APPENDIX 1 (Continued)

	FY	Date of Signing	Project	US$ Millions		Subtotal by FY		Total
				Bank	IDA	Bank	IDA	
26.	85	08/26/85	Railway II	235.0	—			
27.	85	08/26/85	Fertilizer Rehab. & Energy Saving	97.0	—			
28.	85	09/05/85	Forestry Development	—	47.3			
29.	85	10/08/85	PiShiHang-Chaohu Area Develpmt.	17.0	75.0			
30.	85	08/26/85	Weiyuan Gas Field Tech. Assist.	25.0	—	654.1	442.3	1,096.4
31.	86	01/03/86	Rural Credit II	—	90.0			
32.	86	04/16/86	Industrial Credit III (CIB III)	75.0	25.0			
33.	86	04/16/86	Technical Cooperation Credit II	—	20.0			
34.	86	07/01/86	Provincial Universities	—	120.0			
35.	86	10/16/86	Third Railway	160.0	70.0			
36.	86	10/16/86	Tianjin Port	130.0	—			
37.	86	09/26/86	Freshwater Fisheries	—	60.0			
38.	86	07/01/86	Beilungang Thermal Power	225.0	—			
39.	86	07/01/86	Yantan Hydroelectric	52.0	—			
40.	86	07/01/86	Liaodong Bay Petroleum Appraisal	30.0	—			
41.	86	01/15/87	Rural Health & Preventive Medicine	15.0	65.0	687.0	450.0	1,137.0
42.	87	12/18/86	Red Soils	—	40.0			
43.	87	01/15/87	Shuikou Hydroelectric	140.0	—			
44.	87	03/16/87	Industrial Credit IV (CIB IV)	250.0	50.0			
45.	87	10/08/87	Shanghai Machine Tool	100.0	—			
46.	87	09/14/87	Xinjiang Agricultural Develop.	—	70.0			

No.	FY	Date	Project			
47.	87	11/23/87	Shanghai Sewerage	45.0	100.0	
48.	87	09/14/87	Beijing-Tianjin-Tanggu Expressway	25.0	125.0	
49.	87	09/14/87	Gansu Provincial Development	20.0	150.5	
50.	87	12/28/87	Fertilizer Rationalization	97.4	—	
51.	87	02/03/88	Wujing Thermal Power	190.0	—	
52.	87	09/14/87	Planning Support & Special Studies Tech. Assist.	—	20.7	
				867.4	556.2	1,423.6
53.	88	06/22/88	Huangpu Port	63.0	25.0	
54.	88	02/29/88	Rural Credit III	—	170.0	
55.	88	07/15/88	Dalian Port	71.0	25.0	
56.	88	08/11/88	Northern Irrigation	—	103.0	
57.	88	09/16/88	Coastal Lands Development	40.0	60.0	
58.	88	08/11/88	Teacher Training	—	50.0	
59.	88	12/22/88	Pharmaceuticals	127.0	—	
60.	88	Not yet signed	Sichuan Highway	75.0	50.0	
61.	88	Not yet signed	Shaanxi Highway	50.0	—	
62.	88	07/15/88	Daxing An Ling Forestry	—	56.9	
63.	88	10/20/88	Beilungang II	165.0	—	
64.	88	01/31/89	Phosphate Development	62.7	—	
65.	88	07/15/88	RSAL	200.0	100.0	
66.	88	01/25/89	Railway IV	200.0	—	
				1,053.7	639.9	1,693.6
67.	89	02/13/89	Ningbo & Shanghai Ports	76.4	—	
68.	89	Not yet signed	Xiamen Port	36.0	—	
69.	89	Not yet signed	Highway VI-Jiangxi Prov.	—	61.0	
				112.4	61.0	173.4
			Grand Total including all FY89 projects	4,486.8	2,883.3	7,370.1

APPENDIX 2

World Bank Publications Dealing with China

Balassa, Bela. *China's Economic Reforms in a Comparative Perspective*. World Bank Development Research Department Discussion Paper no. 177. Washington, D.C.: IBRD, 1986.

Birdsall, Nancy, and Dean Jamison. *Income and Other Factors Influencing Fertility in China*. World Bank Population and Human Resources Division, Discussion Paper no. 81-24. Washington, D.C.: IBRD, 1981.

———. *Income and Other Factors Influencing Fertility Decline in China*. World Bank Population and Human Resources Division, Technical Notes, no. GEN 12. Washington, D.C.: IBRD, 1983.

———, et al. *Alternative Projections of the Chinese Population*. World Bank Population and Human Resources Division, Discussion Paper no. 81-24. Washington, D.C.: IBRD, 1981.

Byrd, William A. *The Shenyang Smelter: A Case Study of Problems and Reforms in China's Nonferrous Metals Industry*. World Bank Staff Working Papers, no. 766. Washington, D.C.: IBRD, 1985.

———, et al. *Recent Chinese Economic Reforms: Studies of Two Industrial Enterprises*. World Bank Staff Working Papers, no. 652. Washington, D.C.: IBRD, 1984.

Colletta, Nat J. *Worker-Peasant Education in the People's Republic of China: Adult Education During the Post-Revolutionary Period*. World Bank Staff Working Papers, no. 527. Washington, D.C.: IBRD, 1982.

Evans, John R. *Medical Education in China*. World Bank Population, Health and Nutrition Department Technical Notes, no. GEN 15. Washington, D.C.: IBRD, 1983.

Feltenstein, Andrew, et al. *Savings, Commodity Market Rationing and the Real Rate of Interest in China*. World Country Policy Department Discussion Paper no. 1986-27. Washington, D.C.: IBRD, 1986.

———. *Savings, Commodity Market Rationing and the Real Rate of Interest in China*. World Bank Development Research Department, Discussion Paper no. 243. Washington, D.C.: IBRD, 1987.

Henderson, John Vernon. *International Experience in Urbanization and Its Relevance for China*. World Bank Staff Working Papers, no. 758. Washington, D.C.: IBRD, 1986.

Hill, Kenneth. *Demographic Trends in China, 1953–1982*. World Bank Population, Health and Nutrition Department Technical Notes, no. 85-4. Washington, D.C.: IBRD, 1985.

———. *Demographic Trends in China from 1950 to 1982*. World Bank Discussion Papers. Washington, D.C.: IBRD, 1988.

Ho, Samuel P. S. *The Asian Experience in Rural Nonagricultural Development and Its Relevance for China.* World Bank Staff Working Papers, no. 757. Washington, D.C.: IBRD, 1986.

IBRD. *The Peoples Republic of China: Environmental Aspects of Economic Development.* Washington, D.C.: IBRD, 1982.

———. *China: Industry and Development Banking Course.* Washington, D.C.: IBRD, 1983.

———. *China, Socialist Economic Development.* 3 vols. A World Bank Country Study. Washington, D.C.: IBRD, 1983.

———. *Primary Health Care—The Chinese Experience: Report of an Inter-Regional Seminar.* Geneva: World Health Organization, 1983.

———. *Seminar on Chinese Accounting and Financial Reporting Systems, September 11–13, 1984.* Washington, D.C.: IBRD, 1984.

———. *China: Long-Term Development Issues and Options.* Washington, D.C., IBRD, 1985.

———. *China, Agriculture to the Year 2000.* A World Bank Country Study. Washington, D.C.: IBRD, 1985.

———. *China, Economic Model and Projections.* A World Bank Country Study. Washington, D.C.: IBRD, 1985.

———. *China, Economic Structure in International Perspective.* A World Bank Country Study. Washington, D.C.: IBRD, 1985.

———. *China, Issues and Prospects in Education.* A World Bank Country Study. Washington, D.C.: IBRD, 1985.

———. *China, the Energy Sector.* A World Bank Country Study. Washington, D.C.: IBRD, 1985.

———. *China, the Transport Sector.* A World Bank Country Study. Washington, D.C.: IBRD, 1985.

———. *China: Management and Finance of Higher Education.* A World Bank Country Study. Washington, D.C.: IBRD, 1986.

———. *China, the Livestock Sector.* A World Bank Country Study. Washington, D.C.: IBRD, 1987.

———. *China: External Trade and Capital.* Washington, D.C.: IBRD, 1988.

———. *China: Finance and Investment.* Washington, D.C.: IBRD, 1988.

———. *China: Growth and Development in Gansu Province.* Washington, D.C.: IBRD, 1988.

Jamison, Dean. *Child Malnutrition and School Retardation in China.* World Bank Population and Human Resources Division, Discussion Paper no. 81-27. Washington, D.C.: IBRD, 1981.

———. *China, the Health Sector.* A World Bank Country Study. Washington, D.C.: IBRD, 1984.

———, and J. van der Gaag. *Education and Earnings in the People's Republic of China.* World Bank Education and Training Department, Discussion Paper no. EDT 56. Washington, D.C.: IBRD, 1987.

———, and F. L. Trowbridge. *The Nutritional Status of Children in China: A Review of the Anthropometric Evidence.* World Bank Population and Human Resources Division Technical Notes, no. GEN 17. Washington, D.C.: IBRD, 1983.

———, et al. *Food Availability and the Nutritional Status of Children in China.*

World Bank Population and Human Resources Division, Discussion Paper no. 81-26. Washington, D.C.: IBRD, 1981.

Khanna, Anupam. *Issues in the Technological Development of China's Electronic Sector.* World Bank Staff Working Papers, no. 762. Washington, D.C.: IBRD, 1986.

King, Timothy. *Population Policy in China Since 1950 and Its Demographic and Economic Implications.* World Bank Population, Health and Nutrition Department Technical Notes, no. GEN 11. Washington, D.C.: IBRD, 1983.

Knight, Peter T. *Economic Reform in Socialist Countries: The Experiences of China, Hungary, Romania, and Yugoslavia.* World Bank Staff Working Papers, no. 579. Management and Development Series, no. 6. Washington, D.C.: IBRD, 1983.

Lardy, Nicholas R. *Agricultural Prices in China.* World Bank Staff Working Papers, no. 606. Washington, D.C.: IBRD, 1983.

Lewis, C. M. *Emerging Issues in China's Food Trade and Distribution System.* AGREP Division Working Paper no 91. Washington, D.C.: IBRD, 1984.

Li, Xuezeng, et al. *The Structure of China's Domestic Consumption: Analyses and Preliminary Forecasts.* World Bank Staff Working Papers, no. 755. Washington, D.C.: IBRD, 1985.

Lim, Edwin. *China, Long-Term Development Issues and Options: The Report of a Mission Sent to China by the World Bank.* A World Bank Country Economic Report. Baltimore, Md.: Johns Hopkins University Press, 1985.

Lin, Justin Yifu. *Rural Factor Markets in China After the Household Responsibility System Reform.* World Bank Agriculture and Rural Development Department, Discussion Paper no. 61. Washington, D.C.: IBRD, 1986.

Moock, Peter, et al. *Childhood Malnutrition and Schooling in the Terai Region of Nepal.* World Bank Education and Training Department Discussion Paper no. EDT 17. Washington, D.C.: IBRD, 1985.

Muller, Manon, and Mary E. Young. *Health Care in China: The Availability, Utilization and Cost of County Hospitals.* World Bank Population, Health and Nutrition Department Technical Notes, no. 86-16. Washington, D.C.: IBRD, 1986.

Nickum, James E. *Irrigation Management in China: A Review of the Literature.* World Bank Staff Working Papers, no. 545. Washington, D.C.: IBRD, 1982.

Orr, Ann C., and James A. Orr. *Economics of Worker Education and Training in China: Lesson from Japan.* World Bank East Asia and Pacific Projects Department. Washington, D.C.: IBRD, 1985.

Piazza, Alan Lee. *Trends in Food and Nutrient Availability in China, 1950–81.* World Bank Staff Working Papers, no. 607. Washington, D.C.: IBRD, 1983.

———. *Trends in Food and Nutrient Availability in China, 1950–81.* World Bank Population, Health and Nutrition Department Technical Notes, no. GEN 16. Washington, D.C.: IBRD, 1983.

Prescott, Nicholas, and Dean Jamison. *Health Sector Finance and Expenditures in China.* PHN Technical Notes, no. GEN 14. Washington, D.C.: IBRD, 1983.

Prost, Andre, et al. *Health Sector Issues in Shandong Province (Peoples' Republic of China).* World Bank Population, Health and Nutrition Department Technical Notes, no. GEN 18. Washington, D.C.: IBRD, 1983.

Rawski, Thomas G. *Industrialization, Technology and Employment in the People's*

Republic of China. World Bank Staff Working Papers, no. 291. Washington, D.C.: IBRD, 1978.

——. *Economic Growth and Employment in China.* New York: Oxford University Press, 1979.

——. *Croissance et Emploi en Chine.* Paris: IBRD, 1979.

——. *Crecimiento Economico y Empleo en Chine.* Madrid: IBRD, 1981.

Sheahan, John B. *Alternative International Economic Strategies and Their Relevance for China.* World Bank Staff Working Papers, no. 759. Washington, D.C.: IBRD, 1986.

Taylor, Robert P. *Decentralized Renewable Energy Development in China: The State of the Art.* World Bank Staff Working Papers, no. 535. Washington, D.C.: IBRD, 1982.

Tidrick, Gene. *Productivity Growth and Technological Change in Chinese Industry.* World Bank Staff Working Papers, no. 761. Washington, D.C.: IBRD, 1986.

Tschannerl, Gerhard, and Kevin Bryan, eds. *Handpumps Testing and Development: Proceedings of a Workshop in China.* World Bank Technical Paper no. 48. Washington, D.C.: IBRD, 1985.

van der Gaag, Jacques. *Commune Health Care in Rural China.* World Bank Population, Health and Nutrition Department Technical Notes, no. GEN 20. Washington, D.C.: IBRD, 1983.

——. *Fertility Correlates in China.* World Bank Development Research Department Discussion Paper no. DRD 99. Washington, D.C.: IBRD, 1984.

——. *Private Household Consumption in China: A Study of People's Livelihood.* World Bank Staff Working Papers, no. 701. Washington, D.C.: IBRD, 1984.

Wood, Adrian. *Economic Evaluation of Investment Projects: Possibilities and Problems of Applying Western Methods in China.* World Bank Staff Working Papers, no. 631. Washington, D.C.: IBRD, 1984.

Wulf, Luc-Henry de. *International Experience in Budgetary Trends During Economic Development and Its Relevance for China.* World Bank Staff Working Papers, no. 760. Washington, D.C.: IBRD, 1986.

Yenny, Jacques, and Lily V. Uy. *Transport in China: A Comparison of Basic Indicators with Those of Other Countries.* World Bank Staff Working Papers, no. 723. Washington, D.C.: IBRD, 1985.

Young, Mary E. *The Barefoot Doctor: Training, Role, and Future.* World Bank Population, Health and Nutrition Department Technical Notes, no. GEN 19. Washington, D.C.: IBRD, 1984.

——, and Andre Prost. *Child Health in China.* World Bank Staff Working Papers, no. 767. Washington, D.C.: IBRD, 1985.

Yusuf, Shahid. *Enterprise Control in the Soviet Union and China and the Futility of Lessons.* Domestic Finance Studies, no. 40. Washington, D.C.: IBRD, 1977.

Zaidan, G., and E. K. Hawkins. *The Treatment of Population in Bank Economic Work.* World Bank Staff Working Papers, no. 16. Washington: D.C.: IBRD, 1968.

Zhang, Jun. *Urban Construction Reconsidered: China's Cities, Issues and Solutions.* World Bank Water Supply and Urban Development Department, Discussion Paper no. UDD-101. Washington, D.C.: IBRD, 1986.

Questionnaire: Substantive Questions

2. Here are certain opposing adjectives that could describe the present international economic environment. Could you tell me in your opinion whether one or the other, or both or neither adjective accurately describes the contemporary international economic environment?

	BOTH		NEITHER
Static	——	Dynamic	——
Satisfactory	——	Unsatisfactory	——
Nationalistic	——	Globalistic	——
Hierarchical	——	Egalitarian	——
Low interdependency	——	High interdependency	——
Democratic	——	Undemocratic	——
Exploitative	——	Unexploitative	——
Violent	——	Nonviolent	——
Fragmented	——	Integrated	——
Has a gloomy future	——	Has a bright future	——
Competitive	——	Cooperative	——
Just	——	Unjust	——
Stable	——	Unstable	——

4. I am going to read to you several opinions that have been expressed about the world economy. Could you indicate to me the extent to which you agree with each of them. 1 indicates that you strongly disagree and 5 indicates that you strongly agree.

	STRONGLY DISAGREE				STRONGLY AGREE
	1	2	3	4	5
Changes in the international order have to be made gradually.	□	□	□	□	□

There is a growing
consensus among nations

	STRONGLY DISAGREE				STRONGLY AGREE
	1	2	3	4	5
about global problems and how to cope with them.	☐	☐	☐	☐	☐
There will always be conflict among nations about economic problems.	☐	☐	☐	☐	☐
To be effective, decisions in international relations have to be made by mutual consent, without sacrifice to one or the other party.	☐	☐	☐	☐	☐
Ideology is a declining factor in international relations.	☐	☐	☐	☐	☐
The most important obstacles to economic growth are internal ones.	☐	☐	☐	☐	☐
It is legitimate to introduce political questions into international economic negotiations.	☐	☐	☐	☐	☐
Generally speaking, in international economic negotiations extreme positions should be avoided.	☐	☐	☐	☐	☐
We should opt for a faster economic growth rather than for a redistribution of wealth and income to solve the poverty problem.	☐	☐	☐	☐	☐

	STRONGLY DISAGREE				STRONGLY AGREE
	1	2	3	4	5
Developing countries should pay greater attention to market forces in managing their economies.	☐	☐	☐	☐	☐
Economies of individual countries throughout the world are becoming more interdependent.	☐	☐	☐	☐	☐
Insistence on national sovereignty is increasingly an obstacle to international economic stability and growth.	☐	☐	☐	☐	☐

I am going to read you several statements that pertain to China's entry into and participation in the World Bank (IMF, GATT). Could you indicate the extent to which you agree with each of them. Again 1 indicates that you strongly disagree and 5 indicates that you strongly agree. After you tell me the extent to which you disagree or agree, I will ask you why you hold your view.

	STRONGLY DISAGREE				STRONGLY AGREE
	1	2	3	4	5
5. The entry of China into the World Bank (IMF, GATT) is an important development.	☐	☐	☐	☐	☐
6. Why do you hold this view?					
7. China undertook (will undertake) significant change in its economic policies in the process of entering the World Bank (IMF, GATT).	☐	☐	☐	☐	☐

	STRONGLY DISAGREE				STRONGLY AGREE
	1	2	3	4	5

8. Why do you hold this view?

9. The World Bank (IMF, GATT) made (will have to make) special arrangements to facilitate China's entry.   ☐   ☐   ☐   ☐   ☐

10. Why do you hold this view?

11. Since accession to membership in the World Bank (IMF, GATT) China has sought to be treated as a special case.   ☐   ☐   ☐   ☐   ☐

12. Why do you hold this view?

13. China's membership has led (will lead) the World Bank (IMF, GATT) at least in some respects to fundamentally alter the nature of its policies and practices.   ☐   ☐   ☐   ☐   ☐

14. Why do you hold this view?

15. China's membership in the World Bank (IMF, GATT) has had a profound effect on the way the Chinese manage their own economy.   ☐   ☐   ☐   ☐   ☐

16. Why do you hold this view?

17. China has played an active and influential

	STRONGLY DISAGREE				STRONGLY AGREE

role in shaping the
long-term direction
of the World Bank's
(IMF's, GATT's)
policies.   □   □   □   □   □
18. Why do you hold
this view?

Questions specifically designed to deal with the individual's own experience

As you reflect on your involvement in China's participation in the World Bank (IMF, GATT), what are the major lessons that you have learned?

References

Aggarwal, Vinod. *Liberal Protectionism: The International Politics of Organized Textile Trade.* Berkeley: University of California Press, 1985.

Aho, C. Michael, and Jonathan David Aronson. *Trade Talks: America Better Listen.* New York: Council on Foreign Relations, 1985.

Amin, Shamir. *Unequal Development: An Essay on the Social Formations of Peripheral Capitalism.* New York: Monthly Review Press, 1976.

Assetto, Valerie J. *The Soviet Bloc in the IMF and the IBRD.* Boulder, Colo.: Westview Press, 1988.

Ayres, Robert L. *Banking on the Poor: The World Bank and Poverty.* Cambridge, Mass.: MIT Press, 1983.

Banno, Masataka. *China and the West, Eighteen Fifty-Eight to Eighteen Sixty-One: The Origins of the Tsungli Yaumen.* Cambridge, Mass.: Harvard University Press, 1964.

Barnett, A. Doak. *China's Economy in Global Perspective.* Washington, D.C.: Brookings Institution, 1981.

Batsavage, Richard E., and John L. Davie. "China's International Trade and Finance." In *Chinese Economy Post-Mao,* U.S. Congress, Joint Economic Committee, 95th Cong., 2d sess. Washington, D.C.: GPO, 1978.

Bauer, Peter T. *Reality and Rhetoric: Studies in the Economics of Development.* Cambridge, Mass.: Harvard University Press, 1984.

Baum, Warren C., and Stokes M. Tolbert. *Investing in Development: Lessons of World Bank Experience.* Washington, D.C.: IBRD, 1985.

Beijing Review. Various issues.

Borg, Dorothy. *The United States and the Far Eastern Crisis of 1933–1938.* Cambridge, Mass.: Harvard University Press, 1964.

Broad, Robin. *Unequal Alliance: The World Bank, the International Monetary Fund, and the Philippines.* Berkeley: University of California Press, 1988.

Burki, Shahid Javed. "Reform and Growth in China." *Finance and Development* 25, no. 4 (December, 1988): 46–49.

Chen, Dezhao. "China and the GATT." Paper prepared for presentation at the 14th Congress of the International Political Science Association, August 28 to September 1, 1988, Washington, D.C.

Cheng, Nien. *Life and Death in Shanghai.* New York: Grove Press, 1987.

China Business Review. Various issues.

Chinese Communist Party, Central Committee Party History Research Office. *Zhonggong dangshi dashi nianbiao* (Chronology of major events in the history of the Chinese Communist party). Beijing: People's Press, 1987.

Cohen, Paul A. *China and Christianity: The Missionary Movement and the Growth of Chinese Anti Foreignism, 1860–1870.* Cambridge, Mass.: Harvard University Press, 1963.

Colton, Timothy J. *The Dilemma of Reform in the Soviet Union.* Rev. ed. New York: Council on Foreign Relations, 1986.

Cox, Robert W., Harold K. Jacobson, et al. *The Anatomy of Influence: Decision Making in International Organization.* New Haven, Conn.: Yale University Press, 1973.

Dam, Kenneth W. *The GATT: Law and the International Economic Organization.* Chicago: University of Chicago Press, 1970.

————. *The Rules of the Game: Reform and Evolution in the International Monetary System.* Chicago: University of Chicago Press, 1982.

Dernberger, Robert F. "The Resurgence of Chung-hsueh wei-t'i, Hsi-hsueh wei-yung' in Contemporary China: The Transfer of Technology to the PRC." Paper prepared for the Conference on Technology and Communist Culture, Bellagio, Italy, August 22–28, 1975.

de Vries, Margaret Garritsen. *The International Monetary Fund, 1972–1978: Cooperation on Trial.* Washington, D.C.: IMF, 1985.

————. *The IMF in a Changing World, 1945–1985.* Washington, D.C.: IMF, 1986.

de Wulf, Luc-Henry. "Financial Reform in China." *Finance and Development* 22, no. 4 (December, 1985): 19–22.

———— and David Goldsbrough. "The Evolving Role of Monetary Policy in China." *IMF Staff Papers* 33, no. 2 (June, 1986): 209–42.

Domes, Jurgen. *The Government and Politics of the PRC: A Time of Transition.* Boulder, Colo.: Westview Press, 1985.

Eckstein, Alexander. *China's Economic Revolution.* Cambridge: Cambridge University Press, 1977.

Emmanuel, Arghiri. *Unequal Exchange: A Study of the Imperialism of Trade.* New York: Monthly Review Press, 1972.

European Communities Commission, "Commission Decision of 15 June 1987 Changing the Import Arrangements Established by Council Decision 87/60/EEC and Applied in the Member States in Respect of Imports of Various Agricultural and Industrial Product from the People's Republic of China (87/392/EEC)." In *Official Journal of the European Communities*, no. L 206/34. Brussels: EC, 1987.

Fang, Weizhong, ed. *Zhonghua Renmin Gongheguo jingji dashiji* (1949–1980) (Chronicle of the economy of the People's Republic of China). Beijing: Chinese Social Science Press, 1984.

Feeney, William. "Chinese Policy in Multilateral Financial Institutions." In *China and the World*, ed. Samuel S. Kim, 266–92. Boulder, Colo.: Westview Press, 1984.

Fei, John C. H., Gustav Ranis, and Shirley W. Y. Kuo. *Growth with Equity: The Taiwan Case.* Washington, D.C.: IBRD, 1979.

Finger, J. Michael, and Andrzej Olechowski, eds. *The Uruguay Round: A Handbook on the Multilateral Trade Negotiations.* Washington, D.C.: IBRD, 1987.

Fox, William T. R., and Annette Baker Fox. *NATO and the Range of American Choice.* New York: Columbia University Press, 1967.

Fried, Edward R., and Henry D. Owen, eds. *The Future Role of the World Bank.* Washington, D.C.: Brookings Institution, 1982.

General Agreement on Tariffs and Trade. *International Trade: 87–88.* 2 vols. Geneva: GATT, 1988.

———. *GATT Activities, 1987.* Geneva: GATT, 1988.

———. *The Texts of the Tokyo Round Agreements.* Geneva: GATT, 1986.

———. *Newsletter: Focus.* Various issues.

Gold, Joseph. *Membership and Nonmembership in the International Monetary Fund: A Study in International Law and Organization.* Washington, D.C.: IMF, 1974.

Goldstein, Steven. "Chinese Communist Policy toward the United States, 1944–1949: Opportunities and Constraints." In *Uncertain Years: Chinese-American Relations, 1947–1950,* ed. Dorothy Borg and Waldo Heinrichs, 235–78. New York: Columbia University Press, 1980.

Gordenker, Leon. *International Aid and Development Decisions: Development Programs in Malawi, Tanzania and Zambia.* Princeton: Princeton University Press, 1976.

Gowa, Joanne. *Closing the Gold Window: Domestic Politics and the End of Bretton Woods.* (Ithaca, N. Y.: Cornell University Press, 1983.

Guitian, Manuel. *Fund Conditionality: Evolution of Principles and Practices.* IMF Pamphlet Series, no. 38. Washington D.C.: IMF, 1981.

Haas, Ernst B. *Tangle of Hopes: American Commitments and World Order.* Englewood Cliffs, N. J.: Prentice-Hall, 1969.

Haggard, Stephan. "The Politics of Adjustment: Lessons from the IMF's Extended Facility." In *The Politics of International Debt,* ed. Miles Kahler, 157–86. Ithaca, N. Y.: Cornell University Press, 1986.

Halpern, Nina. "Economic Specialists and the Making of Chinese Economic Policy, 1955–1983." Ph.D. diss., University of Michigan, 1985.

Hao, Mengbi, and Duan Haoran, eds. *Zhongquo gongchandang liushinian* (Sixty years of the Chinese Communist party). Beijing: People's Liberation Army Press, 1984.

Harding, Harry. *China's Second Revolution: Reform after Mao.* Washington, D.C.: Brookings Institution, 1987.

Hartland-Thumberg, Penelope. "China's Modernization: A Challenge for the GATT." *Washington Quarterly* 10, no. 2 (Spring 1987): 81–98.

Herzstein, Robert. "China and the GATT: Legal and Policy Issues Raised by China's Participation in the General Agreement on Tariffs and Trade." *Law and Policy in International Business* 18, no. 2 (1986): 371–415.

Hewett, Ed A. *Reforming the Soviet Economy: Equality versus Efficiency.* Washington, D.C.: Brookings Institution, 1988.

Ho, Samuel P. S., and Ralph Huenemann. *China's Open Door Policy: The Quest for Foreign Technology and Capital.* Vancouver: University of British Columbia Press, 1984.

Horsefield, J. Keith. *The International Monetary Fund, 1945–1965: Twenty Years of International Monetary Cooperation.* 3 vols. Washington, D.C.: IMF, 1969.

Hsu, Immanuel C. Y. *The Rise of Modern China.* Oxford: Oxford University Press, 1982.

Hufbauer, Gary Clyde, and Jeffrey J. Schott. *Trading for Growth: The Next Round of Trade Negotiations.* Washington, D.C.: Institute for International Economics, 1985.

Hyde, L. K., Jr. *The United States and the United Nations: Promoting the Public Welfare, Examples of American Cooperation*. New York: Carnegie Endowment for International Peace, 1960.

International Bank for Reconstruction and Development. *World Bank Atlas 1979*. Washington, D.C.: IBRD, 1979.

———. *Annual Reports*, 1980–88. Washington, D.C.: IBRD, 1980–88.

———. *World Bank Atlas 1980*. Washington, D.C.: IBRD, 1980.

———. *World Bank Annual Report, 1981*. Washington, D.C.: IBRD, 1981.

———. *China: Socialist Economic Development*. 3 vols. Washington, D.C.: IBRD, 1983.

———. *China: Long-Term Development Issues and Options*. Washington, D.C.: IBRD, 1985.

———. *China: Management and Finance of Higher Education*. A World Bank Country Study. Washington, D.C.: IBRD, 1986.

———. *China, the Livestock Sector*. A World Bank Country Study. Washington, D.C.: IBRD, 1987.

———. *World Development Report 1987*. Washington, D.C.: IBRD, 1987.

———. *China: External Trade and Capital*. Washington, D.C.: IBRD, 1988.

———. *China: Finance and Investment*. Washington, D.C.: IBRD, 1988.

———. *China: Growth and Development in Gansu Province*. Washington, D.C.: IBRD, 1988.

———. *World Development Report 1988*. Washington, D.C.: IBRD, 1988.

———. *World Tables, 1987*. 4th ed. Washington, D.C.: IBRD, 1988.

———. *The World Bank: Annual Report, 1988*. Washington, D.C.: IBRD, 1988.

International Finance Corporation. *International Finance Corporation: Annual Report*. Washington, D.C.: IFC, 1988.

International Monetary Fund. "How Countries Use Resources through Tranches, Facilities," *Survey*, January 5, 1976, 2–3.

———. *The Fund and China in the International Monetary System*. Washington, D.C.: IMF, 1983.

———. *Direction of Trade Statistics Yearbook, 1987*. Washington, D.C.: IMF, 1987.

———. *Direction of Trade Statistics Yearbook, 1988*. Washington, D.C.: IMF, 1988.

———. *International Monetary Fund: Annual Report, 1988*. Washington, D.C.: IMF, 1988.

Jackson, John H. *World Trade and the Law of GATT*. Indianapolis: Bobbs-Merrill, 1969.

Jacobson, Harold K. "The Soviet Union, the UN, and World Trade." *Western Political Quarterly* 11, no. 3 (September, 1958): 310–14.

———. *The USSR and the UN's Economic and Social Activities*. Notre Dame: University of Notre Dame Press, 1963.

———. "ONUC's Civilian Operations: State Preserving and State Building." *World Politics* 17, no. 1 (October, 1964): 75–107.

———. *Networks of Interdependence: International Organizations and the Global Political System*. 2d ed. New York: Alfred A. Knopf, 1984.

Keohane, Robert O. *After Hegemony: Cooperation and Discord in the World Political Economy*. Princeton: Princeton University Press, 1984.

Kim, Samuel S. *China, the United Nations, and World Order.* Princeton: Princeton University Press, 1979.

Kindelberger, Charles P. *The World in Depression, 1929–1939.* Berkeley: University of California Press, 1973.

———. "Dominance and Leadership in the International Economy." *International Studies Quarterly* 25, no. 3 (1981): 242–54.

Kissinger, Henry. *The White House Years.* Boston: Little, Brown, 1979.

Kostecki, M. M. *East-West Trade and the GATT System.* London: Macmillan, 1979.

Krasner, Stephen D. "The Tokyo Round: Particularistic Interests and Prospects for Stability in the Global Trading System." *International Studies Quarterly* 23, no. 4 (December, 1979): 1–22.

———, ed. *International Regimes.* Ithaca, N.Y.: Cornell University Press, 1983.

———. *Structural Conflict: The Third World against Global Liberalism.* Berkeley: University of California Press, 1985.

Kuznets, Simon. *Modern Economic Growth: Rate, Structure, and Spread.* New Haven, Conn.: Yale University Press, 1966.

Lardy, Nicholas R. *China's Entry into the World Economy: Implications for Northeast Asia and the United States.* New York: University Press of America, 1987.

Lee, Chae-Jin. *China and Japan: New Economic Diplomacy.* Stanford, Calif.: Stanford University Press, 1984.

Leslie, Winsome J. *The World Bank and Structural Transformation in Developing Countries: The Case of Zaire.* Boulder, Colo.: Lynne Rienner, 1987.

Levenson, Joseph R. *Liang Ch'i-ch'ao and the Mind of Modern China.* Berkeley: University of California Press, 1970.

Levi, Werner. *Modern China's Foreign Policy.* Minneapolis: University of Minnesota Press, 1953.

Lieberthal, Kenneth, and Michel Oksenberg. *Policy Making in China: Leaders, Structures, and Processes.* Princeton: Princeton University Press, 1988.

Long, Olivier. *Law and Its Limitations in the GATT Multilateral Trade System.* Dordrecht, The Netherlands: Martinus Nijhoff Publishers, 1985.

Ma, Shu-yun. "Recent Changes in China's Pure Trade Theory." *China Quarterly*, no. 106 (June, 1986): 291–305.

Ma Hong. *New Strategy for China's Economy*, trans. Yang Lin. Beijing: New World Press, 1983.

McDonnell, J. E. D. "China's Move to Rejoin the GATT System: An Epic Transition." *World Economy* 10, no. 3 (September, 1987): 331–50.

Mancall, Mark. *China at the Center: Three Hundred Years of Foreign Policy.* New York: Free Press, 1984.

Mason, Edward S., and Robert E. Asher. *The World Bank since Bretton Woods.* Washington, D.C.: Brookings Institution, 1973.

Moser, Michael, ed. *Foreign Trade, Investment, and Law in the People's Republic of China.* Oxford: Oxford University Press, 1984.

Nixon, Richard. *RN: The Memoirs of Richard Nixon.* New York: Grosset and Dunlap, 1978.

Oksenberg, Michel, and Steven Goldstein. "The Chinese Political Spectrum." *Problems of Communism* 23, no. 2 (March–April, 1974): 1–13.

————. "*Tzu-li Keng-Sheng:* China's Developmental Principle." Manuscript.

Organization for Economic Cooperation and Development. *Geographical Distribution of Financial Assistance to Developing Countries, 1980–1983*. Paris: OECD, 1984.

————. *Geographical Distribution of Financial Assistance to Developing Countries, 1981–1984*. Paris: OECD, 1985.

————. *Geographical Distribution of Financial Assistance to Developing Countries, 1982–1985*. Paris: OECD, 1986.

————. *Geographical Distribution of Financial Assistance to Developing Countries, 1983–1986*. Paris: OECD, 1987.

Patterson, Eliza R. "Improving GATT Rules for Nonmarket Economies." *Journal of World Trade Law* 20 (1988): 185–205.

Payer, Cheryl. *The Debt Trap: The IMF and the Third World*. New York: Monthly Review Press, 1975.

————. *The World Bank: A Critical Analysis*. New York: Monthly Review Press, 1982.

Please, Stanley. *The Hobbled Giant: Essays on the World Bank*. Boulder, Colo.: Westview Press, 1984.

"A Review of China's EDI Program: Looking Back," in *EDI Review*, April, 1986, 1–3.

Reynolds, Bruce L. "Reform in Chinese Industrial Management: An Empirical Report." In *China under the Four Modernizations*, pt. 1, U.S. Congress, Joint Economic Committee. Washington, D.C.: GPO, 1982.

Reynolds, Lloyd G. *Economic Growth in the Third World, 1850–1980*. New Haven, Conn.: Yale University Press, 1985.

Ruggie, John Gerrard. "International Regimes, Transactions, and Change: Embedded Liberalism in the Postwar Economic Order." In *International Regimes*, ed. Stephen D. Krasner, 195–232. Ithaca, N.Y.: Cornell University Press, 1983.

Soeya, Yoshihida. "Japan's Postwar Economic Diplomacy with China: Three Decades of Non-Governmental Experiences." Ph. D. diss., University of Michigan, 1987.

Sutter, Robert G. *The China Quandary: Domestic Determinants of U.S.-China Policy, 1972–1982*. Boulder, Colo.: Westview Press, 1983.

Tidrick, Gene, and Chen Jiyuan, eds. *China's Industrial Reform*. Washington, D.C.: IBRD, 1987.

Thomson, James C., Jr. *While China Faced West: American Reformers in Nationalist China, 1928–1937*. Cambridge, Mass.: Harvard University Press, 1974.

Tsao, James T. H. *China's Development Strategies and Foreign Trade*. Lexington, Mass.: Lexington Books, 1987.

United Nations. *International Trade Statistics Yearbook 1965*. New York: United Nations, 1966.

————. *International Trade Statistics Yearbook 1985*. New York: United Nations, 1985.

United States, Congressional Budget Office. *The GATT Negotiations and US Trade Policy*. Washington, D.C.: GPO, 1987.

United States, Department of the Treasury. *United States Participation in the Multilateral Development Banks in the 1980s*. (Washington, D.C.: GPO, 1982.

United States, Office of the Special Trade Representative. *National Trade Estimate: 1986 Report on Foreign Trade Barriers.* Washington, D.C.: GPO, 1987.

Wang, Yi Chu. *Chinese Intellectuals and the West, 1872–1949.* Chapel Hill: University of North Carolina Press, 1966.

Williamson, John, ed. *IMF Conditionality.* Washington, D.C.: Institute for International Economics, 1983.

Winham, Gilbert R. *International Trade and the Tokyo Round Negotiations.* Princeton: Princeton University Press, 1986.

Wolf, Thomas A. "Economic Stabilization in Planned Economies: Toward an Analytical Framework." *IMF Staff Papers* 32, no. 1 (March, 1985): 78–131. Reprinted in IMF, *IMF Survey,* November 1986, 357.

Wu, Friedrich W. "Socialist Self-Reliant Development within the Capitalist World-Economy: The Chinese View in the Post-Mao Era." *Global Perspectives* 1, no. 1 (Spring 1983): 8–34.

Yeats, Alexander J. "China's Recent Export Performance: Some Basic Features and Policy Implications." *Development and Change* 15, no. 1 (1984): 1–22.

Young, Arthur. *China and the Helping Hand, 1937–1945* Cambridge, Mass.: Harvard University Press, 1963.

Yue Daiyun with Carolyn Wakeman. *To the Storm: The Odyssey of a Revolutionary Chinese Woman.* Berkeley: University of California Press, 1985.

Zhou Enlai. Report on the work of the government, delivered to the First Session of the First National People's Congress, September 23, 1954. In *People's China,* October 16, 1954, 3.

Index